# LIFE UNKNOWN

## A PASSAGE THROUGH INDIA

# KARTIKEYA LADHA

# LIFE UNKNOWN

## A PASSAGE THROUGH INDIA

WILD AMBRO

Dream Beyond Shadows
Kartikeya Ladha

WILD AMBRO

in collaboration with EB Press

ISBN - 978-93-89160-17-8

*For the people who inspired me and continue to do so.*

# INTRODUCTION

*A* *SURFEIT OF NOISE WAS* holding my heart. I was unable to see through the unknown ahead of me. My mind was losing its grip on reality; I could not understand what was happening to me.

I stood still in my body, not knowing how I had arrived in it. I stood beyond time, unaware of my existence.

Unexpected events had begun manifesting every second, confounding my spirit and keeping it in a constant state of awe. They were enticing my senses to leave my body behind and follow an unknown path, to unravel the truth of what held me together.

Death of my sins was precipitating the dawn of my sorrows.

I was downright lost and seeking a life beyond misery.

Chasing joy and happiness, I was running wild in my intentions, hoping deep in myself that it would lead me where I needed to be. I was living in the darkness, waiting to see the light at the end of the tunnel. My eyes were sobbing with excruciating pain, while my body could not feel a thing.

There I was – standing by a lone mountain lost in my vanity and looking for answers beyond the cause of humanity.

Ceasing to triumph over the land, I was letting go of the blood splashed on my skin from the wars of my ancestors. The waves of my mind were guiding me along the sea to open the hidden doors concealed within my being's depths. I was learning to fly with the wind as the shadows began to disappear, and the sun became visible.

The stars were daring my eyes to leave it all behind. I climbed alone in a darkened valley, about to lose myself in the absoluteness of this world.

It was time to connect with the roots of my spirit, so that I could let go of that what made my heart forget how to beat.

India was calling my heart.
My heart was responding.

India was screaming at my soul.
My soul was missing.

India was coming my way.
My way was unknown.

The words relayed in this story will carry you through a stormy burial that induced a man to reignite his spirit and rebreathe with an exposed heart.

For life, beyond and above us.

For the shades, lost and beneath us.

For the dead, that found and proclaimed us.

# TABLE OF CONTENTS

# PART ONE
## RETURN TO THE MOTHERLAND

# I. THE ALIEN LAND

*I N A DARKENED HOLLOW* night, I stood in the middle of an empty street, wondering what had happened.

The weight of the sky burdened my shoulders. My feet were being drawn beneath the land to hold me tight.

My whole body felt encased by the conditioned layers hovering around it after having been previously struck down by them and was now slowly drowning beneath a bottomless surface.

---

I had only recently returned to India for an indefinite period. I had been in the United States for many years, followed by a vividly expansive time in Peru, South America. Moving back to India after years of letting go of my immaturely constructed Indian identity led to a crisis- my mind was unwilling to accept an identity based on my body's appearance and the infinite delusions projected onto it by the human world.

This identity crisis seemed grave at the time as I was losing a sense of where I belonged and who I was in the relative sense. I was slowly being pulled away from everything and converging with a strange feeling of nothingness, which presented me with an outsider's perspective to all my encounters in India.

An unpredictable and exasperatingly chaotic country, India is where I was born and grew up in before leaving for the US. I went there as a young man to follow my naively ambitious drive to "conquer the world," without ever really having grasped the short-sightedness of that profoundly ignorant and egotistic goal.

It was not until I had my feet on the land of woven treasures again that I felt a sense of completion within me, which had dissipated somewhere in the darkness where I had managed to consistently and continuously delude myself, for a long time previously.

Until I returned to it, I never really understood the significance of the land on which India emerged over thousands of years ago, having lost all that I thought was mine. The only thing that remained was the fire burning within me and the desire to free myself from the core of my vitality.

Encompassing a history probably as complicated and complex as any other country's, India has had a convoluted history. Over numerous years, it has given birth to all kinds of ideologies, belief systems, rituals, religious practices, and countless other variables, and they all play their unique roles in composing the symphony of modern-day India.

On a piece of paper, India seems to be a country. However, it is an incredible amalgamation of many diverse kingdoms brought together by the admirable idea of building a new nation based on a single identity, whose substantial weight is carried by the broadened shoulders of the term "Indian."

Each state preserves its history, language, culture, dialects, religious preferences, assorted practices, belief systems, and the implications of its topography to form its identity-subset within the vast Indian identity – whatever that is.

The country of India is nothing short of a universe. A person would have to devote multiple lifetimes to understand it truly and would eventually realize that the attempt will still fall short of understanding the whole breadth and length of this multi-faceted and colorful country.

What makes India so fascinating isn't solely its rich cultural heritage or illogical operational arrangements. Its fascination derives from mystical phenomena showcasing their presence as you move around the country, observing yourself through the eyes of other people.

—— ⬦ ——

In a senseless undertaking to break my hidden walls and face my never-ending dark self, my return to India was followed by me being teleported to the alien land of Ladakh. All I wanted to do was lose myself in the remoteness of the deserted area, whose naked and unkempt setting in the distant mountains inescapably provided for reflection.

Several months had passed since I had moved to Leh in the summer of 2017 to Leh, a significant district situated in the then-emancipated and isolated region of Ladakh.

Far away from the ashes of burdened, civilized societies, Ladakh was a region standing beyond time, even in the 21$^{st}$ Century. Sharing its borders with Chinese occupied Tibet on the eastern side, Ladakh was the northern-most part of India. It is the home of the Indus Valley, named after the Indus River. This is one of Asia's longest rivers and the lifeline of the archaic Indus Valley civilization.

Hiding its vastness in the glorious Himalayan mountain range, Ladakh was nothing less than a desert at an extremely high altitude. It produced a drunken sensation in the minds of outsiders – and sometimes nausea in their bodies – as soon as their feet stood on this outwardly-expanding, empty land.

With vast mountain ranges encompassing panoramic vistas, nothing but absoluteness characterized this magnificent region of Ladakh. However, it was in the process of becoming the latest victim to the virulent spread of the human condition known as greed.

The most addictive of all drugs, once we humans get a taste of it, we can't get enough of greed. Elusively, it drives and empowers us and corrodes us internally without us even being aware of it. Then it slowly takes over every cell of our bodies to govern all our actions, leaving us utterly fractured at the core of our existence.

As most of Ladakh's population identifies themselves as Buddhist devotees, Buddhism's influence could be seen and felt everywhere. It started from the moment I stepped out of Leh's dated airport and was hailed by the sun's rays, piercing my skin and inciting my cells to reckon how high my body was, in comparison to sea level.

The simple architecture of most buildings, even ordinary houses, was inspired by monastic structures. Amidst Buddhist prayer flags hanging everywhere and mimicking the land's physical terrain, I was transported in an old van by a *Ladakhi*[1] man I met outside the airport.

He said, *"Jullay,"* to me as I was looking around for a taxi and simultaneously taking deep breaths so I could inhale enough of the thin air of that ancient land.

*Jullay* was the word used by the *Ladakhis* to greet one another. It would become my go-to word in *Ladakhi* for the entire time that the powerful land embraced me.

He had a big smile on his shiny face, which for a second, I thought, looked very much like the people I had come across while trekking in the Andean mountains in Peru, South America. A few months previously, I had been led to the mysticism of the Inca legacy in those mountains. They were also located at a high altitude, but on the opposite side of the globe from where I had just landed.

While sitting inside the van, my eyes were glued to the windows on both sides, getting hints of the amplified, ancient significance of the place.

Distant from the road we were cruising on, I could see some age-old, flat-roofed Buddhist monasteries sited at regular intervals on top of the rocky, magnetic mountains showcasing their mammoth presence. In contrast, on the flat, deserted land, there were many traditional, mud-brick houses constructed of locally sourced materials. It roused the sense that I had landed in an offbeat, mythical kingdom on another planet altogether.

<hr />

Ladakh was the home to myriads of ageless and magical Buddhist monasteries, architectural wonders in themselves, on the top of an endlessly abundant, vast, and magnificent terrain encompassing an enticing landscape. In just the last few decades, it had become a popular site for tourists, backpackers, adventurers, motorcycle riders, and Buddhist devotees from across the world with its outlandish natural beauty.

---

1 Ladakhi is the term the people of Ladakh use for identifying themselves – and their language.

With none of those identities attached to my body any longer, I found myself involuntarily hitched to the roots binding the land of Ladakh. I was not trying to find anything, I was trying to lose it all- everything I foolishly thought I had gained in life because of the systematic, predictable chain of events that goes into the making of someone's life in our present-day world.

Drowning beneath the searing sun, my eyes mislaid their ability to capture the ascendant scenery. On my way into Leh, construction sites started to emerge on both sides. I was in touch with the vanguard of change materializing in Leh – greed was dissolving in people's veins.

The pulsing of each breath provoked me to let go of everything that had previously mattered to me – or i naively thought had – before choosing to walk down this unknown path. It took me to faraway lands and a distant place within myself, where nothing seemed to exist anymore.

I was loosening my grip on the illusion that I was breathing through every single day.

## A. Why Ladakh?

I flew into Ladakh from New Delhi, India's capital, where I had just spent a few weeks with my parents. They lived in a comfortable apartment in Noida, a commercially active city in the south-east corner from New Delhi's center point.

Noida was among the four cities surrounding New Delhi that make up one of the busiest combinations of endless waves of millions of people bustling ceaselessly from one point to another, trying to make a living. The other neighboring cities to New Delhi are Gurugram, Faridabad, and Ghaziabad.

The whole National Capital Region is an over-populated and ever-growing, human-derived reality. It drove millions to get up in the morning and strive for a better life than what they have. They do not have the luxury of retaining the physical or mental space to investigate the question: "What are we running this race for?"

They are simply synching into the capitalist mindset, which has scaled-up tremendously worldwide over the last several centuries and toxically infiltrated our minds with thoughts of furthering our selfish needs. We are to achieve this mindset by continually creating material wealth using a superficial and short-sighted economic system that has devastated our planet's natural state of being. This has unleashed the global environmental crisis our planet is currently going through. However, it still hasn't affected our species' skewed ambitions to gain evermore superiority. The superiority seems to magically arise from the sheets of a blank canvas, whereas, in fact, an unforeseeable picture is being painted that we fail to acknowledge.

I had only just returned to India a few weeks previously after traveling around Peru for many months. It was in Peru that I decided to let go of my initial life plan of building a life in the United States.

Taking that momentous step of abruptly leaving the United States left my mind in a state of utmost confusion. That continued until my liberating time in Peru's Amazon Jungle, where facing my innate fears about death dragged me down to my weakest moments ever. Those moments forced me to lose my pride and arrogance at every step and took me closer to being in tune with the wilderness of the world. Those moments shook my system apart and provoked my mind into questioning everything I had been brainwashed into believing all my life.

Bit by bit, the image I had wrongly formulated about myself got tarnished, as my ego drained down the sewers of misery. Enclosed by the jungle, I begged the Peruvian shaman[2] helplessly in an urgent attempt to save me from the constant stream of torturous flashes that there seemed no return from.

I was stuck in the prison of my mind, which was producing pain throughout every nerve. It made me susceptible to the slightest suggestions from the darkened shadows hovering around my body, waiting to encompass me and prevent me from seeing past my insecurities and fears.

---

2  Shamans are medicine men/women who can access and influence the world of the spirits through an elevated state of consciousness, which they then channel to heal people in the material world.

These were the insecurities and fears we all share but fail to acknowledge – or purposely choose to ignore because of the anxiety arising from accepting our flaws. They tie us to our inferior selves, which then sit uncomfortably in the presence of past grievances and present sorrows.

It was amid my carefree living with an indigenous tribe in the Amazon Jungle that a vision showed me that I needed to return to India and visit the Himalayas.

As soon as I finished traveling in Peru, it was clear to me that I had to get to this ancient Himalayan region of Ladakh, where something beyond me was pulling me.

## B. What Called for the Seeker's Path?

What I am doing now is considered far from normal in modern-day India, where people have been blindly following in the footsteps of the western world and adopting a one-dimensional way of looking at life. Such a life only looks through the prism of creating material wealth while ignoring the rest of what goes into a balanced, nourishing life.

As I was born in India, I was raised in a system that acquints children with the military-style regime of the country's educational system, from the moment of their first breath. It is designed to make robots out of children. In a devious manner, the system forces them to compete with each other after continuously being fed the fearful possibility of becoming a failure in life. In my initial days of schooling, that fear certainly goaded me into doing what everyone else was doing. I devoted countless hours studying irrelevant material so I could get top grades in exams and be admitted into a good university.

Fortunately, I got the opportunity to move to the United States after finishing my schooling in India, and that provided my younger self some hope of gaining what I had lost over the years of being told what was right and wrong.

That way of functioning conditions the mind so profoundly, without us having any awareness of what is happening. We can be easily controlled, steered, and manipulated by people sitting at the top of the food chain.

I didn't know it at first, but when I left for the US, there was an urge to be free somewhere deep within me. Even though I wasn't consciously aware of it at the time, it worked as a hidden gem by subconsciously emboldening my mind to go on a wild crusade to experience life and tenaciously open myself to the world exuberantly.

Who knew that that infinitesimal spark would eventually not only lead to the quest of a lifetime but truly invigorate every part of my body and mind into gradually unleashing it and letting it become the source of an ever-blazing fire. That fire burns deep down through every cranny of my unbreakable spirit, making it stronger with every annihilation along the way.

The countless daring and risky steps I took in the years following my first flight from India to the US led me to ultimately becoming a trusting, intuitive, and self-assured person, someone who could gear up the courage to welcome unexpected and unimagined future events.

And even though it was not the usual path or the easy way, I began trusting something beyond myself in the process, until a storm surfaced in New York through the wounds in my heart. I felt totally broken despite having achieved the things I had always been made to believe life was for.

I felt wrecked in myself.

The self-assurance and confidence in my abilities that had been building throughout my years in the United States died in a flicker. Even when my mind was trying to reassure my heart that what I was doing was the way forward, it did not seem to help.

I could see my future going along a specific course based on the projections and stories I had been brainwashed into believing from the start of my life, but at that moment, I knew I couldn't be a part of that.

I had no idea what I wanted to do. My entire being felt wholly shattered at that moment of vulnerability. While the storm raged, I struggled to accept the reassurances from my defense mechanisms but only experienced wreckage without any clarity whatsoever.

I had no idea who I could listen to at that moment, so I put my deep trust in the voice emanating from somewhere beyond me that was guiding me to leave everything behind and embrace the unknown path.

The voice encouraged me to become a seeker in life. It piloted me to the mysterious land of Peru, where I was forced to drop my unhinged guards and come face to face with my darkened self. Eventually, I realized that I had to return to the mystical land of India, not as a visitor or countryman – but as an individual who no longer had an identity.

All I carried was the pure intention of rediscovering my true self without any strings attached to the previously fabricated image I had developed over the years of soulless expansion.

Having been born and raised in India, I left the country as a young man thinking I would only return during vacations to see my family. I never considered the possibility of returning to it so I could go past all my innate fears and learn to live beyond measures of time and space to bring about a massive change within me – to transform my whole outlook on life and walk on a nameless path.

I returned to India in a state of utmost uncertainty about what the future held for me.

I just knew one thing – that I needed to follow through with my new-found purpose of becoming a writer, which is possibly one of the least respected fields of choice for a young, independent, and highly educated Indian man.

Initially, and rightly so, people in India, including most of my family, dismissed my intention to write. Whenever I spoke to anyone about it, my voice was not heard. I could imagine what I was saying made no logical sense to the ears of other people.

I was being shut down by people just because I dared to think atypically and wanted to pursue something unique in life. Even though I sometimes felt like I was speaking to walls, not people, I understood that their concern for me originated from a good place.

So, even though it was tough to keep on being denied by people, I tried to not take it personally and kept on practicing the art of "letting it go."

Instead of worrying about what people thought of what I was doing, I focused on silencing the external noise, and at the same time, acknowledged the inner voice. I wanted it to keep on challenging me into bringing out the more authentic version of myself, which had been suppressed somewhere within my many layers of human madness.

And even though I was unsure about what was to come, I was somehow convinced that my inner being needed strengthening. I was also convinced that the only way to do that was to dive deep into the darkness within me and deal with it, no matter how excruciating it seemed.

I did not return to India to be with my family or to work with them so I could make a living and have a secure job title to my name. I came back to live through the streaming of an endless dream, which had begun on that darkened winter's night in New York City and began to manifest itself in the depths of the Amazon Jungle.

All that led to me standing in front of countless people, able to withstand their demands. I solidly held to the truth of the fire that wanted to burn through my core.

I had decided to go to Ladakh even before I boarded my flight to India from Peru because I knew how exposed my heart was. I also knew I had to follow through with my vision of going to the Himalayas.

Ladakh seemed like the perfect option. I had heard about it before and somehow knew it was the place I had to go to so I could keep on expanding within myself while being on my ever-evolving journey.

# II. LOST IN THE DESERT

*I* ARRIVED INTO THE CURIOUS presence of my immediate family in India – my father, mother, and sister.

All of them were happy to have me back but were quite anxious about what I was going to do next. My parents had been scared the whole time I was in Peru. They had been especially concerned about the security of my future. After all, they had worked their entire lives to provide security for my sister and me.

Seeing me throw it all away in the blink of an eye prompted pervasive unease in their minds. Although I understood where their fear stemmed from, I could not withhold myself from the rampaging internal calamity I found myself in.

I had no choice but to fully give in to the intricacies of my unwinding nature, which was providing a lifetime of performances. I needed to cut the strings to find my way out.

Only with complete immersion in the ongoing internal cataclysm would I have an honest chance of taking on the world. There was no way I would settle for anything less than that, and neither could I give up. Even without any clarity about what the future held in store, I had made up my mind to enter whatever it was that I was getting into, without holding back.

I got to spend some time with my immediate family before leaving for Ladakh, but it was merely a break from facing the turmoil of darkness within me.

That darkness had started spreading its roots in me when I was part of many shamanic ceremonies in the depths of the Amazon

Jungle. With time, it brought out more fears and insecurities about the future, as well as grievances about my past and present close personal relationships.

In the company of my parents, I rested my mind from wallowing in the depths induced by my unhinged darkness and took a slight breather from battling the unexpected challenges that the world was throwing at me. For the time being, there was no more shedding at the boundaries of my torn layers and no looking past my buried grave to bring about a transformed version of myself.

That's a version of yourself you are not aware of – or even know the existence of – until you get a taste of it, and when you do, your whole world changes like never before. You're driven to seek more from life than its usual charade, which keeps you from finding out why you took birth on this land in the body of a conscious human being.

---

On my heat packed days of roaming around the dusty streets of Leh, I always wore a red baseball cap over my long, thickened hair and a brown silken shawl sliding around the back of my neck to complement the hat. The shawl was always slipping down the front of my body. I would then grab it, prompting mild pressure on the back of my neck.

In the evenings, I would loosen the hat and use the shawl to cover my body. I did not want to shiver from the sudden temperature drop triggered by the sun's drowning below the high-altitude desert or from the mountain breezes striking numbness into the night.

A loose t-shirt and a stained pajama on my body were enough clothing to make my days go by without having to worry about what I would wear the following day.

Lost in a desert at an altitude of over 11,000 ft (3,350 m), I was present among the rawness of nature by myself.

Hiding in the daylight, I would find shade in the silence that rested in the vast space surrounded by the immense number of mighty, color-altering mountains. And in the night, I found light beneath the infinite number of glowing stars, which greeted my eyes in seclusion and nurtured an expansive moment of unanimity through my veins.

Before I found myself a temporary home for my stay in Ladakh, I spent ten days in complete silence in a small, unfinished meditation center located at a tiny village, Saboo, near Leh.

I'd only just arrived in Ladakh and went there before getting any idea of the land. It was primarily set up for people to practice Vipassana, a widespread meditation practice from the Buddhist tradition. It empowers a person to see things as they are in the present moment.

I had been constantly moving for many months and meeting tons of people every day. Being able to sit in silence at one place for innumerable hours each day without any external distractions helped mellow my mind's busyness. My mind could then submerge into the depths of its vitality and indulge itself without any external stimulus.

Ten days seems quite trivial in the so-called "real world." However, when you are by yourself in the remoteness of nature with no technology at your disposal and no human distractions surrounding you, you can reckon on an interminable storm bursting in your mind. Uncontrolled and untouched, this storm overpowers you by demonstrating its dominance over you.

While you are busy thinking you are in control, the truth of the matter is that you are only living an illusion of being in control. Your ability to interact with the material world and generate wealth for yourself may seem like the appropriate measure of your grasp of yourself and everything else in your life. However, that is the biggest illusion we've created for ourselves in this world.

This illusion makes us distance ourselves from ourselves and lose touch with that curious childlike spirit, which bubbles in all of us but dies down when we give in to the grandiosity of adult life, bound by life's seemingly significant but irrelevant complexities.

The meditation center, consisting of a small meditation hall, two dormitory wings, and a dining hall, was situated on a flat, Mars-like surface, with nothing around it for many miles. There were two bathrooms in each wing. Segregated *Ladakhi* toilets – the composting toilets that local *Ladakhis* have been using for centuries – were up the hill above the dormitories.

The center was not linked to the outside world by water pipelines, so we received water every few days by a delivery tanker. There were solar heaters outside the dormitory wings to fill a bucket of hot water every once in a while. It was basic, and much of the center was not fully constructed.

I can not imagine how difficult it would be to survive in Ladakh during winters. Numerous mountains were located around, but they seemed too far away for my body to get a hold of them, and only consented to my eyes receiving their grace in which they humbly and unshakably stood in the ground.

After a wild ride in Peru, I found that the many days of complete silence in this isolated Ladhakhi spot triggered deep introspection.

Everything I had done in my past took over my mind in a manner I had not experienced before. I was forced to face my fears. They sprang to the surface in an overwhelming arc of visuals that induced sensations throughout my body. They made me question my attachment to all of life's sensory pleasures.

Vivid images of my past experiences, be it women, food, alcohol or chemical drugs – basically anything that made my mind and body feel good in the short term – kept me connected to my senses and dictated my mind to work with them.

Images of my past experiences and lust for indulging in life's sensory pleasures played in my head, regenerating the essence of the human emotions that had been aroused within me the multiple times I had indulged in those pleasures to make myself feel good.

The feelings initiated by our actions govern our whole lives. Knowingly or unknowingly, those feelings control us. We spend our time trying to move away from feeling awful to feeling elated. It doesn't matter who the person is – even if it is the President of the United States – no one is an exception to this. Feelings govern our actions our whole life.

In silence, exiled in a desert in the far-fetched Himalayas, I wrestled with an obnoxious dilemma. I was trying to detach myself from these past experiences, and additionally, trying to understand how I would become more relieved and joyful in life if my inner world became independent of the external world.

I saw that by standing free from being driven by this world's externalities, I would not give anyone other than myself the privilege of reacting to any situation or circumstance. This would initiate the birth of inner freedom during every external expression.

———∞———

Days seemed like years, and hours seemed like days while I navigated past the human clock to revolt against my mind's wishes, and let the silence take over and welcome the darkness flooded by my waterless tears.

All those days of sitting in solitude brought a sense of immersion in myself. I was compelled to take a good look in an imaginary mirror at the stranger standing before it. He had buried a lot of his past and had withheld from projecting a false future. He was learning to break away from the vicious cycle of entrapment by past and future atrocities so he could focus on the present.

Moment to moment is what my life became as I prepared to end my silent days and make my way back to the entrancing, dream-like district of Leh.

I shed many concealed layers of misery. With minimal food supporting me through those days, my body lost a lot of its muscular strength, and was symbolic of the loss of my old internal heaviness. With no external voices demanding my mind's attention, I was gripped only by my unfiltered voice.

Hearing myself speak after ten days of complete silence left me awestruck. I felt great unfamiliarity in recognizing my vocal cords. I could now communicate with others around me and express in words the enthralling, natural beauty of the primordial land enfolding us.

My attempt to capture the surrounding magnificent land in a few words did not do it justice; however, it did provide some restoration. My mind could take in the beauty consuming it while unreservedly appreciating Ladakh for providing my eccentric idyl.

## A. Rulers of the Human World

I sat in the front seat of the old van, which had come to pick me up along with some others from the ten-day silent meditation course.

We were heading back to Leh and humoring one another with a fruitful dialogue after not having spoken for those days. Nationals from Switzerland, the U.S.A., and India were with me. We drove through Saboo's empty streets toward Leh, and the cars grew in number as we got nearer to human civilization.

It was a civilization changing as western influences had overtaken the younger generation's minds, forcing them to move away from Ladhakh's previous, agrarian society toward a more capitalist one. Once joyful communities of *Ladakhi* people who did not understand the difference between rich and poor were now drained by the consumerism mindset and the influx of advertising.

They were persuaded to think of themselves as poor for not owning a bigger house, not wearing the latest fashionable clothes, not riding the best motorcycle in town, or not boasting a white-enough skin. From childhood onward in India, one sees advertisements about different brands defining beauty based on skin color. As a result, we think that pale skin "obviously" makes a person better looking than darker skin.

In other parts of India, especially in major cities like Mumbai, Delhi, Bangalore, or Chennai, the change from natural to artificial living has already occurred; people are blindly following in the western world's footsteps. People there are living lives more distanced from the reality of existence and closer to ones based on the illusion of a structural framework.

These major Indian cities have already become living cages where people are welded into the fabric of a broken system that has historically produced wealth by the exploitation of people, land, and natural resources.

Our desire to own and rule over more has led to a willingness to infinitely expand our economies at whatever finite expense is required; the world's systems are a time bomb waiting to explode. Ladakh was now being brought into this equation. The change was not as visible there as it was in the macro-settings of India's big cities. Still, it could be observed in the micro-elements – an entire culture altered in a few years after humans had a taste of greed.

India's economy opened to the world in the early 1990s, allowing us to become the global economic powerhouse we currently are – almost equal to, if not bigger than, our erstwhile ruler, the United Kingdom.

And with the changing times in this globalized world, we can only comply by joining the power game and by giving in to what the current times demand, so that the new 21$^{st}$ century civilizations can be built. In the process, we have lost sight of why we were born in the first place.

Our blind strife to amass vast amounts of material wealth has allowed massive ignorance to settle within us. We have become more successful at calling ourselves futurists but struggle to own our present.

We Indians may think that we gained freedom from the British in 1947, but we have only lived an illusion of owning our liberty since then. Instead, like the rest of the world, we are ruled by the world's current largest corporations. Governments do not look after the people; they look after the interests of the few sitting at the top of the food chain.

The contemporary world's real rulers are not the leaders we are familiar with or used to seeing on television. They have hidden faces that we do not even know of.

These people somehow govern everything we do in our relative world. They use us as pawns to do what helps them further their vision of the future. And I am nobody to say whether this is right or wrong – it is merely how our external world functions today.

Every century has an empire and its rulers, as capitalism is not just about gaining capital. It is about delivering power to the hands of those who own the most capital. Because humans have changed the rules over the centuries, we now have large corporations with immaculate sums of capital as our rulers. Who is to say if that's good or bad? I guess we will find out with time, but it sure controls a whole lot of what goes on in our external world today.

Demand and supply. These two words have made our minds lose grip of reality and cave into the external influencers that continually encourage us to react and act in ways not aligned with our highest forms of functioning.

## B. The Need for Human Introspection

The van entered Leh's tapered, busy streets full of vehicles and seething with people. The month of June had just ended and ushered in the most active months of Ladakh's tourism season.

In July and August, rain takes over India's land, except the region of Ladakh, which is in the rainshadow because of its high altitude. The extensive Himalayan range secludes the land from everything, including the water-filled clouds.

So, in July and August, Leh attracts many tourists from around the world- Indians, and foreigners alike – many of the foreigners, of course, being white-skinned. They are referred to as *firangi* or *angrez* in Hindi by many Indians, words holding a similar connotation to that of *gringo*, the Spanish term used by Latin American locals to identify white westerners.

That's a response triggered by European colonization over the last several centuries. In the last century, Europeans went around the globe, intending to conquer more land to extend the reach of their empires. By asserting their dominance, based on their being a "superior race," they could enslave and exploit others and accumulate wealth for their empires.

Most Western nations let go of their colonies by the end of the 20th century and ended colonization. The British did the same and left India in 1947, just after World War II. By then, they had extracted all that they could from India, leaving it shriveled to its roots.

In many subtle ways, colonial heritage still plays a unique role in the world today. Certain privileges accrue to being a national from a European nation or other nations considered to be "highly developed," such as the United States, Australia, or Canada. These were all formed by European migrants, who were white-skinned and used their skin color to control other lands and natural resources while exploiting and killing their indigenous populations.

For the last several centuries, white Europeans left Europe to bring wealth back to their nations or to establish colonies elsewhere. At the same time, they battled with one another to maintain and extend their empires in order to own more material wealth and land and control more natural resources. These resources spurred constant economic growth while ignoring inner wellbeing.

In the process of conquest and acquisition of power, these nations ruled by white men accumulated prodigious wealth. They strengthened their economies, oblivious to the significance of the actions they took to satisfy their greed and hunger for more.

Today we refer to these nations as "highly developed." They used the wealth accumulated over centuries of colonial rule to build modern infrastructures and provide their citizens with a better quality of life by securing their physical needs and creating economic opportunities. However, we have failed to ask ourselves why we refer to these nations as "developed" and what we define as "development."

Is development just about expanding the economy and material wealth? Or should it also address the development of mind and inner being?

In just the last few centuries alone, human activity has resulted in enormous destruction in the world. It has also established economies based on the exploitation of natural resources and investment in weapons of mass destruction. Sadly, in the 21$^{st}$ century, this defines which country is the most powerful.

As a result, a constant geopolitical battle plays out between the nations considered as the most powerful because of their military capabilities. The United States, Russia, and China are the key contenders, while India, France, Japan, South Korea, United Kingdom, Turkey, and Germany do not hold back as they do not want to be left behind.

Humans have established a world based on fear and exploitation.

Is this development – or mental regression? These are the questions we need to ask ourselves.

Humans around the world are categorized according to which country they belong to. Based on their passport, they have certain privileges determined by the power of their respective country.

One of the perks of power for a "developed" country's passport is that it allows holders visa-free travel and ease of access when moving around the world. Those passport holders have fewer obstacles to worry about than people from, what is termed, "developing countries." This occurs even though Asian nations are no longer far behind their western counterparts – the 21$^{st}$ century is now referred to by many economists and world leaders as "Asia's century."

These "developing" countries are spread out across the continents of Asia, South America, and Africa. Their rulers from the west exploited them over a drawn-out period. Subsequently, residents responded to white-skinned people from the western world with an unspoken but tainted power dynamic, predominantly based on their race and nationality.

It plays out differently in various parts of the world but can be clearly seen around India. While moving around the country as a wanderer, I noted how local people's treatment of visitors changes according to their skin color and nationality.

It is something we humans respond to, without thinking about it consciously. No matter where I have been, I saw that. It started with my physical appearance; then, there were biases based on how I spoke or where I came from. Even the equations of class and caste played their silent roles. Being able to speak fluent English and having lived in the U.S. created a different perception of me in eyes of people.

In major tourist areas, the biases became more prominent because of the locals' plentiful exposure to all kinds of people. Stereotypes were formulated in their minds depending on which part of the world the visitor came from. This, of course, happens everywhere as we humans love to categorize people based on where they come from and how they look.

Even though there were significant biases based on my skin color and other factors when I was moving around India, I somehow managed to get away from them most of the time because of how indifferent I had become to how people perceived me.

I wandered on my own in my casual attire with nothing to hold me back and with no ulterior motive. My aim was to focus on immersing myself within my inner world's unintelligible chatter. I lost myself in the fleeting passing moments and postponed reacting to the conditioning of the many people I came across.

Their response was founded on many facets that contribute to the shaping of a personality. This included understanding derived from their place of birth; the values inculcated in them by their parents; the social environment and the religious identity they grew up in; their socio-economic status; the culture they adopted depending on their geography, and so on.

Being on my own after having left behind my previous identities, I didn't fall into a known category anymore. Many a times, the locals I came across were flabbergasted when I passed by their land as a rover. My usual response was: "I'm a writer, and working on my book." That was a part of the whole story, but the whole story was something even I was unsure of – I was discovering a little more of it with every new day as the plot unfolded.

I was always open and distinctive in myself and provided space for locals to feel at ease when they interacted with me. They bubbled with curiosity as to why I was alone. That was a question I heard many times, regardless of where I went in the country. "Don't you get bored by yourself?" or "What do you do for work?" or "How come you are not married?" or "What does your family think about what you are doing?" or "Why are you doing this?" or "Aren't you worried about your future?" These are just a few of the many questions I got used to hearing wherever I went and whoever I interacted with.

Untouched by all their questions, I would only respond when it seemed fit. I had already dealt with the gravity of the existential crisis that these questions had brought to my mind, and I had become quite detached from the answers that followed. No matter what I said, none of it was significant – until I was living by those words.

So, rather than focusing on the questions or the answers that followed such questions, I started summoning my whole attention to the present moment and learning to embrace life as it happened. I indulged by engrossing myself more with the ongoing, rather than the upcoming. This brought a nurturing space to my mind where I could keep harnessing the power of now.

The van dropped the four of us on Changspa Road, a busy, disrupted street leading away from the main market in Leh and extending as far as Yurthung Road. The presence of the renowned Buddhist landmark of Shanti Stupa on top of the mountain at the end of Changspa Road and parallel to Yurthung Road marked the meeting of the two roads.

A gigantic, colorful statue of Buddha was positioned on top of Shanti Stupa. Plenty of tourists were attracted to the landmark and its other features, such as an open-to-all meditation hall and a Buddhist temple – along with mesmerizing views of Leh.

We got off on Changspa Road and found ourselves in the presence of many backpackers, hikers, motorcycle riders, and other assorted groups walking around the area and chilling out in the umpteen cafés lining the whole street.

It was quite an overwhelming sight after having spent the last several days in silence in an isolated, vast land, not so far away from here.

Those who had accompanied me on the van ride dissipated into the crowds. I trailed past the many cafés with the task of finding a tranquil place to stay in – away from the clatter of Changspa Road – where I could continue living my newly adopted simple life.

—❦—

# A DYSFUNCTIONAL WORLD

Learning to brush the floor
into bringing peace through my fingers.
Moving away from sundry misconceptions,
about how we are supposed to live and be
amidst the madness entailed in being born as a human being
in today's deceptively connected but highly dysfunctional world.

~~~

# III. CHOW CHOW

**"** *HOW GUEST HOUSE," IT* said, the name engraved on a metal board hanging by a small wooden door. It was at the edge of a narrow street, extending further away from Changspa Road's busyness toward the interior of Leh, where *Ladakhi* families lived in serenity with the land.

Leh, with its growing popularity as Ladakh's tourist hub, had become a heavy construction site. Most *Ladakhi* families in Leh had built large houses to accommodate the influx of outsiders with no foresight about the destruction that wrought on their very ecologically sensitive land.

Once in a while, when I was strolling in and around Leh's district, I saw some traditional *Ladakahi* houses built using sun-dried mud-brick, stones, rammed earth, timber, and straw. Still, it was mostly square concrete buildings with flat roofs often painted white. Traditional houses could mostly be found in the old town of Leh or villages away from Leh.

Families kept many rooms in their homes for travelers who came to their land looking for solace. Renting rooms was a source of income for many locals, who depended on tourism for their continued financial security.

I had been walking on a stony, narrow alley with mud-brick walls beside me. A slender canal rolled by my feet with cold water briskly flowing through it and generating a poetic sound for my ears.

The alley was taking me away from Changspa Road. The concrete houses built beyond the walls on both sides ultimately fashioned this slender space for passers-by, which I was walking along in search of a temporary home.

That was when I saw the sign with Chow Guest House written on the outside of the old wooden door. My mind straightaway recollected a specific memory of an interaction with a traveler at the meditation center shortly before we went into complete silence.

He told me he had been staying in Chow Guest House just beforehand, and the woman who owned it was wonderful. He said she had also provided him with a discounted rate on finding out that he was going to be doing a ten-day silent course at the Vipassana Meditation Center.

Recalling that, I followed my impulse to enter the wooden doorway and found myself in the presence of two stylish white buildings designed in a box formation, contrary to traditional *Ladakhi* houses.

I was standing by the door looking at the ample space between them that was being used as a passageway. Further away in the distance was an open sitting area next to a striking garden. The garden included a small amount of vegetation and colorful flowers, whose soothing presence further enhanced the whole atmosphere.

*Quite a setup!* I thought to myself, and straightaway knew that this was where I wanted to stay. I started wandering around, looking for the woman I had been told about. Ladakh was a melting pot for travelers, who like me, came to lose themselves in the wondrous, spacious beauty of the land.

It was afternoon time, so the sun was shining at its zenith, and being at such a high altitude, I could feel its harmful rays on my skin as usual, much more than if I had been stranded at sea level.

I couldn't find the woman anywhere, but a short guy with dark skin came to address my curiosity. His features and skin color were a clear indicator that he wasn't a native from Ladakh, so as he came closer to me, I asked him in Hindi, *"Tum yaha kaam karte ho?"*[3] He had a confused look on his face.

---

3    Some short dialogues are written in Hindi, the language they were originally spoken in, to maintain a sense of authenticity.

With big round eyes, he asked me in a *Bihari*[4] accent, *"Haan, aapko room chahiye?"*

I replied, "Yes," and when I asked where the aunty was, he told me she was inside the house.

I asked him while pointing my index finger toward the rectangular white building to my left, "Is that the house?" He replied with a wobble of his neck, indicating a confused *yes*.

"Can you call the aunty, please? And tell her somebody is here to see her."

He stood there for a second, still looking confused, and then walked away toward the house, looking inside the sizable, spotless windows enclosed between thick, wooden frames. They overlooked the garden and the far-reaching mountain range at a distance.

Later, I realized this man, whose name is Umesh, was generally confused.

He waved through the windows to call somebody, and soon enough, I saw a tiny *Ladakhi* woman walking in my direction carrying a bright young smile. Her grey eyes were filled with joy and the sparkle of life. Her face, wrinkled though it was, reflected a sense of childishness. Her hazy, white hair was tightly tied on the back of her head, and her face reminded me of the Andean people from Peru.

She wore the traditionally crafted, simple Indian attire of *Salwar Kameez*, an outfit commonly worn by women around North India. Its trousers are loose and cover the legs. The cloth for the upper body, referred to as a *Kameez,* is generally adrift and cascades down to the knees.

She was not wearing the traditional outfit worn by *Ladakhi* women, who mostly wear a robe-like attire, a *Kuntop*, the weight of which is more suited to winter. As I would be told later by some locals, *Ladakhi* winters are a testing time, and mere physical survival becomes daunting.

---

4   Bihari is used among Indians to identify people who come from the state of Bihar. Their Hindi accent and pronunciation differ from people from other Hindi speaking states. Those other people can easily hear if someone is from Bihar, especially if the person has a strong Bihari accent.

She said to me in a reassuring tone of voice, "*Jullay ... Aapko room chahiye? Kitne time ke liye chahiye?*"

I responded, "*Jullay ... Jullay,*" and then continued. "I just got back from a ten-day silent Vipassana course at Saboo and will be staying here for a while. Can I get your cheapest room?" As soon as she heard that I had just come back from the ten-day silent retreat, her eyes emitted more sparkle than before.

*Jullay* is the only word that most *Ladakhi* visitors pick up and quite frequently use when interacting with the locals. Saying *jullay* along with a slight bow of your neck and with one palm held on your chest is the most fitting way of greeting locals.

"I can give you a room for as low as Rs 300 ($4) a night, considering you just got back from the retreat." She added in a lower tone of voice, "Just don't tell any other guests about that rate." I smiled amiably and thanked her for the kind gesture.

She then asked me, "How was it?"

"Very intense and powerful, but so worth it. I most definitely got a lot out of it," I replied.

She said to me, "*Acha hai na bohat?*" and continued, "It's good that you have already started at a young age ... by the time you reach my age, it's difficult to get all the trash out of your mind."

"It's difficult already," I said to her, "because our whole lives we've been filling our minds with rubbish and unnecessary crap."

"That's very true," she agreed. "I'm glad to hear that you already understand this. Let me show you the room."

I followed her tiny figure into the other building, which stood across from the main house. This one was purposely set up as a guesthouse with about eight rooms.

She took me to the first floor after slipping past several rooms on the ground floor and climbing the narrow, wooden, ladder-like steps. The room was just next to the stairs. She opened its door to show me the small interior, with a single bed and a square window that exhibited a view of the neighbor's charming farm. There was nothing else in the room; it was a tiny rectangular box with no attached bathroom.

Some of the other rooms came with an ensuite, but they were more expensive.

"There's a common bathroom at the end of the passageway. You can use that." Then she added, "a room downstairs will open up in a few days once the guest who is there leaves. I can move you there afterward. It's a little bigger than this one, so it has a bit more space."

"That sounds perfect. All I need is a room and a bed, and I'll be happy. Nothing fancy is required," I replied.

She agreed with a tender smile on her face, and just like that, I had found a home for myself while also making a connection with an exquisite *Ladakhi* woman. *Aunty*, she became to me.

Never during my long stretch at that place would I know her first name. To me, she was just *Aunty*, a term that instantly turns strangers into family members in India. Indians commonly refer to strangers as *aunty* and *uncle*. So, she became *Aunty* and her husband – *Uncle* – while I stayed with them.

Her beautiful presence and divine eyes were assurance enough for me to ground myself at a simple place for a while. There I could focus my resources and keep feeding a once-diminished fire. It had only been reignited in the recent past, as I let myself break apart into tiny particles of unanimity and relinquish the many slavish beliefs I had initially stood for.

That old belief system was not built on the truth of my existence but on the muddle of conflicting ideas systematically installed in our minds during our lives. It is a system that only makes our present moments more deceptive than ever.

## A. A Day in the Life of Leh

I stayed in Aunty's guesthouse for the whole month of July and the beginning weeks of August. Every day was an imitation of the others. I followed the simple routine of waking up early in the morning to meditate and then attended a group yoga practice led by a yogi named Mike, originally from Germany who had been visiting Ladakh for almost two decades.

The 1990s was a time when sizable numbers of western explorers came to Ladakh. It was challenging to reach Ladakh then because of its isolation. Only the very adventurous could dare to get there.

That must have been an exciting time for westerners, following the roaring wave that started in the 1960s when people from the west began traveling across Asia looking for meaning in life.

We refer to them by the familiar word of hippies, which represents the kind of free-flowing lifestyle these people adopted to, after getting struck down by the brutalities of greed struck capitalism with its heavily integrated, materialistic mentality. Those original hippies broke away from the standard life path that had been shoved down their throats by the benefactors of a superficial, wealth-creating system skewed toward benefitting those at the top. The striking of an internal chord made them recognize that something was missing, something that neither money nor anyone else, for that matter, could furnish them with.

They found themselves traversing Asia and other parts of the world where they were far removed from that uni-dimensional thought process, even though it enabled people in the western world to procure a comfortable life for themselves.

Seeking joy, meaning, peace, and purpose in life, those hippies went on the adventure of a lifetime. They didn't know then that by advocating a lifestyle inspired by ancient Eastern values, emphasizing the need to focus on inner wellbeing rather than solely growing material wealth, they were setting off a torrent for many in the future.

An inner fountain of joy is the key for humans to be living balanced lives for their brief existence on this planet.

Even though Ladakh is in a very remote part of India, it still managed to attract many western travelers back in the day. It offered a dateless, secluded location with a culture that was unique to India. It held on to its Buddhist roots, which were a source of fascination for many. Because of its strategic position on the map, close to China-occupied Tibet and Central Asia, Ladakh possessed a manuscript full of appealing history chapters about what had ensued there in the preceding centuries.

It must have thoroughly lived up to its image of being an isolated desert back then.

Individuals such as Mike, who first arrived in Ladakh in the 90s, started building their lives around practicing and teaching yoga to other westerners, who traveled to Asia seeking answers that they could not find in the west.

Mike was a whimsical yogi, who conducted his classes in English with a funny German accent that we chuckled about, while practicing with him. He had traveled around India for several decades, learning and practicing yoga from a range of Indian yogis before he began teaching yoga around the world. His classes were no less than any intense physical workout routine that I had done in the past. Being at such a high altitude, doing countless Sun Salutations before getting into the rounds of the elongation poses, tested the bodies and minds in his classes.

The yoga took place in a spacious meditation hall at the edge of Changspa Road that Mike rented from the owners of a very commercially active organization, utilizing spiritual tourism as a good source for generating income.

Following that extensive yoga session, I would then make my way back to Aunty's guesthouse after a quick stopover at one of the many cafés hovering around Changspa Road for a simple meal. I usually had a *thali* (a round platter serving a combination of Indian dishes), which generally consisted of a *dal* (a dish made with lentils), some rice, two pieces of *roti* (a round flatbread made from wheat), and a *sabji* (cooked vegetables with specific Indian spices). The *thali* counter-balanced the extensive yoga session with Mike. My body was always rejuvenated and refurbished for the remainder of the day.

By the time I returned to the guesthouse, I would see Aunty working in her garden while wearing a huge round hat to protect her skin from the sun's severity. Many *Ladakhis*, especially those who worked in the open fields, had deeply wrinkled skin because of the strength of the sun's rays at that high altitude. Some locals, in their 40s, looked like they were in their 70s because of how the sun's UV rays along with Ladakh's dry air aged their skin.

Aunty's husband, Uncle, was the most genial man I have ever come across. He would usually be sitting outside their main house, reading something, or doing some household chores. He always ferried the happiest smile on his face, and together they were the cutest pair a visitor could ask for as hosts.

After a quick bath using a bucket filled with frigid cold water to awaken all my cells, followed by a rapid change of clothes, I headed out the house's front metallic gate, across from the tiny wooden door past the garden area. I was on my way toward the main market area of Leh.

Like most other houses in Leh, this guesthouse was also equipped with a rooftop solar heater that provided hot water for guests. But I fancied my cold bucket baths, which triggered sudden activation in my body.

I avoided the organized chaos whipped up by the coalition of traffic and all kinds of people, including beggars and street sellers, a well as animals, such as cows and dogs, and any other possible calamity brewing in the inescapable chaos in every part of Leh. I had found a combination of internal, meandering routes away from Changspa and Zangsti Roads. They all led me to Leh's main market.

If you are walking towards the central part of Leh, you will reach Zangsti Road after wandering through Changspa Road. Zangsti Road formed a curvaceous junction of sorts with two options.

One direction led toward Old Fort Road and the Leh Market, built on an added street called the Main Bazaar Road that led upward at a right angle away from Old Fort Road. Only pedestrians are permitted through Main Bazaar Road, which takes them away from the traffic into a broad pebbled footpath with buildings on both sides.

The main market of Leh had been renovated not so long ago. Right away, pedestrians were thrown into the tide of modernization heaving its way through Ladakh.

The market followed its course along Main Bazaar Road, which is built in an L-shape to encourage the union of people, traders, food outlets, clothing, and jewelry shops – among other amusements – spread right throughout. Leh's main market is a bustling jumble in an appealing space, impregnated with the imaginable and unimaginable.

The market further uplifted its inhabitants with views of Leh Palace, a historical sound-proofed fortress firmly positioned up in the mountains above the main market where it could extend its dominance over the vast spreading land. A troop of mountains encircles Leh Palace with the old town of Leh and a multitude of traditional *Ladakhi* houses settled beneath. A reasonably obvious distinction exists between the old and new towns of Leh for the eyes of enamored beholders.

It offers an amalgamation of the modern and the archaic.

The pathway to the Old Town of Leh and Leh Palace is on an extra extension away from Main Bazaar Road, heading upward toward the mountain. The vast, ancient Palace stands at a distant height, and further up from the Palace, a small Buddhist temple stands on top of the mountain.

That Buddhist temple, with its serene atmosphere and elevated position delivering a resplendent view, was to become my treasured spot in Leh. I could look at the entire district of Leh and some nearby villages from it. The landmark of Shanti Stupa was visible from the top of the temple, too, along with the quintessential, animated mountains surrounding the interstellar, boundless space.

The other direction on Zangsti Road past the curvaceous junction led downward to Fort Road, diverted traffic away from Leh's main market toward the southern end of the town.

Through the inner ways, my route passed through empty areas and narrow alleyways, with mud-brick walls separating traditional but mostly newly established, *Ladakhi* houses, guesthouses mostly.

My mindless stroll through the inner routes would ultimately bring me to the beginning of Upper Tukcha Road, where it joined with Zangsti Road and was closer to the curved intersection. There, I would decide if I wanted to go toward the main bazaar or away from it toward the southern side of Leh.

The Original Ladakh Café rests at the curving intersection, where Zangsti Road diverged in two directions. This place operated as my anchor during my whole stay in Leh. I spent many afternoons writing, or reading there, or mingling with miscellaneous individuals who took a break at that café to simmer down in the heat brought upon them by the sun god.

I had come across that café at the beginning of my time in Leh, just before I was about to leave for the meditation center in Saboo Village to be sent by eternity into the outer world's silence.

It was a hard place for human eyes to miss, that café, because of its location. People had to pass that intersection many times a day while getting around Leh. Because of its convenient position, many travel agents operate there – including Tashi, a Tibetan refugee, whose travel agency was an extension of the Original Ladakh Café.

Ladakh hosts many Tibetan settlements, one of them near Leh. Tibetans had been escaping from Tibet since the Chinese government began clamping their grip on Tibet while robbing Tibetans of their fundamental rights and freedom to practice their desired faith.

Each – the travel agency and the café – complements the other by offering travelers everything they desired at one spot. They could make their travel bookings for getting around Ladakh at Tashi's place and then sit back and take a breather afterward at the café, which offered refreshments for simmering down in the heat.

The café is run by two young *Ladakhi* men, Tani and Rigzen, and even though it is a compact setup next to Leh's busiest streets, I somehow found it a perfect outlet for me to frequent.

Maybe it had something to do with the courteous *Ladakhi* men who run the place, or the fascinating characters I met there, or how it had become a space for many artists to work in. Whatever the reason, I ended up spending a lot of my afternoons in that café during my stay in Leh.

There are two entrance points to that tiny triangular setup. One entry is right at the curved intersection next to Tashi's Travel Agency. The other from a slender road that goes down toward the southern part of Leh. Even though it is a tiny café, its interior comprised two floors, with both entrances curving up to both levels via a few timber steps.

With limited seating available to accommodate passersby in such a compact space, a conversation could be easily carried out between people sitting at its farthest ends, thereby allowing the space to have a cozy and intimate setting for all participants.

Somehow, I always managed to find such places for my disposal. I would spend hours of my time enlarging my internal world to create something out of pure expression. I was also drawn by a few characters who always left a permanent imprint on my being.

Just before I left to immerse myself in the ten days of silence in Saboo, I had stopped there and briefly met the two people who would come into my life again during my stay in Ladakh. Something or the other would bring us together to deepen our pure bond with each other.

## B. The Monk's Way?

When I vanished into silence in Saboo and dealt with the storm tearing my being apart, I considered renouncing everything in my life to go down the monk's path.

I had a profound realization relating to my existence. Whatever I had thought I was doing earlier in my life about "driving change in the world," or "making a difference of some sort," or "building something out of myself" was nothing more than the fermentation of my ego.

The need to have a female companion to serve my physical or emotional needs seemed trivial. Every single aspect of my interaction with the material world became inconsequential. I drifted apart in a figment of my imagination and visualized a life that would require me to become a renunciate by taking the monk's vows.

Alongside cutting the strings with the superficial, material aspects of life, I would also have to do the same with my family and friends, which seemed possible enough in that moment of complete detachment from the world. Still, the thought of my parent's pain on knowing that their only son had become a monk was something I found difficult to put aside.

I was born in a culture where the term "monk" was not unfamiliar. Many revered it because of the implications ascribed to somebody renouncing everything and living a meticulous life. However, it would not be easy for any parent in the world, no matter which culture they were from, to accept their child going down that path.

That would especially be the case in a family surrounded by peers, where striving for financial security and creating wealth seems to be the most critical aspect of personal life. Breaking away from all of that required that I be in a very distant place within myself. It would also beget an unexpected turn of events for my family and friends to deal with. It was something they had probably never thought they would have to deal with, given that their expectations for their children were very much in congruence with the standard Indian mindset. Every Indian parent's goal is for their children to get a good education, do well in business or any other high-profile job, earn a reasonable sum of money, get married, have children, and continue living.

Anything other than this life-pattern is unfamiliar for modern-day humans.

It brings them to a place of uncertainty where they don't know how to react. They can't understand the reasons for someone pursuing a life outside our civilization's typical framework.

It is just this enslaving framework that may have caused our species to lose sight of the simple reasons why we took birth on this land in the first place.

Seeing the events of my past unfold until that moment, no one – including myself – would ever have imagined that I, of all people, would seriously consider the path of a renunciate at some point in my life.

It felt like an assured thing to do as monkhood continued to resonate more within myself. The silence amplifying through my veins only prompted me to distance myself from the world's human-made complexities and move toward the simpler ideal of what appears to be a true reflection of our selves.

I could feel a roar in my chest that caused me to go through this analysis genuinely. Was I being called so that I could become a monk on my return to India?

Family, friends, lovers, work, wealth, travel – none of it could hold the intensity fluctuating through every corner of my body in those ten days and making me go through the possibility of renouncing the last little bit that I could.

I had already given up the idea of living what we consider a "normal life" even before arriving in India. Not much attached me to the "default world" other than the people in my life. Cutting my strings with them was the only thing holding me back from becoming a monk.

I had previously let go of the false story that had been braided into my head by the limited unfolding of reality we get accustomed to, growing up in our little bubbles. We think that is all there is to life. We are not aware that what we understand about the world is as limited as our one-dimensional take on our entire continuation.

# IV. THE ISRAELI CONNECTION – SHALOM

"*HOW ARE YOU?" SHE* asked. We hear this phrase all the time from strangers. But this time, it came floating in my direction with a hint of genuine curiosity and an Israeli accent. The words were spurred by a gentle separation of red lips dreaming on a surprisingly smooth face.

A few weeks into my rambles around Ladakh, I realized how India's travel scene was strikingly dominated by Israelis. They were, by far, one of the largest groups of foreign nationals visiting India.

The primary reason was that Israel had a big traveling culture, especially for young Israelis. After their mandatory military service – which both Israeli men and women are obliged to complete – they traveled to either South America or Asia in large numbers for a lengthy period of time. India is one of their prime Asian destinations.

I came across many Israelis while traveling through India. It helped me gain insight into the unique culture and the complicated political dynamics of Israel and form profound bonds with some Israeli travelers.

Her face was radiating in conjunction with the rays of the sun filtering through the striking rectangular glass windows, loosely attached to the narrow door with decayed nails on the lower floor of the Original Ladakh Café.

A pair of earthy, brownish-green eyes kept looking into my large, brown eyes, silently waiting for me to respond to her question.

"I'm good," I said, "and what about you?"

"I'm good as well," she replied with a much more noticeable Israeli accent. "My name is Shira, and this is Dan," she said, pointing her finger toward the man seated next to her on the long wooden bench.

Behind their backs was the ordering counter with its closet-like kitchen, Tani and Rigzen's esteemed domain.

Dan, the Israeli fella sitting next to Shira, had a thick, long beard dangling down his face. It almost kissed the top of his chest and hid most of his face, but his sparkling eyes took more of my attention than any other part of his face.

He stayed silent while Shira continued with her curious questioning about the "whats" and "whys." It was a quick stopover for me at the café before I went to the meditation center in Saboo. Our encounter was brief but filled with a sense of deep familiarity as if it had been a reunion between old friends.

As I was setting foot outside the café door, I told them, "I think I'll be back here after ten days. Not sure, though ... let's see what happens." I was not thinking ahead, as I knew there was already a lot that my mind had to process before making any decisions; I was allowing my mind space to simply be.

Shira said to me as I was heading out the door, "Maybe we'll see you when you come back. Who knows where we'll be then!"

I replied, "Yes. Hopefully, I'll see you again!"

———

The days after this encounter with Shira and Dan, I was fading away in a turmoil of rage. Everything I had been holding back for the last few weeks since my return to India from Peru came thundering to the surface, making me go through all aspects of human emotion in a blistering sensory torrent.

It encouraged my whole being to form a faithful alliance with the deep-seated, reassuring voice within me. It was the only thing I could still trust, as no other aspect of the world seemed to hold onto my craters of swelling darkness, which time and again encompassed my mind and carted it off to a place where return seemed implausible.

That place, existing far away from my mind's conceivable limits, had no name or appearance reverberating with what my external eyes saw. It was formless, knew no boundaries, and provided no scope for my human mind to project it onto an external object. Consequently, my mind felt shattered as it had no purpose or direction to live for – it had been left jobless in a job-seeking world.

The space-less space evolved, so my mind was further removed from the alone-ness of my visceral self and forced to dismantle itself from the entrapping delusions of its self-construed images of reality.

Being introduced to this darkened space initially left me flabbergasted by its cruelty, as nothing seemed to matter anymore because my mind could not comprehend anything. Then with time, I learned to move past my mind's apprehensions. I allowed the darkness to sink in and let my mind become familiar with that space where nothing ceases to exist – where existence has no significance whatsoever.

All my mind knew then was nothingness. The possibility of uncovering the mysteries surrounding our honest transformation arises from knowing that.

Transformation is a loose term, which has been overused plenty of times to describe the change within us. With no precise quantitative means to measure such internal change, our understanding of it is still quite limited.

Skeptics who need proof are too restricted in their minds. The ones who think they know all about it easily fall into the trap of arrogance and ego and start preaching their techniques and methods to reap the benefits from those looking for a quick fix to their problems.

And so begins the enchainment in which our own limitations consume all of us, though we confuse it with transformation because we arrogantly think we know it all. This confusion is validated by our modern, human systems, as they only function for business transactions, in which everything you provide to others takes the form of a product or a service. Only then is there said to be a "value" in the economy – one which can be maneuvered and make cash flow in society.

And when the cash flows at a phenomenal rate, as we generate more and more of this "value," we feel like we are the gods of the system and doing something worthy in life. The system validates us and decrees with approval that we have finally made something of ourselves.

We further magnify our arrogance and illusion by bundling that sense of validation and approval into a self-image while thinking it applies to everything we do. Doing this makes us project an inflated image of ourselves, which further serves our pride and distances ourselves from embracing the unknown path that demands we give it all away. Only then are we aided in seeing things clearly with a broadened perspective.

This picture's clarity, invisible to the corrupted human eye, can start the transformation we all seek, either consciously or subconsciously.

## A. Understanding Not Governed by Externalities

When I arrived back in Leh after being engulfed by the emptiness of the desert, I had forgotten about my brief encounter with Dan and Shira.

I followed a simple routine of a low-key life so I could build on the work I had put in over those ten silent days and the many prior months in Peru.

The sublimity of the thought convincing me in my days of silence that my path ahead was as a monk de-escalated by the time I ended my silence. I was left with a clear realization that being a monk did not matter as much as being internally free at all times regardless of the external world.

I started to embrace an unconditional state of being and to nurture a mindset in which I could continue engulfing myself in the joyfulness of an extraordinary life, impartial to what was bred into me based on where I was born.

I did not fall into the trap of germinating my ego by dressing a certain way or by turning into a specific religious identity. India already had a large market for the many self-proclaimed gurus and political leaders who were busy deceiving people while furthering their selfish agendas.

I did not want to play that game – or be part of it. I just wanted to keep on living freely by experiencing the rawness of our creation.

Dogmatism based on religion is difficult to avoid in India, particularly if you are an Indian wanting to go down the seeker's path. You are bound to come across countless preachers who are busy preaching how to live and who to pray to. Those very same people fail to acknowledge the beauty and power of the moment with us now, where the answers to our questions truly rest. These are answers that no external object – be it a large statue of an esteemed god or a revered ancient text – can provide.

Dogmatism isn't about spreading knowledge; it's about a blind set of "how-tos" based on a specific ideology, where everybody tries maneuvering the market to convert the masses into believing what they want them to believe. That way, the masses can be controlled as desired, so they do what is required ... as and when needed.

People are being drenched in disempowerment in the name of God, religion, and belief systems. It was explicitly clear that I was not to fall into that trap and was to stay away from all forms of institutionalized religious propaganda. They only turn us apart from the actual path of truth.

## B. When the Days Go By

The current in my body fired along with Ladakh's stormy winds for the whole of July.

I visited some stunning sites, such as Pangong Lake, Nubra Valley, and Tsomoriri Lake, before practicing the virtues of my sensitively designed, simple life in Leh. It was easy to find other travelers going to these spots. All I had to do was tag along with them in shared car rides while we drove through many well-known, high altitude passes, such as Khardungla, Changla, Bara-lacha, and Tanglang la. The elevation of Khardungla was the highest of them all in Ladakh at about 17,500 ft (5,360 m).

The drive to these principal attractions took in the most outrageous mountain ranges and breathtaking views I had ever laid my eyes on in my life. The beauty of these spectacular and grand sites was unquestionably out of this world. Historic monasteries and unseen nature hypnotized my eyes.

My time in Ladakh wasn't defined by trips to these prime tourist sites but by the day-to-day changes that I noticed within myself while I was learning to breathe through my new, simple life.

Remaining hidden to the eyes of the people, I continued to breathe. Wearing standardized clothing, which was considered normal by the people around me, allowed me to be unnoticed among the crowd's busyness.

I could get lost amongst the madness, and no one would notice.

Although my days were based on a set routine, there was always a sense of spontaneity attached to everything I did. From early in the day after I concluded my yoga practice with Mike, a day full of brimming possibilities would alter its shape organically.

I would leave the gates of Aunty's house to begin each new day with the sun transmitting its verve on all the life shooting around the simplicity of that endless desert.

I would meet strangers from all walks of life throughout my days in Leh – Ladakhis, Indians from other states, and foreigners of varying nationalities. Perceptions in the minds of people based on my external appearance would alter. Some locals thought I was a foreigner. Some foreigners thought I was a jobless Indian seeking money from them. Some thought of me as a yogi. Some as a traveler.

People interacted with me, perceiving what they wanted to perceive, believing what they wanted to believe. I neither corrected nor wronged anybody but played along with the characters I was regularly seen as.

Wandering through my usual array of concealed routes thru Leh, I would make my way toward the main town only to take a breather at the Original Ladakh Café and get on with some writing for the day. While writing for hours, many people would enter and leave the squashed café. I would converse with some as I pleased, talking about life, Buddhism, traveling, India, politics, relationships, art, business, philosophy, spirituality, love, etc.

The point of a discussion did not matter as much as its integrity, as we could forgo putting up our superficial guards and connect on a human scale without expecting anything in return from each other. In a fleeting moment, we shared the causality that brought us together in a particular time and place.

I didn't indulge in any conversation just for the sake of it. I only found myself in one when the person who stood in front of me stood there for the same reason as I did. I was open and honest about who I was, without trying to impress anyone but simply wanting to enlarge my authentic self while learning from those who came by to share their wisdom and legion of stories.

---

It was just another afternoon in Leh, and I'd come back to the Original Ladakh Café after hiking up to the small Buddhist temple on top of the mountain above Leh Palace. I used to sit in silence on the narrow verandah behind the temple, which had a timeworn statue of Buddha resting inside.

I could see far into the horizon from there – the whole of Leh along with some nearby villages and the diverging mountain ranges. Barely anybody came to that spot, so it was a perfect hideout on top of Leh.

I could let my eyes drop into the spaciousness of the land and let my mind expand with the enormity flourishing in the limitless sky.

After trekking back down back from the *Gompa*[5], I would usually stop for a cup of mint tea at a traditional *Ladakhi* house in the old town that had been renovated into a café and was run by an adorable *Ladakhi* family. It was adorned with the title, Lala's Café.

Entering inside its slim wooden door carried me back in time right away, with its narrow stairs leading me to a darkened floor, a compact space, and limited seating options.

A small ordering counter was on the right side, where usually a young *Ladakhi* woman stood to say *"Jullay,"* as soon as you ceased climbing the stairs. A much narrower, tiny wooden ladder to the roof, hooked to the left away from the ordering counter. Climbing that ladder, leaning forward and with a lowered neck, I finally stepped onto the brightened roof for some respite.

Most traditional houses and ancient architecture in Ladakh are designed for the dimensions of *Ladakhis*, who usually have small bodies.

The roof of Lala's Café is what everybody goes there for, as it grabbed a picturesque view of the old town of Leh.

In a secluded corner, part of the roof is covered by a shed to provide daytime shade. A long wooden table is fixed under it with benches

---

5   A *Gompa* is what locals called all Buddhist sites, including monasteries and small temples.

to balance on. The benches and the table are quite dwarfish in their dimensions. They made me feel smaller and made the view even more overwhelming.

I usually sat in the shed drinking a mint tea while simply gazing far away into the horizon. It was designed for observers to attend to the length and breadth of Leh.

Lala's Café always had a bunch of young *Ladakhi* men seated in that secluded corner. Most of them would be smoking *charas*[6] and playing card games. They would timidly smile at me as I sat in the corner across from them engulfed in my private world – reading a book, writing, or simply observing everything while sipping my cup of mint tea.

Following a reclusive time at Lala's, I would then make my way around the market or head directly to the Original Ladakh Café, where Tani and Rigzen would be running their usual daily chores. At some point, they got so used to having me there that they would leave the café under my supervision and go shopping for ingredients. Amusingly, frequent visitors to the café started assuming that I was partly running the place.

It had become a very intimate space for me, where I wrote extensively about my travels in Peru.

Other outsiders spent extended time there too: Dan and Shira, Dan more than Shira, as Shira traveled around other parts of Ladakh quite frequently, but she always regrouped at the café to make her next plan.

Dan was more like me in that we both rejoiced in our simple routines in Leh and didn't worry at all about where we wanted to go next. We made no plans but merely lived day by day immersed in whatever was happening around us.

As I wandered through Leh's spirited market toward my home base, the Original Ladakh Café, most of that day had already gone by in accommodating the various indeterminable rituals that had somehow artlessly become a part of my life. In it, I was learning to break away from the shackles of the past, present, and future.

I enlivened my life by resonating with timelessness and without interference from anything human-made that encouraged my mind to

---

6    Charas is the hashish form of cannabis.

operate as part of a mechanized system. That would have made me the same as any machine, whose system propels us, so our bodily organs work merely to keep us alive –even though we would be far, far from being truly alive.

It saddens me at times when I observe the world's nuances and see how we've been primed to overthrow ourselves in the madness of a race; we continuously strive to become a winner because we are so afraid of being a loser.

In the external world, we spend our whole lives trying to project ourselves as a front-runner, without ever questioning: "Why are we trying to win?" or "What are we trying to win?" or "What is it that we are trying to achieve by becoming a winner?"

We know in our hearts that we are trying to hide our fears and insecurities, as we continue scrambling to establish our egos. We know too that we are giving in to a system that benefits no one in the long run. Instead, it perpetually taps into our unidentified fears and overrides our actions.

Instead of merely carrying out a task with complete surrender and devotion, we are purely concerned about its results and consequences.

Why can't we allow ourselves to experience life in its purest form in the rising of every moment without any presumed inhibitions attached to what is to come?

# V. HOW ORIGINAL

*T*HAT DAY, I ENTERED the doors of the Original Ladakh Café and saw Dan sitting at the table by the ordering counter. His back was resting on the wall, and his legs were spread out on the extended wooden bench. He was intensely gazing at the pages of a book held right in front of his eyes. His neck was quite upright. I had forgotten about him since my return to Leh as I'd been absorbed in my private world and leading a simple life.

I went and sat next to the table placed beside him, mirroring his posture. He saw me and acknowledged my presence.

Right away, I said, "How are you doing, brother? Still here, huh?"

He smiled affectionately and replied, "Good ... yes, I went around Ladakh for a few days checking out new places, and now I'm back in Leh." Then he inquired, "How was Vipassana?"

"Very intense ... you know how it is ... you've done it before, right?" I said.

He replied, "Yes ... I know what you mean ... it really takes you very deep."

"It sure does," I agreed.

I asked him about the book he was reading. The letters on the cover were in Hebrew, so I could not read them.

Dan said to me, "Let me try and translate it for you in English. It means something like 'the wise heart.' It is written by Jack Kornfield and talks about Buddhist psychology. He was one of the pioneers from the western world who first introduced such eastern concepts of spirituality into the west." After a moment, he continued. "Everything in the book is thoroughly described, and I like how he uses western ways of logical thinking to make sense of things."

I replied, "That's great! I'll have to read it at some point."

We continued our conversation as if we had known one another for a long time and shared some very deep and personal things we were both going through. He had been moving around India for over eight months already. Starting from the southern part of the country, he had traveled to the Himalayan nation of Nepal. He crossed the border into Nepal for a visa run, and then, after spending some time there, made his way back to India.

I asked him about Shira during our conversation. "So, where is your girlfriend/partner?"

He replied with a smirk on his face, "Who? Shira? Shira and I don't have anything going on. We just met a few times while traveling and decided to come to Ladakh together ... that's it."

"Ahh... " I said, and continued, "You guys looked so comfortable together; I thought you were together. Sorry about that."

He replied composedly, "That's OK... We met in the south and then randomly ran into one another again on the streets of Nepal. Both she and I had been thinking of visiting Ladakh, and somehow it just worked out."

"That's great!" I said. "So, where is she now?"

"She's gone to Nubra Valley with some other travelers ... and I decided to stay here and take it easy."

"I really know what you mean, brother ... I've been taking it easy as well. Just trying to keep it simple," I replied.

As the hours went by and we talked more, we found out that we had both recently considered taking the monk's path and renouncing everything in the world. But, then decided not to because of how we felt – that what matters is not so much about what we do externally, but how much we float internally, developing ourselves toward freedom from within, regardless of whatever appears in the external world.

The fluctuation of our words corresponding with our thoughts led to the sun almost drowning behind the remarkable mountains, which suddenly reminded me of something I had told Aunty earlier. She and I had agreed to meditate together that evening. That was one of the other undetermined matters that occasionally transpired while I stayed at her house.

Aunty was a very keen meditator and dedicated an hour every morning and evening to her practice. An isolated room had been set up by her, primarily devoted to meditation and prayer. This was quite commonly seen in most parts of India. Despite the contrary faiths that people practiced, I could always find a space in a house set aside, specifically for a sacred purpose. It worked as a sanctuary where a person could distance himself or herself from day-to-day activities for a brief period to focus on a higher cause beyond the physical self.

That was probably the original reason for such sacred spaces in homes, but it has somehow turned into a sort of a blind faith thing in this age. People have such spaces in their castle-like houses more for display – as status symbols – to their peers or for asking god to solve their problems and help them get what they desire. Primarily, this involves the goddess *Laxmi,* commonly referred to as the God of Wealth in the Hindu tradition.

Instead of this sanctified space being used for purifying the self, it has unfortunately been converted into a commercialized business transaction just like everything else. Many priests around the country prescribe millions of rituals to please the gods rather than suggesting a remedy that could initiate actual personal transformation. For this, you do not have to pray to a symbolized version of a specific god or carry out any rituals – you only need to resonate in connection with your true self.

Aunty's meditation room was on top of a tall building, attached to the main section of her house. Three blocks had been put on top of each other to construct the meditation room. The doors of each floor were accessed by climbing a fire escape-like metal staircase at the front. There was no need to go inside her house to get to this specific room, it was was thus an independent kingdom.

When the imminent sunset reminded me of what I had told Aunty earlier that day, I had to interrupt my in-depth conversation with Dan to say, "I gotta go back to my guesthouse. I told Aunty I was going to meditate with her this evening." With surprise in his eyes, Dan questioned, "Meditate with Aunty?"

I told him how she was like a pure soul and how I'd developed a deep admiration for her because of how devoted she was to her meditative practice, and how she did long silent retreats every year to keep growing within herself. I said to him, "I think she's enlightened." Surprised by that comment, even more, he said, "Really?"

"Yeah, man, I really think so. Her simplicity is what gives it away, and she doesn't know much of what's happening in the world, but her joyful presence makes me think so," I replied.

"Hmm ...." said Dan, with a deep look in his eyes, visible through the thick-framed glasses he was wearing while holding onto his chin with his left hand thoughtfully.

I asked him, "Do you want to join us?"

"Yeah? Can I?"

"Of course, she'd love it!

"Let's do it!" he answered.

We left the café together for my guesthouse on the cusp of sunset. I took Dan through the inner routes away from the main streets of Leh. By then, I had gotten very fond of those amorphous little ways, which always made it seem like I was on a treasure hunt in an Indiana Jones movie.

On the whole way back to Chow Guest House, our conversation simmered about how our lives would change if we became monks and what it was in us that had us contemplating becoming one. It was interesting talking to somebody in a similar pair of shoes mulling over complete extraction from the havoc of our primal instincts.

We arrived at Chow Guest House by concluding our walk along the widened, parched road that led straight to the metallic gate. Beyond that point, only a forced right, which curved into a much smaller street, could accommodate only foot traffic.

Further along, that smaller street was paved in a snake-like rhythmic pattern, and it led toward Changspa Road, which is where most Israeli travelers hung out.

I sometimes felt as if I had been transported to Israel in the matter of a few seconds because most people hanging around Changspa Road were Israelis – to the extent that many cafés and eateries offered menus written in Hebrew. However, the external setting remained that of Ladakh, which made a fascinating conundrum for the mind to observe.

We entered the silver-colored metallic gate only to find Aunty working in her little garden. She said to me, "*Aap aa gaye? Saath main dost bhi laye ho?*"

I replied, "*Haan*[7] Aunty. I asked him to join me as well for a meditation session with you."

She said, "*Bohat acha*," and while smiling wholeheartedly, she added, "*Chalo.*"

We waited for her to come out of her garden onto the paved pathway leading toward her house. When she stood in front of us, we followed her little figure up the metallic, blackened, fire escape-like stairs to the topmost room, which could be mistaken for a small monastery.

When I entered the tiny room, it seemed like a whole monastery had been gift-wrapped to fit inside it – various gold-plated, shiny little ornaments, an infinite number of Buddha statues in all sizes, and many photos of the Dalai Lama and other Buddhist monks were nestled inside the room.

I had been inside several times before. Sometimes to meditate with Aunty and sometimes by myself. When I first saw it, I told Aunty, "You have fitted a whole monastery in here!" She laughed about it quite joyfully and replied, "*Ho jata hai.*"

I playfully told Dan, as we were walking up those trembling stairs, that he was in for quite a treat when he sees the room.

"How so?" he asked, and I replied with amusement, "You'll see! This room is like a Buddhist museum."

And not to my surprise, his lips opened to whisper, "Wow!" as soon as we entered.

We then sat down on the floor, using a cushion to support our buttocks to get into a correct lotus posture. We meditated with Aunty for about an hour.

It was always pleasant meditating in Aunty's presence as her humility made her so purifying. She was like an enlightened being hiding in daylight as a householder, who managed the guesthouse, her own

---

7    *Haan* means "Yes."

house, her little farm, and was apparently a grandmother to many. I found that out later – and was also shocked to learn that she was a 70-year-old whose own children were as old as 50.

## A. Breaking Barriers

Aunty's involvement in society was unlike what happened in other parts of modern India, where women are still suppressed and disempowered by the restricted mindsets of men and women. Misinterpreted and misunderstood, countless old traditions and norms – and other factors – have produced a society where millions of women and girls in 21st century India are still constrained by a distinction between male and female children.

Depending on their sex, children are treated differently. They are conditioned, so they grow up with a set of ideas about how each should act and react in a society based on their sex. They don't get to grow in a society that provides all with equal opportunities.

Of course, this phenomenon applies worldwide to all countries and cultures in distinctive ways. It's quite ironic to see this divide between men and women in India, though. Many Indians consider themselves devotees of goddesses such as *Kali* and *Durga,* among the pantheon of highly empowered female goddesses. The latter splendidly showcases the strength of a mother and female embodiment's divine spirit in a human body. However, the devotees still fail to practice the essence of what these powerful incarnations represent in their daily lives.

Millions consider themselves pure devotees of highly revered Gods such as *Rama* and *Krishna* but fail to adopt the pure virtues these gods represented in the triumphant mythological stories Indian children are introduced to while growing up.

The embodiments of such godly figures are so dear to millions of Indians that you can hear many people quoting the texts and preaching the stories, even as they fail to enact the words in their real lives.

It can be confusing to witness because it makes you think that we are just a bunch of hypocrites preaching what sells, without acting on the words we so busily quote or preach.

This is not dissimilar to what happens in other parts of India. Rules and structures have been formed so the men can stay in charge and continue asserting their dominance. They steer the wheel, so it automatically puts them in a position of power and allows them to do as they please, without thinking about the consequences of their actions. Because of how imprudently men are raised, their power lets them falsely assume that they have the right to dominate women. Purely because they are men, they think they have the right to tell women what they can or cannot do, how they should live, and how they should be no more than caricatures in society!

Ladakh is an aberration to this trend. Most of its cultural and social organizations are quite equally apportioned; women's involvement in society is evident. You could even see women working as construction workers around Ladakh while glamorously displaying their traditional attire. Their involvement in decision making, ranging from household to business activities, is reasonably commonplace and perceivable by outsiders.

For instance, contrary to the common trend established around most of India, where a woman moved in with her husband's family after an arranged marriage, that is not necessarily the case in Ladakh. On some occasions, men moved in with the woman's family, and although it led to some playful teasing by their male friends, it was not seen as shameful. In other parts of India, if a man goes to live with his wife's family after marriage, it would not be considered "manly" at all and could bring shame to his family.

The older generation of Ladakh had readily accepted women and men dating and separating before marriage. It is not considered a taboo, as it was in many other parts of the country, where men and women are carefully segregated from childhood until they are married off by their parents in an arranged marriage.

I'm not saying that this is all that is needed for women to be empowered and for society to be equal. What struck me in Ladakh was that there was less unnecessary tension and division between men and women. There is space for a lot more intertwining, understanding, and correspondence to emerge between them, which allowed things to flow better. Their thought processes are quite progressive.

It was refreshing to perceive such a trend in an ancient, deserted land, whose ageless culture was now being tormented every step of the way by the mass infiltration of a novel set of belief systems.

Part of the vicious cycle of living as a human being involves continually having external forces changing and manipulating our identities to suit what is best for the people in power to control the masses. In the past, dictatorial and colonial rulers heavily imposed certain doctrines in the name of one godly figure. These doctrines then decreed what was good or bad for a person.

Nowadays, it's more of a subtle trajectory. We are manipulated and influenced by the current newsmakers, advertisers, politicians, and marketers, who busily exploit social media platforms that are already used by almost every human on the planet.

This has created a data-driven, scientific method that accounts for all the necessary variables – location, ethnicity, religion, caste, age, gender, class, political affiliation, etc. The method strategically employs analytical tools with the help of artificial intelligence to predict, manipulate, and influence the population in whatever way is desired.

Social media marketing has become a huge tool in today's technologically driven world. Media outlets, political campaigns, corporations, and non-governmental organizations around the globe have successfully been able to use platforms such as Facebook. Through them, they propagate and perpetuate their agendas to get people to do what they want them to do and believe what they want them to believe.

This practice works like silent poison. It concocts a lot of havoc in our mind by encoding it in ways we cannot understand.

The fundamentals of "divide and rule" are practiced in a concerted approach as never before. It generates a mounting sense of outrage and anger among many groups because its propaganda incites fear within people by emphasizing what could happen.

It is ingeniously targeted marketing. People's nerves are besieged directly via their survival instincts and their established identity. Rising confusion destroys clarity; people cannot make decisions for themselves with a sound understanding of the full picture. Their minds can be easily molded into whatever seems fit for the discreet, external forces, inconspicuously working on cloaked agendas.

—⊗—

After meditating together for about an hour, the three of us went our separate ways. Aunty went on to her remaining tasks for the day. Dan left for his guesthouse, situated near the Original Ladakh Café, and I went on my usual evening walk.

Walking along Changspa Road in the direction of Shanti Stupa, I turned right after passing a red-colored Buddhist prayer wheel situated just before a tiny bridge over a vigorously flowing river. Most Buddhist devotees circled this wheel at least three times to vibrate with the chanted mantra's essence.

The deviation before the bridge in the direction parallel to the Shanti Stupa took me toward a more secluded area away from the hustle of Changspa Road. After walking away from Changspa with the stream flowing by my left shoulder, I came to bountiful willow trees grown in sufficient number to cultivate an oasis-like space, which enclosed me inside a magical forest. The sun sank behind the extravagant, established mountains located at a distance from the stream. Shades of red bounced off the water and reflected on the surrounding rocks.

Not many people come to that part of Leh, so it only felt more enchanting as I sat under one of the trees firmly grounded next to the stream, waiting for the blackness of the sky to take over my sight and let my unhinged darkness consume me.

# NECTAR OF CLOUDS

Weeks had gone by in a matter of flickers,
Leaving me drunk from the nectar of clouds.
Still holding onto me even though I had let go of time.
Dragging me away from the encores of a life, which had
no truth in it –
Only lies, wrapped up in shiny packages, calling for illusive
ties with the devil.

# VI. A CAGED PALACE

*I* WAS SEATED ON THE ground beside a cobbler, who used to set up his portable shoe repair business at a spot on Changspa Road. During my stay in Leh, he and I had developed a fond friendship free of judgments or expectations.

We had *chai* together several times, while he would tell me about his roots in Rajasthan while simultaneously fixing somebody's trekking shoe or backpack. He journeyed from Rajasthan to Ladakh every year to work in the tourist season.

He would always joyously shout out, *"Aur kya haal hai? Theek hai?"* while looking in my direction with his twinkling eyes and a brown face stylishly sporting an unbelievably-long curved mustache.

I had become friends with a *Nepali*[8] fellow named Luv Bhaiy[9], the owner of a restaurant called "Oh La La La," over the road from where the cobbler sat fixing every little object that needed repairing.

So, whenever I stopped to sit with Luv Bhaiy, a cheerful man from Kathmandu, who invited me to have a *chai* with him every time he saw me pass his restaurant, I would also take a moment to share some unadulterated accord with the cobbler.

I never found out what his name was. He was referred to as *Chacha* by everyone, which means "Uncle" in Hindi. We never asked each other our names, as it was an eye-to-eye kind of a relationship, which needed no introduction of any sort.

---

8   *Nepali* is the word used to identify people from Nepal.
9   *bhaiy* means brother in Hindi.

I had an on-going relationship with others too. There were many shopkeepers and other people – including a few beggars – who had gotten used to seeing my face whenever I was on my solitary walks.

I would sit with them whenever I could to share a moment of solidarity and humanity, especially with a few of the beggars who were always roaming around Leh's markets and targeting foreigners to extract money from.

They used to ask me for money when they first met me but then eventually stopped when they realized that I didn't think I was better than them or didn't feel guilty about not handing out cash.

Instead, I sat with them as an equal, without trying to give them anything or receive something to serve my pride or guilt, but simply to be there with them as a fellow human being.

By treasuring the virtues of the renunciate in my everyday life, I was learning to detach myself from my pride and ego and understand the elemental certainty that no one on this planet is genuinely independent and cannot ever be independent. This perception allowed me to condone the possibility of accepting donations from people if the situation ever demanded it.

I comprehended that we are all dependent on something or someone else for operating as a society.

From the old barter system to the current cash-based one, we have relied on one another to keep our vitalities functioning from the beginning of our history. Let's suppose I was living as isolated as a farmer in the distant mountains of Ladakh. I would still depend on the benevolence of nature to provide me with water and suitable farming conditions. I could not reap my crops to fulfill my basic survival needs.

The labels of "self-made" and "independent" are two of the most egocentric tags we put on ourselves. They undermine the reality that we are where we are and doing what we are doing because a lot of conceivable and inconceivable factors have played their parts in bringing about a pathway that supports the progression of our ideas, agendas, concepts, and aspirations.

In many ways, we are simply the products of our environment. We are wholly dependent on both natural and human ecosystems for our survival. Even if, let's presume, we are able to distance ourselves from the human systems and live off-grid, we would still depend on nature and can not survive without its unconditional support.

So, it is arrogant to proclaim: "I am self-made" or "I am independent" in a world where our mere survival is dependent on the proper functioning of our natural ecosystems.

I wonder what would happen if the trees started taxing us for their provision of breathable air, or the rivers started charging us for the water we consume from them. Would we then consider covering them by governmental policies and preserving them as a priority?

Because we are so disconnected from our natural state of being and thrive in an artificial way of living, we can't see past our world's comforts and conveniences to acknowledge how insignificant as a species we are in the grand scheme of things.

Nowadays, we take our much more easily manageable survival for granted. Our caveman ancestors weren't able to do that in their severe circumstances. They spent energy on securing their necessities while simultaneously avoiding being consumed by the wilderness.

In today's large, mega-wealthy cities, the wealthiest people breathe away their lives trying to become more prosperous than they already are – based on their skewed understanding of wealth. Yet, these so-called influential individuals are utterly dependent on others for just food and water.

State-supplied water and outsized supermarkets fulfilling our dietary requirements are everyday things we take for granted. These are two essentials for physical survival of millions living in the dense human concrete jungles – our cities.

Even though the world may sometimes feel as if it is in a disastrous condition, the reality is that a large proportion of our species' physical survival is more secure today than ever. This affords us the possibility of centering our energies on raising our collective consciousness.

Many humans are going as far as consciously choosing not to procreate to control the birth rate. They realize our planet is overpopulated – not because it is unable to provide for people's needs, but because it is not equipped to provide for our endless greed.

If you think about it, we are programmed biologically to procreate as much as possible to survive in eons past. That brought us to where we are now. It was a simple matter of probability – having as many children as possible was imperative to ensure that some of the offsprings survive, and the species could continue.

In the past, many new-borns died because of human ineptitude in fighting a multitude of lethal scenarios. Disease, famine, war, drought, and natural disasters were responsible for a great many deaths. Even though we continue to whip up a torrent of conflict and unrest around the globe, we have undoubtedly attained a marvelous feat – because of human advances in technology, science, medicine, and infrastructure, we have now secured the physical survival of vast numbers of our species.

With the climate changing so dramatically and many of our water sources having either dried up or become contaminated, water continues to be a significant worry for our species. Unpredictable climatic patterns and increasing natural disasters will no doubt test us immensely in the approaching years. However, terrifying as this sounds, we have unquestionably made a lot of progress in securing our physical survival.

There is plenty of work still to be done, to assure the physical survival of an outsized population living in extreme poverty. They have no escape from being battered by the cruelty of life in such animal conditions.

In India itself, millions of people still live in the primitive, survival stage of having to secure their physical needs daily. They do not have the luxury of the mental and physical space required to think beyond physical survival.

This is where we lack understanding. Those people who are not limited daily by having to secure their physical survival – a decent percentage of the world's population – are automatically placed high on the food chain. They could consciously choose to move beyond their encoded survivor mentality.

People at the top of the food chain – the world's controllers – consistently promote a false version of the survival mindset. They want people to aspire for enormous wealth to access romanticized versions of worldly pleasures, material luxuries, and desirable social approval.

Massive endorsement has made such instant gratification the denominator of success and it directly promotes consumerism. In turn, consumerism has become the base of the GDP of significant, world economies. It is either this or exploitation of natural resources to keep furthering the economy's growth.

There has been a slight shift in this trend currently. A lot of people realize how short-sighted we are about this human-designed madness. They are calling for a phased transition in our external systems as we cause our planet to suffer while failing to find real happiness, joy, and peace in ourselves.

This changeover from the old systems of exploitation and destruction is happening in rich, western countries, particularly those with small populations and strong social systems such as Norway, Sweden, and Denmark. They have already seen the ups and downs of this foolishness and realize we are living in a bubble – a bubble that is waiting to explode if we continue to rear populations that are not joyous and content with what they have.

Adopting a minimalist approach to living with a renewed focus on environmental preservation and instantaneously addressing the rise in mental health issues are the needs of the hour. More and more people across the world are struggling with their mental health than we realize. It only shows the short-sightedness of what we have been trying to do over the last many centuries – our actions are more destructive than constructive.

We have failed to learn from the mistakes of our past. We are still creating a present that corresponds with needing to secure our survival. Instead, we need to establish a world where we can strive to understand the fundamental reasons of our existence. That is preferable to being borne along by a system that makes humans behave like mechanized robots. Those humans will soon be left out of jobs when Artificial Intelligence takes over.

Unfortunately, India and most Asian countries are not learning from the mistakes already made by the western world.

We do not realize that we must change our whole concept of "success" and reshuffle our entire system. People must no longer work like mechanized robots to promote the growth of large corporations. Some of those corporations are already economically more valuable than many countries combined. Without any change, populations will continue to grow, and an outdated economic system will move closer to collapse.

It is a recipe for disaster. If the planet does not collapse and Artificial Intelligence doesn't overtake us, we may be able to secure the physical needs of all our population fifty years from now. Still, we must consider why we were born and what we should be doing.

Is it merely to survive, give birth, and then die? Is that all? Or, is it to have a high-profile job, own the fastest car, build a luxurious house, score a dazzling partner, and other such distracting illusive goodies – all of which enslave us more than they free us?

These illusions contain us inside a palace-like cage. The cage may be equipped with all the latest toys to please our senses and occupy our thoughts. However, those toys are not – and never will be – the answer to a question we fail to ask ourselves. Or do we purposely choose to ignore it because of the unendurable burden of not knowing the answer?

What are we really born to do?

I had lived and worked in other parts of the world and was now grounded in India, where I had considered becoming a monk. Yet, every cell in my body was driven by a thirst to know the answer to this question. I was raging within myself to find it.

Listening to the theories of other self-proclaimed gurus – who were preaching a way of life without experiencing the real thing – only increased my rage.

I was frustrated by the jargon used in the name of truth, religion, and spirituality. It only made me realize that those people had not obtained freedom. They only got further enchained by another institution. It bolstered their egos and led them to portray the false self-image produced by their mind's deception.

In this chaos, the essence of experiencing life in its absolute entirety is lost. It is not about being enchained by an institution. It is about being able to live a life full of unyielding potential.

The seeds of freedom are precious – they must be nurtured – not caged.

When the roots of such trees slowly spread deep into the ground, they will have a durable foundation that nothing can break, a foundation for abundant wisdom and truthful realizations.

Therefore, let the mind break out of its cruel cage and fly away into the widened sky with no goal in mind but complete immersion in living a life with no need to hold onto any fear or any bribe.

## A. Itchy Nerves

Several weeks had gone with me in Leh and thoroughly indulging in a simple life. It roused me to live my every day creating something new while learning to deconstruct the ironclad parameters set by my previous self. That self was being let go of naturally as the days grew in number, and hours became irrelevant.

Another typical day of walking around Leh followed by sitting in the Original Ladakh Café was in order, except a familiar face was now back in Leh. Shira was sitting on one of the benches going through her thick Lonely Planet Book of India, with all its Indian routes, maps, and destinations. That book was overwhelming, and Shira being a fanatic explorer, wanted to go everywhere. She was unlike Dan and me – we would go to one place and stay there for a long time, get into our rhythms, and just let life happen to us. She was the opposite – she wanted to see everything. During July, she had managed to get around almost all parts of Ladakh, except one located south from the border district of Kargil, Zanskar Valley. It was considered one of the most superb regions in Ladakh.

After entering the café, I interacted with Shira, who was delighted to see me. I noticed the marked locations on the uncovered pages of her guidebook. She was going through the book when I sat down in front of her. She had marked the name Zanskar on the map inside the book.

Dan was sitting next to her, reading his book. I said to Shira while looking through her glittery eyes, "You're already thinking of going somewhere, even before you're back?"

She smiled flirtatiously and replied, "Yes!! India is so amazing. I can't get enough of it."

I agreed with her and asked, "You're thinking of going to Zanskar?"

"Yes, and I think Dan is also going to come with me."

I looked at Dan and asked him if he was going. He replied casually, "Maybe ... let's see how I feel in a few days."

I laughed, looking at Dan, who was wildly amused and then asked Shira about Zanskar. She told me that not many people go there. It was far away and difficult to get to, but it has an old monastery built inside a cave that she wanted to go to.

"That sounds really cool!" I said and asked what it was called.

"Phuktal."

I briefly looked at the map of Zanskar and somehow felt the urge to go there. I asked Shira out of sudden curiosity, "How do you get there?"

"First, you go to Kargil ... and then you go south from Kargil toward the main town of Zanskar called Padum, then you figure it out from there."

"Hmm ...." I said.

I spent some time talking with Shira and Dan afterward and later made my way back to my guesthouse. A few days passed while I again went into my little private shell detached from everything happening around me.

One morning after these overwhelming days, I somehow knew I had to get out of Leh. I wanted to go away on my own and get lost in the absoluteness of the far-reaching mountains. It was time for me to break away from my little routine, time to be taken back to the solidity of the towering mountains. They were such mammoth, living organisms that always made me reckon how negligibly I stood in my own body when my eyes drifted away from gzing at them.

Later that day, I asked Tashi, whose travel agency was next to the Original Ladakh Café, "How can I get to Zanskar?"

"The cheapest way would be for you to take the local bus from the bus station tomorrow morning."

"Perfect," I said and asked him where the bus station was.

"There are two bus stations. If you keep walking down from Main Bazaar Road away from Leh Palace, the main bus station is down near Khardungla Road. Just ask anybody, and they will tell you. A bus for Kargil driving along the Leh-Srinagar Highway leaves every morning around 6."

That was enough information for me to get going the next morning.

I told Aunty later that evening. "I am leaving for Zanskar tomorrow. Will probably be gone for some time. I'll be back here afterward."

"How are you getting there?" she asked.

"A bus goes to Kargil tomorrow. I'll get on it and then figure out the rest as I go."

She chuckled and said, "*Zanskar kehte hai bohat khoobsurat hai.*"

"Have you been there?" I asked.

"*Main nahi gayi par uncle gaye huye hai.*"

Her motherly zeal started to surface as she told me to be careful on the way. I said to her in a reassuring voice, "Don't worry, Aunty, I'll be ok."

---

I was awake and up the next morning, ready to go to the bus station. A few trekkers I'd met the previous day had also decided to join me. They intended to get off somewhere on the Leh-Srinagar Highway to go on a trek, which started near Lamayuru Monastery and ended back in Leh.

The trekkers were from all over the world, and I didn't mind having some company for the bus ride. I had been told that Lamayuru Monastery was in the middle between Kargil and Leh. I was considering getting off there for a night instead of going all the way to Kargil. Lamayuru was known as one of the most prominent monasteries around Ladakh, so it only seemed fitting to do that on the way.

The local Leh bus station had a basic construction. I felt transported back in time with the buses being as old as they could be.

We made sure we got to the bus station before 6 am as we still had to figure out which bus to take and all the other logistics that went along with that. With fewer people moving around Leh in the morning, it felt fresher than it would have felt in the afternoon or evening.

In my state of mind, it did not matter which bus I took and where I went. I just wanted to move and get lost in the mountains. I didn't care about any whats, whys, and wheres – so much so that I hardly had any cash on me. I hadn't even considered taking cash out from an ATM the day before – I didn't care, I suppose.

I didn't think about whether I would come back or what I would do once I made it to Zanskar. Nothing was going on in my mind – everything had been abolished by the constant battle going on within me.

I didn't care if some of the cash I had left on me ran out, or anything else for that matter. Such issues usually arise from the doubts in our mind that begin with the phrase "What if ...?"

"What if" was no longer there because I did not care about anything.

The difference between thinking you don't care about anything to living it separates one person from another.

When you think about it, it does nothing for you. Arriving at a point in your self where you don't care that you are not thinking about applying that statement is when you start living it and do not care that you're doing so.

It's not a fearful state to be in, but most liberating. Nobody in the world can hold anything over our minds then. Instead, our minds stand utterly free from all the rubbish that holds us back from experiencing this hitherto concealed power - power that got sidelined when we gave away our freedom to those who took it from us and shackled our throats. Those people control us and let us be dominated by the cruelty of what slowly and carelessly kills life in us every single day for the rest of our bleak lives.

# VII. MAN IN A RED ROBE

*S EVERAL BUSES STOOD ON* that empty surface, but only one had hoards of people standing around in a crowded jumble waiting to board.

The trekkers with me wanted to make sure it was the right bus for where they wanted to go. I found the lurking bus conductor to confirm that it was going toward Kargil and stopping close to Lamayuru Monastery.

He told me in quirky, fast speech, "*Haan haan ... Jaldi betho ...* we leave soon."

"Perfect. *Yeh bags kaha rakh sakhte hai?*"

Each of us had an adequately sized backpack with us. Even though the bus's exterior skeleton was large, it offered minimal leg space inside as all the seats were bolted very close to one another to maximize occupancy. That is what matters most in a country home to more than a billion people.

Any where you go in India, the concept of physical space is something that people don't understand, so travelers from the western world – or from countries with a small population and large areas of empty land – get overwhelmed. They come from a setting where you must find people to fill a space; in India, it is the opposite – you must make space to fit people in.

A car meant for holding four can have a village riding on it. A motorcycle designed for two has a whole family racing on it. A bus intended for fifty has almost double that number sitting inside. Only in flights can you see the exact number of people as the designated seats because more are not allowed to board – though it wouldn't surprise me if more people start to be allowed to board flights in a few years.

With such densely populated regions spread throughout the country, India can only function if people are sincerely connected and work with one another. Synchronicity in the minds of people allows the organized chaos to operate.

Even in Ladakh's vast space, somehow, we were stuck in a thick cluster of people at six in the morning waiting for a bus to start its engine and get on the road.

Half an hour of waiting for the bus driver to start the engine went by. And when the ignition was pushed to let a big blob of thickened black smoke discharge from the bus's tailpipe, the driver started beating his palms on the steering wheel to honk energetically. It was like a thunderstorm, but this forewarning was used across the country.

As soon as the honking began, the bus conductor started acting as if a bomb was about to be dropped, and the bus had to leave right away. It was hysterical – nothing had happened for about half an hour, during which time all the passengers had been waiting silently, and in just a second, it was now-or-never!

I had to act quickly, climb up the bus using the rigid ladder attached to its rear and put our backpacks on the roof. One of the trekkers, a man from the Czech Republic, quickly threw the bags in my direction, so I grabbed them and secured them on a metallic stand purposely fixed there for holding luggage.

The conductor threw an old rope in my direction, which allowed me to secure our bags so they wouldn't fall off the moving bus.

Somehow, adrenaline rushed through everybody, even though the bus was supposed to have started half an hour ago, and nothing had happened during that time. Now, all at once, the stillness was replaced by a legion of throbbing hearts.

And just like that, we were on our way out of Leh toward our destinations. I still was unsure where I was going – I simply wanted to get out of Leh. The rest I had left on the nameless denominators which carry you through your ride and get you to where you're supposed to be, when you're trusted to be there.

The bus drove slowly, going up and down the epic mountains on which the Leh-Srinagar Highway was built. It took us away from Ladakh's desert-like terrain toward Kashmir's lush, green, sublime valleys. Both were part of the single state of Jammu and Kashmir but were divided by religion, geography, history, ethnicity, and other such variables used for distinguishing people based on the land they occupy. (This changed a few years later, in August of 2019, when the Indian government bifurcated the state of Jammu and Kashmir into two Union Territories – and separated the Kashmir and Ladakh regions.)

In detaching ourselves from Leh, we were passing through one of the most scenic highways in the world, where sometimes it feels like we are flying up in the air along with the massively up-thrust mountains.

A tape playlist of worn-out funky Bollywood songs was pumping out of the ancient stereo inside the old bus. That combined with bodies sticking together in the cramped space. The bus moved at a snail's pace across an altitude of 11,500 ft (3,500 m) and over extreme ups and downs on a highway through the tenaciously deep-rooted mountains. It sure was one hell of a ride.

I talked with a few trekkers who had found one another in Leh and had decided to go on a trek together. But mostly, I was immersed in the beauty of the landscape that escorted the highway. We drove past small villages and Buddhist landmarks on the way, but nothing seemed to stand out more than the natural scenery of the outrageous mountain range revealed vividly to our eyes.

Hours went by in no time, and soon enough, the trekkers got off at the point where their trek commenced, and just when they were leaving the bus, I asked the conductor about Lamayuru Monastery. He told me, "*Bas pohachne wale hai Lamayuru.*"

"Please, can you drop me there?" I asked. He waved his head in agreement and continued looking out the open door of the bus stylishly, as he stood on the steps while passengers got on and off the bus.

I did not keep track of time and arrived in Lamayuru just when the afternoon kicked in. The bus dropped me off a few hundred yards from the Lamayuru Monastery. It was on a plateau with mountains encircling it in a captivating loop, whose wondrous authority demanded awe.

The monastery was next to the highway, so it was easily accessible by vehicles. Many houses offering cheap accommodation were situated where the bus dropped me off. I went to one right next to the highway and inquired about a room.

I didn't think about what kind of room I wanted. I just wanted a place to crash, not knowing when exactly I would be leaving. A young Ladakhi man who was the caretaker of the house and the small eatery linked to the highway approached me. He asked how long I would stay. I said, "Possibly one night, but it could be two nights. Let's see how I feel tomorrow."

It was an interesting mental space to be operating in. Not knowing what the future held for me and breathing absolutely detached from the world and myself, I was traversing away from Leh toward an unknown destination. With Zanskar in the back of my head, I had some idea about where I wanted to go. But in terms of absolute reality, the "where" did not matter.

So long as my body kept moving, my eyes were entertained by the sight of unseen images. The curvatures of their depths absorbed my mind, but nothing seemed to move my spirit. It was learning to burn past its motionless flames.

The intensity of the mix had been flavored. I was letting go of the unwanted desires that usually hold us back from asking the essential questions in life. Following that, I was developing the courage to follow up on those questions by voluntarily leaving behind life's comforts.

Pursuing a quest throws more than unexpected challenges at us, but also paves the way for the mind to be genuinely broadened by taking on immeasurable perspectives. Those perspectives can't be obtained by carrying out life's usual chores, but can only be when our mind is forced to deal with unfamiliar situations with nothing to lean onto.

Only surmounting the atrocities of unhinged darkness can revive our mind after it has broken past its old, habitual patterns. Only facing those atrocities can provide a space that lets us rewire our minds to see a different reality from what they originally saw.

When we are continuously streaming on a very shallow scale, we not only distance ourselves from life's actualities that have existed in this universe for millions of centuries but we also concoct an experience that doesn't relate to, or intertwine with, fundamental aspects of our creation.

——❧——

I rested for a bit after eating. I'd treated my taste buds just after arriving in Lamayuru with the usual Maggi noodles and bread – the customary affordable diet people wandering in the Himalayas get used to. It left me with hardly any cash, as I had not been thinking about money when leaving Leh, and was still unconcerned about what would happen if I ran out of it. I just did not care.

I walked up the road toward Lamayuru, one of the most ancient monasteries of Ladakh. While my feet were carrying my body upward, I could hear monks chanting the evening prayers in unison. Following the sound, I climbed up the stairs of that colossal monastery and found them vibrating out from the main temple.

Snowcapped mountains neared the monastery, and barely anybody could be seen there. I was one of the only few visitors there, other than some tourists and locals. They were visiting for their usual evening ritual of receiving blessings and participating in a short pilgrimage around the monastery, while spinning the countless small prayer wheels on the main temple's periphery, a familiar sight in most Buddhist monasteries.

I felt like I had been transported back in time and was moving around some ancient palace with massive gateways and everlasting architecture supporting the rock-bound monastery on top of a mountain far removed from our soulless, thriving metropolitan cities.

I slowly made my way up while engrossed by the unique ambiance surrounding me and finally made it to the main temple. Its large gates were open, and I solemnly entered the presence of a golden statue of Buddha and many monks, seated on the floor in their usual linear pattern and reading from ancient Buddhist scriptures.

They were being read with thorough comprehension. I sat on the floor just next to the main gate directly at a right angle to the monks and went deep into a meditative state while absorbing the vibrations resonating from the monks' chanting.

I didn't understand the meaning of the chant. Still, I liked being in the presence of people who wholly devoted their lives to being liberated from the catastrophe of our derailing civilization.

Soon enough, I heard the echo generated by gongs denoting the end of the evening prayers. All the monks started making their way out of the temple. They included a young, white-skinned male, seemingly in his late 20s, dressed in a red robe like the other monks. He had long red hair falling all the way down to his middle back, in contrast with all the bald heads around him.

I left the main temple along with the monks and stood by the balcony where I could see the mountains on the other side of the valley.

The white-skinned man came and stood next to me. He said, "Hey, how are you?"

"I'm good, and you?"

"Very good!" he said and asked me where I was from.

"Right now, nowhere," I said.

He laughed childishly with placidity streaming from his crystal blue eyes.

I asked him with curiously, "Are you a monk? Or something else? A student, maybe?"

"We are all students of life. You could think of me as a yogi. I have been living here for many years studying and practicing Buddhism."

"And where are you from?"

"I was originally from America, but now I am more from here than anywhere else. My name is Ryan," he said to me and asked me my name.

"Kartikeya."

He then requested that I join him for evening tea in his room, and so I did.

We scrambled down the main temple, passing other buildings inside the Lamayuru Gompa and then climbed the section containing the monks' residential area.

Ryan lived on the topmost level in a tiny rectangular room with a large window looking far into the mountains on the other side of the valley. His room was filled with all kinds of books, ancient scriptures, a single-framed bed, a little kitchen packed with assorted snacks, and a fine tea collection.

I sat down on his single bed and looked out the window as he poured some water into a kettle and asked me a few minutes later, "Would green tea be ok with you?"

"Yes, of course," I replied.

He selected the packet of green tea from the options on a small wooden table next to the bed. Its surface was not visible as it was crowded with a mixture of random stuff – just like his room. It was equipped with all the basics needed for somebody to survive countless days cast away high in the mountains.

Soon enough, we were sitting on his bed, facing one another, sipping our hot tea and conversing about other facets of life. He was especially keen on talking about Indian politics, which I thought was hilarious since he was living such a secluded life as a yogi in the mountains.

One of the great things about being in Ladakh was that, because of its far-distant location, it was difficult to get internet or phone services – which I thought was one of the most blissful things I'd come across in my life. It allowed me to feel connected with the natural world around me in the sense the word *connect* truly stands for.

It wasn't "connecting" based on the superficial concept used by the tech companies and digital world to amass enormous amounts of wealth while contributing to the development of a tool that has become a serious, propaganda-floating machine.

I was not connected to the world technologically anymore, but felt more connected than ever before.

Our lives have become so dependent on technology and gadgets that it is difficult for us to spend a day without them. Our minds always want some external stimulus and distraction to keep them busy while operating on a very compact level.

Phrases such as: "What are these monks doing sitting all day with closed eyes and wasting time?" or "They are not really doing anything, or being productive at all," are frequently articulated by many around the globe who live in large cities driven by a very capitalist mindset. In many ways, that mindset has caused far more destruction in the last several centuries than during the previous thousands of years of evolution of our species.

These were phrases that I used to proclaim until a year before, when I was part of that typical mentality – all about selling stuff, creating more wealth, and working hard to keep growing and become successful.

The meaning of "successful" is flawed and skewed by our limited understanding of the word "success." Not that the earlier version of myself – or people who think like that – are any more wrong than people who do not, but it certainly lacks foresight and conviction about the force of true human spirit.

In its purest form, the human spirit can never be destroyed. It stems from the seeds of creation that enabled us to be born as living beings, creatures who can eventually expand our mind's ability to transcend our physical nature and realize the truth of our existence.

We can have insights that allow us to break our self-induced artificial barriers and move beyond our limiting selves to see the world and ourselves for what they indeed are, which is without any of those common barriers attached to them.

The cup of tea ran its course while we continued conversing about topics ranging from the current political events to the life of a yogi in the modern world. I was not aware of the political scenario at that time, so I chose not to speak much about it but just listened to what this yogi in red robes had to say.

It was also interesting to hear his story about his decision to become a renunciate several years previously. As I had recently considered becoming one, it was fascinating to be sitting in front of someone who had consciously chosen this path for himself.

I could relate to him in many ways, and he could relate to my story as he'd already been through that process in his own way. I told him that the path he was on was not for me because I had realized during my previous several months of doing such far-reaching work that I didn't want to be bound by anything – or anyone for that matter.

"My freedom won't be based on a label I choose to live by. It will be independent of everything and everyone and allow my mind to hold a space that extends to nobody, including myself."

I could not have asked for a better way to end my first day away from Leh than sharing an amazing evening with the man in a red robe and looking at the scenic view surrounding Lamayuru. After sharing a wholesome moment of fellowship, I left his room and headed downward in the direction of the unnamed house that I was staying in.

The night was on its course to take over the luminous sky.
The mountains started glowing from the touch of light
reflected by the moon,
showcasing their mighty presence even more than in the daytime.
The mountains around me were hanging by my side as I walked
alone in the solace of the sky,
without a clue about what the coming days held in store for me.

# VIII. WHERE ENEMIES MEET

*I*T WAS BREEZY THE next morning, and as soon as I woke up and regarded the stillness of the seductive mountains around me, I knew right away that I had to keep moving. With no cash in my pockets, I decided to hitchhike onward.

The house owners provided a light morning meal, and soon afterward, I was standing by the highway below Lamayuru while the sun exhaled its colors onto my face.

I had my backpack strapped on my shoulders, and I was waving my right arm to the vehicles passing by me. A truck driver soon stopped for me. I asked him, *"Bhaiya Kargil tak chodd sakte ho?"*

He replied in his heavy Punjabi accent, *"Ohh, aaja!"*

I hopped quickly onto the truck's metallic front seat. It was screwed in beside the large gearshift that he maneuvered with his left hand. Soon enough, we were on our way to Kargil.

The truck's interior was rugged, charcoal-colored, and metallic. I almost felt as if I was inside some hoary factory, in company with a lean aging Indian man sprouting a white stubble and crooked teeth. He now had control over my life's fate as we drove through the high-altitude mountain region of Ladakh on a highway where people drove with excessive enthusiasm – as if it was going to be their last time driving a vehicle.

He was a nice guy, that driver, and as we drove through the hours, he told me all about himself and his family, who lived with him in

Jammu, another specific region in the State of Jammu and Kashmir. Most of the population in Jammu[10] identified themselves as Hindu.

One of the things I find fascinating about India is that no matter which part of the country I visit, I always find an interesting mix of identities that people label themselves with. It prompts a question in my mind: "What is the identity attached to being Indian?"

What I have realized from years of moving around the country is that the idea of India – or of any country for that matter – is simply an idea. With it, we humans try to build a nation or a community or a tribe by giving its people a collective identity, ideology, and purpose to believe in, so they can work together in unison to build upon that idea – whatever it might be.

This is generally how humans have devised everything in the exterior world. Leaders come into the picture and specify a set of rules, values, and doctrines, so the populace can focus their energies on a single purpose and mission that delivers the human mind a sense of meaning in life and provides a direction for moving forward.

If we have no ideas and identities attached to our physicality, we feel downright lost and confused. We do not know what to do or how to deal with situations that subject our minds to abstractions where things are not distinguishable in terms of black or white, right or wrong. Our entire lives are governed by the rules and ideologies we choose – or are forced to assume. They depend on which part of the world we are born in.

It compels us to live in trapped boxes where our minds can only make sense of things when they fit with the external framework we have assimilated over the years – which then commands that we be, and act, in a certain way.

Either our leaders chose the framework for us, or we chose it ourselves. What we chose or who chooses it for us is not as important as living according to its rules and ideas. It's only another form of illusion – mere stories that have been planted in our minds to form our reality.

---

10  In later years, when the State of Jammu and Kashmir was divided into two Union Territories, Jammu became part of the Union Territory of Jammu and Kashmir, which was independent from the Union Territory of Ladakh.

It might be onerous for us to accept this truth because having nothing to work for in the external world can leave us purposeless and feeling meaningless. Still, it can ultimately prompt our minds to let go of every single story that has come from thousands of years of combined history.

In that case, our seeking purpose and meaning in life can propel us to live with the biggest illusion of all.

What if somebody told you, "There is no purpose and meaning to life. The stories we are brainwashed to believe in our lives are only a contrived version of reality. They help our minds feel secure and content; however, they have falsely convinced us to accept this illusion fostered by our minds."?

When I decided to leave New York City, it was in pursuit of finding my heartfelt purpose in life. That got me to travel around Peru in a vulnerable state, forcing me to experience life, by not being afraid of throwing myself into situations that would help me conquer my deep-rooted fears.

That quest to overcome my fears had me go through a transformative and most definitely got me to express myself as a writer and artist. It also instigated within me a spark to return to India and submerge myself more deeply in the process of uncovering the darkness that hindered me from letting go of my most stringent fears.

I chose my initial path because I wanted to find a purpose and have some meaning in life. Although I found my desire to write and serve people in whatever manner I could, I eventually understood from consistently trying to break down all my self-generated barriers that another level existed. That ultimate level involves being able to let go of the idea of striving for a purpose in life and of attaching any meaning to life.

When we start operating in a frame of mind where we are not trying to find any meaning or not working on a single purpose, we begin to extend beyond our delusional stories that attempt to attach meaning. More importantly, we start to clean the slate written inside our heads.

---

It was thrilling to be sitting in the front of that truck with my eyes irrevocably distanced from the road while the truck was free-falling down a mountain. Climbing up the mountain again was a much tardier job – how grueling it was for the engine to carry the truck up against the pull of gravity. Going up and down that rollercoaster surrounded by the endless mountain ranges was a sight my eyes will never forget.

As we approached Kargil, I could see changes in the topography of the land and the religious influence over the architecture. The landscape became greener, and Islamic influences were revealed in people's homes and the increasing visibility of mosques.

Kargil is a name familiar to most of India because of the Kargil War between India and Pakistan in 1999. I noticed the significant presence of the Indian Army in the state of Jammu and Kashmir. It resulted from activities carried out there since the early days of India's independence from the British and its geographical placement. Wherever I went there, I could easily locate an Indian Army base camp with some sort of military exercise going on.

I guess sharing borders with Pakistan on one side and China on the other – neighbors India has always shared – complicates relationships. Unfortunately, these countries have always had border conflicts of some sort with one another. The few people on top of the food chain are always hungry for more power and influence.

If only India, China, and Pakistan could come together and work in unison for the betterment of humanity in the long term. That would solve the numerous problems currently undermining the flawless potential of the people residing in these border regions. Time and again, those people have been victims of the use of brutality and religion as weapons for brainwashing and dividing them, so they act as per their leaders' demands – demands only designed to further their leaders' selfish agendas. If the leaders had cooperated, they could have paved a pathway, so a peaceful and secure environment blossomed for all.

A peaceful and secure future for that entire region would set an affirmative example for the whole world and future generations. It would provide them with the hope that humans from disparate backgrounds can consciously choose to come together and work for the common good. That way, future generations could move ahead with a sense of oneness while learning to let go of the past, accept the present, and flag the way forward to create a better and inclusive tomorrow for all.

This still seems like a dream, but the hope needs to stay alive even though the region has such a complex geopolitical history. It was so complicated that in the early years after India's independence from the British, a special article was legislated in the Indian Constitution specific to the then State of Jammu and Kashmir.

Article 370 granted the State of Jammu and Kashmir a special status. It endowed the state with the liberty to have its own constitution and independent flag. It allowed the state to have autonomy over its administration and room to enact specific laws, to provide its residents with certain benefits that residents of other Indian states did not have. Buying land or property by nonresidents was prohibited, for instance.

The Indian Government revoked this article in August of 2019 (two years after this story) after a heavy debate in both houses of the Indian Parliament and the entire country.

This is very general information about this whole issue, which is excessively complicated and difficult to address. This book is not about the political equation in Jammu and Kashmir. That is worthy of a whole book – and many have already been written on it.

While riding on the truck away from Lamayuru Monastery toward Kargil, I did not think about these issues. I was entranced by the wondrous natural beauty on display around me and I was not contemplating new thoughts, only plainly observing the world around me. Finally, the truck came to a standstill next to the highway at a junction. At this point, a road diverged toward the main district of Kargil.

The driver suggested I get off and find another ride, as he had to continue along the highway toward Srinagar. I thanked him for the ride and yet again stood by the highway. This time I was in front of a *dhaba*[11] and looking for a lift to Kargil.

---

11  A *dhaba* is a roadside restaurant in India commonly found on highways.

I had no money left on me, but luckily, I found a ride shortly. It was a large van filled with many people. I managed to squeeze myself in for free to wherever the van was going.

The van dropped me at a busy bus station just outside Kargil's main market area. There were many taxis there as well, so I got off the van and started wandering around the station. A taxi driver approached me, asking, "*Aapko kal Zanskar jaana hai?*" His accent was a bit of a change from what I was used to in Leh.

I asked, "*Kal?*"

"Yes. I am taking a shared taxi to Zanskar and have an empty seat."

Without knowing why, I said, "Yes," straight away. *He won't take me for free*, I thought to myself, but he did agree to take me for the minimal price of a few hundred rupees. As I was leaving the station, he said he would come to pick me up at 5.45 the next morning and asked me to WhatsApp him my accommodation details.

I said I would and found my way out of the bus station to start walking in the direction of Kargil's main market, which the driver told me was a few miles away. It all seemed to be working flawlessly – I was not thinking about what to do but letting life take me where it wanted.

A river flowed next to me as I headed toward the market. Being out of cash for the whole day and still having made it to Kargil felt quite liberating. However, I was soon to break that redeeming feeling and key my debit card into a money machine to tie myself to the cash cycle again.

The district of Kargil was noticeably unlike that of Leh. Most people there identified themselves as Muslims. The architecture was visibly influenced by Islamic roots. Mosques captured my eyes and the exterior walls of dwellings were painted in green.

Kargil was much lusher than Leh, so it almost felt like I had been beamed into a whole new world in a few days. My eyes loved the soothing sensation composed by the green surroundings. Soon, I was walking uphill away from the river toward Kargil's main bazaar. Eventually, I found myself in the company of a local man from Kargil, who, on seeing me, decided to walk with me and show me around.

He was wearing a loose outfit, a *Kurta Pajama*, with the traditional hat poised on top of his head. Many men in the area adorned one. As we were walking up through the narrow lanes where the butchers had their meat shops with goats hanging by their stands, he started inquiring about my whereabouts.

I told him I had arrived in Ladakh from Delhi. He then started telling me a story about his close relative, who had recently been murdered in Gurugram.

"They cut out his organs and threw his torn body on the railway tracks," he told me.

I said nothing as he continued. "I speak to Allah, wanting to forgive those men who killed my cousin, but I don't understand why somebody would do such a horrible thing."

"Imagine if I did something like that to you here ... what then?" he asked with intensity in his eyes.

I stayed silent while listening to him as he let out his sorrow about the evil havoc that had been carried out by his loved one's killers.

He accompanied me to the main bazaar, where he took me to a guesthouse and helped me get a room. The intensity in his eyes faded away as I listened to him telling me about his cousin's murder. We said *"Khuda hafeez"* to one another and brushed our shoulders with warmth, as he left after getting me a room at a place managed by two young men from Kargil.

The guesthouse was on the main street, also the National Highway. It was bustling with food outlets and people. Barely any tourists could be seen here, in comparison to Leh.

After leaving my bags in my guesthouse room, I went on an aimless wander around the streets. The locals were very welcoming and quite curious about what I was doing there. The hospitality of people who had been through so much in the previous few decades was admirable.

I was glad that I was staying in Kargil for a night before leaving for Zanskar the next day, as it offered a nice change of pace, scenery, and surroundings in contrast to Leh. Having a solitary walk through the streets allowed me to sink into some fragments of the concentrated potency of the place.

The next day would be a long ride to a town called Padum, which was the last stop in the Zanskar region for taxis. They only drove that far. I had messaged the details of my guesthouse to the driver I'd met earlier that day. He texted back, saying he would pick me up at 5.30 in the morning.

## UNCERTAIN

Nothing was certain.
Nothing was clear.
Nothing was dear.
My heart was in a sphere.
Feeding my tears.
Stoking my fears.
Fueling my years.

# IX. THE ZANSKAR RIDE

*T*HE SUN WAS HIDING behind the mountains when I woke up. My eyes opened to receive the blackness of the sky, invading my room's old window. The call for morning prayers with the word *Allah* inserted into Urdu sentences echoed loudly. It was coming from a mosque near me and served as my alarm.

Straight away, I got up from my bed to get ready quickly and make my way down the stairs, so I was waiting for the taxi before the sun could hint at rising. I was not sure if the taxi would come to pick me up when the driver said he would, but to my surprise, he was only a few minutes late. I was waiting outside the guesthouse's main door on some steps linked directly to the street.

It was still dark, but the sun was starting to show its color and bring some light for human eyes. Soon enough, the taxi halted in front of me, with the guy I'd met yesterday at the bus station sitting on the driver's seat.

It was a large vehicle with two rows of seating behind his seat for at least six passengers and one seat next to the driver for another passenger. It was designed for seven passengers. The most surprising thing about the taxi's arrival was two people seated on the last row – Dan and Shira!

"No way!" I said out loud, as they looked at me with eyes captivated by astonishment. None of us could have anticipated such a random encounter at that unexpected time and place. They were not aware that I had left Leh, and I had not been in touch with them since the day we were all seated in the Original Ladakh Café, all those days ago.

And our booking the same taxi out of Kargil for the same day out of so many other possibilities was preposterous.

"I think us going to Zanskar together was inevitable," I said to both of them, while they were as confounded by that moment as I was, and said, "Yeah!" Even the taxi driver was surprised that we knew one another.

I got inside the taxi swiftly, and we drove out of Kargil in the quietness of the morning to the bus station, where he was supposed to pick up more passengers.

By the time we arrived there, the sky was mutating to blue, and we got out of the taxi to get a *chai* as the driver told us we were still waiting for a few more passengers.

An older French guy and several people from Zanskar joined our little crew, and soon after having our morning *chai*, brewed for us by a gentle middle-aged fellow at his modest tea stall, we were on our way to Padum.

I was seated on the middle row next to the window behind the driver. Dan and Shira were on the row behind me. An older Buddhist man from Zanskar, who used to be in the Indian military, was on my left. He had a *jap mala* (prayer beads) tightly held in his hands; many Buddhist devotees in Ladakh always carried a *jap mala* with them for reciting mantras while counting their beads at any suitable time.

The older French guy was seated on the other side of the Buddhist guy, so that put the Buddhist *Ladakhi* in between us, smiling eagerly like a teddy bear.

The French guy's name was Jean Louis. He barely spoke any English and told us at the beginning of the ride in his strong French accent and broken English that he had been visiting India for several decades now. I always found it intriguing whenever I came across people from other countries who barely spoke any English but somehow managed to get around India by themselves.

As it had been a British colony in the past, wherever you travel in India, you can always find somebody who can speak with you in English, if not correctly at least good enough for you to get by and explain what you need.

The British left an important imprint on the country, having infiltrated the minds of the people about using the English language. In Indian cities, higher class people prefer communicating with one another in what is considered to be "proper English." Many a time, it is acclaimed as the hallmark of a person's sophistication and high stature in Indian society.

It can also be used to inculcate a sense of inferiority in those who cannot speak "proper English." The typical trajectory teen students go through in India is that most of India's private schools promote the English language as the medium for conversing with one another rather than their native tongue. Students who struggle to speak English fluently are made fun of by those who can.

There is still a very noticeable power dynamic based on a language, which was foreign to the country hundreds of years ago. It can be easily observed all around India that fluency in English is considered an essential qualification for a person, regardless of how talented he or she may be in other facets of life.

English is thoroughly prevalent across India, with its roots spread deeply. Even if you visit rural villages, where education levels and the use of English may be lower than in urban areas, you will find someone who can at least understand English, if not speak it. Foreigners from countries with a different native language who can, nevertheless, speak English find it relatively easy to get around India. That is more the case now. So many younger people – including those in Indian rural areas – have some exposure to English.

The English language is an esteemed souvenir of what remains of the once-perceived, glorious British Empire. The English may not have a grand Empire anymore, but somehow, they succeeded in getting their language to keep spreading like wildfire across boundaries and continents – India being a prime example of this.

The road to Padum was not concrete but more like a sturdy rocky pathway. Driving required a lot of skill from the driver – it was not just a straightforward drive on a smooth surface. It was another one of those roller-coaster rides but on a nonexistent road. The driver required concentrated focus to make sure the vehicle didn't lose its balance and tip off the road.

Dan, Shira, and I conversed as if our bodies could not feel any of the bus's constant bouncing on the rocky roadway. We were engrossed in our dialogue, as the scenery and picturesque landscape around us kept changing and fluctuating in color.

Our eyes could not comprehend the abounding, faultless expansive nature that was passing by us, as our taxi worked its way toward Zanskar. We left the Muslim dominated area of the Suru Valley and entered a mostly Buddhist occupied region. It was easy to see – mosques and Islamic-influenced architecture had been exchanged with colorful Buddhist prayer flags and ancient Buddhist monasteries secured on mountain tops.

The halfway spot between Kargil and Padum was the village of Rangdum, where we stopped for our meal of Maggi noodles and bread, with the galactic Rangdum Monastery overlooking our shoulders and the silence of that vast land sneaking into our minds.

Past Rangdum, we drove up to Pensi La Pass, considered the gateway to Zanskar as it partitioned the Suru and Zanskar Valleys.

Pensi La Pass, with its encircling snow-capped mountains, sat just below 14,500 ft (4,400 m) above sea level. As we kept going further into Zanskar, we saw hardly any vehicles on the way. It felt as if we were driving back in time, slowly entering the remains of an ancient civilization.

Being with Dan and Shira was like being with old friends. Whenever we were together, it always felt as if we had known each other for many years; we felt so comfortable in one another's presence. Shira was the radiating flower of our bunch. I had never met someone as joyful as her before. She was always happy and talked to every single person with an open heart. On seeing her, men would fall for her charm and do anything to please her. She had something special about her presence. She genuinely cared for everybody and listened to what they had to say without judging them. She was a people-pleaser and would always have everybody surrounding her, all of them wooed by her charisma. I always thought it was a very remarkable trait.

Dan, on the other hand, was of a more relaxed and quiet nature. He was very selective about who he spoke with and took his time to open up with strangers. But once he did become more communicative, he was one of the most loving people to be around.

I fell somewhere in between them on the personality spectrum. I was not as outgoing as Shira but not as selective as Dan either, so the three of us were a good mix.

Somehow that whole uncanny and unplanned trip to Zanskar became about Dan and Shira. We spent all our days exploring the unknown in that untouched land. We formed an unbreakable alliance among the three of us, which my mind could not fathom or describe in words.

It took us over twelve hours to arrive in Padum. We made many stops on the way, some for food and some simply because of the astounding scenic wonders we encountered. Not taking a minute to stop and let our eyes be amazed by the existence of such naturally occurring wonders – the mountains, rivers, hills, lakes, unfilled cosmic spaces displaying altering shades of varying colors from a luxuriant natural prism – would not have been justifiable.

The ride was also packed with heated discussions between the driver and the locals, the numbers of whom grew as we picked up more people on the way and exceeded the vehicle's maximum capacity. The discussions were mostly about politics and religion. That is common from end to end in the country – and worldwide. There were some hysterical conversations with Jean Louis, who was such an amusing character to be around because of his spirited energy, comical accent, and childlike spirit.

In all, it was a fun-filled ride with people from differing walks of life contributing their inimitable part in making a trip memorable out of the spontaneous coming together of strangers from different lands.

## A. When in Zanskar – Time for Wedding Bells

The sun was about to disappear when we entered Padum's main market, where the taxi dropped us off. Without having to speak about it, Dan, Shira, and I just knew we would stay together. Straightaway, we went on a quest to find a place to stay. Jean Louis tagged along too, as we walked away from the market, hoping to find a guesthouse or a local family who could host us.

As not much was going on in the town, it felt as if we'd traveled back in time. Many of the houses were built the old-fashioned way using mud-brick and stones. The locals were used to having trekkers and explorers come by but hadn't gotten a taste of full-blown tourism yet. Greed had not utterly infiltrated their minds, as it had in Leh and other parts of Ladakh and India.

The locals there preferred to identify themselves as *Zanskaris*, rather than *Ladakhis*, even though Zanskar was considered part of Ladakh and was mostly Buddhist. Still, like anywhere in the world, they had a special affection for their land.

Wandering through Padum, we found a newly constructed guesthouse, located away from the the Zanskar Valley Road's main market near the Buddhist temple on top of a hill. It had no name, as it was still under construction, but we found the owner, who resided there with his family.

Not a local, he had moved there from the State of Punjab. He was more than happy to receive us. When I inquired about rooms, he told me, *"Paaji room toh ho sakta hai... par perfect condition nahi hai, abhi construction complete hi huya hai."*

I told him that was not a problem. All we needed was a place to crash. None of us had any explicit requirements.

He told us we were his first customers and gladly gave us the rooms for almost no charge. They were simple rooms built on the first floor of the new communal building. There was only a bed in the room, along with a shared bathroom for the floor.

I think we were glad to have found something because as soon as the sun went down, the temperature in Padum dipped exponentially. It would have been challenging to sleep out in the open without a tent or enough woolen clothing.

After giving us a room, the owner took us to his small eatery in the Padum market, where we had our first proper meal of the day after surviving the long ride on the wayward terrain. There were no streetlights in Padum. Only the moon and stars imposed their presence directly onto the ground, creating a resonating luster, which at night permitted our eyes to see just enough so our legs could walk in the direction our minds desired.

Our night in Padum only got livelier with the passing hours. When we returned after a full meal of *thali,* a wedding was happening right next to where we were staying.

It was a Buddhist wedding. People were dancing and carrying out their traditional rituals on the street around the corner. Many were drinking *chang* (locally brewed wine prepared from barley) and dancing to tunes being played by monks for the villagers who had gathered to celebrate the two souls' union.

Shira took part in some of the dancing with the women, who pulled her and invited us to join them, seeing as we were outsiders.

We could not stay for very long as our bodies were starting to give up after our day of traveling. On returning to our rooms, the guesthouse owner came knocking on our doors to ask if we wanted to drink some *chang.* We had to cheerfully decline and call it a night after reminiscing briefly about how astonishing the day had been amidst all the splendor offered by the ride to Zanskar.

I felt exhilarated by the eventful happenings of the previous few days since leaving Leh, where I had been preoccupied with a simple life and an inward focus while writing a book about my Peruvian travels.

I hadn't moved around much in Leh, and now that my body was being introduced to new surroundings and my eyes were seeing the natural formations of a world they'd not seen before, I felt ecstatic to have left Leh.

My instincts had led me to do that without any cash, and then, I had been unexpectedly united with Dan and Shira. It was part of letting life take control over my every move and sincerely falling prey to the on-going of a nameless phenomenon that drives the functioning of every single aspect of our world.

The music for the wedding celebrations went on all night, but my body was tired enough to sleep through it without being disturbed.

# A VOICE

I hear a voice.
Every night.
Every moment.
Every second.
It speaks to me,
As I speak to you.
It listens to me,
As I listen to you.
We are all part of it, whether we like it or not.
We are all connected through it.
The same voice, which is in me,
Is in you.
Is in everything.
The same voice makes us who we are.
Makes everything around us what it is.
This voice is what we need to listen to.
This voice is what life is.
This voice is what we are.
This voice is what is.

# X. A WRITER'S DILEMMA

*I* *HAD NOT BEEN ABLE* to write a single word since I had left Leh. Without knowing where I was going, I had somehow arrived in Padum and was now with Dan, Shira, and Jean Louis. He was as excited as a young child the morning after our arrival. He wanted to walk to the Karsha Monastery, located in a valley nearby and supposedly one of Zanskar's most eminent monasteries.

Initially, I was not enthused about going to Karsha and wanted to stay in Padum by myself to do some writing, as I didn't want to break my writing pattern. But that did not happen – Jean Louis persuaded me in his broken English to tag along with the three of them for the walk. He also made me realize that the reason I had been carried away from Leh so flawlessly was to take a break from writing and fully submerge myself in the enchanting land of Zanskar. It was time to shift gear away from my usual pattern and let life take over.

I realized it is essential in life not to let our everyday turn into some unconscious mechanical operation. Although it is important to have structure and consistency in our days, when we are trying to do things in the material world, it is equally important that our actions don't become overly repetitive. That way, we can preserve spontaneity in our spines by acknowledging the emanation of a day and simply be and flow along with whatever comes.

I figured that maintaining a delicate balance between having a routine and consistency in my every day and regularly making space for flowing with life's spontaneous occurrences was key to bringing out the best version of myself.

The best of life happens when we balance between the need to sit down and do the work that needs doing and the times when we can simply be and take in what the world has to offer in its limitless potential.

It's equally significant for growth in life to balance our time and energy between what we love doing in the material world and being grateful for the natural world around us.

Spending time by ourselves – or with a few persons we admire – in a place where we are not distracted by the modern world's toys and learning to be completely present in the moment can leave a timeless mark in our hearts. That is especially the case if the natural setting of the place is breathtakingly astounding.

We do more than look back at such moments, thinking, *Wow, how incredible a time that was!* We become more appreciative and understand that life is not worth living if we cannot share it with people we love and care about unconditionally – without any expectations attached to being with them.

---

Dan, Shira, and I followed Jean Louis in walking toward the Kharcha Gompa. It was a hot, sunny day, and dressed in our casual gear, the three of us shadowed the older French man, who in his full-blown trekking gear and heightened spirit got us moving through the beautiful farms lying on Padum's fringes.

We could see only a handful of people working on their fields reaping crops as we let ourselves acknowledge the wind that drew our feet into crossing the farmlands while being waved at by the simple farmers who could see us roving by while they worked.

I remember going past many *Ladakhi*-style, traditionally erected houses on the walk, and being stopped by a few villagers on the way, who on seeing us would cheerfully exclaim, *"Jullay!"*

Everything in Zanskar was far from being urban or modernized – the use of hand pumps was still widespread. On our walk to Karsha Monastery, we saw locals using them to draw water from the ground. We ourselves used them a few times to re-fill our bottles and refresh ourselves from the heat cast by the sweltering sun.

Before we got onto the desert separating Karsha from Padum, we passed a school. All the children came running out of their classes to enclose us.

It was a Buddhist school. The children's tiny bodies in red robes ran in my direction to encircle me by forming a loop of sorts and then started touching my body and investigating the tattoos on my arms. I sat down – not in the least bothered – and let them do whatever they wanted. It was amusing to be the subject of their genuine, playful curiosity.

Shira and Dan could not stop laughing at seeing those feisty little monks taking me hostage. Some took my hat, some grabbed my arms, and some touched my hair. Apparently, it was a hysterical sight.

We played with the little monks for a bit before following Jean Louis. He always walked far ahead of us as he liked reaching the destination, unlike Dan, Shira, and me who were all about relishing the journey for what it was.

This trip to Zanskar got me out of the what-destination mindset into the just-being one. I was not concerned anymore about where I was going – I was learning to welcome every new moment with a sense of openness fastened to it without needing to control everything.

We followed Jean Louis's unmarked pathway on the desert, with his figure walking far off in the distance, until our eyes beheld the light reflecting off the Karsha Monastery from its place on top of a monumental peak.

No people. No vehicles. Nothing could be seen or heard around us. No hint of any other life-form – apart from one another – as we continued to walk on the high-altitude desert toward a fortress.

We arrived in Karsha, an oasis with a few visible locals. We passed its old homes beneath the monastery on our climb.

Being a land of Buddhist devotees for many centuries, the presence of these ancient monasteries in Ladakh's secluded regions always fostered a sense of mysticism and untapped curiosity in my mind. I felt like visiting such human wonders not because that's what people did, but more because I wanted to absorb the essence and history of what must have transpired in such out-of-the-world places over hundreds of years.

We entered past the white walls of the Karsha Gompa only to realize that we could see no monks at all. With its exquisite wall paintings and number of Buddhist shrines situated throughout the monastery, the fortress was empty. Later, when we came across a few monks taking care of the monastery, we found out why it was unoccupied.

They told us that a large gathering of monks from all Zanskar's monasteries was scheduled near Padum for a Buddhist festival, which is where all the monks had gone.

It all made sense then, as we continued wandering around that magical castle with many hidden routes leading to other parts of its configuration holding unusual items in the keeping of a Buddhist monastery. Ultimately, we made our way to the top of the peak by the flat roof from where we could see an expanded view of the whole valley. In the valley's backdrop rested one of the most prodigious views of the Himalayan mountain range.

In that moment of extreme elation, with Dan and Shira by my side, I was sure that this was one of the most memorable moments of my life. Abruptly leaving Leh was the best thing that could have happened. It had brought me to where I was now: on top of this monastery, staring at the Himalayas' wondrous peaks. It also brought a string of realizations.

We are not meant to conform to the prison constructed within our minds. With it, our fears, insecurities, doubts, and anxieties overpower us and don't let us see the world clearly without those filters attached to our perception of the world.

Our freedom is not governed by financial, social, emotional, or any form of security. Our freedom exists beyond everything. Nothing external can stop our minds from breaking away from the prison that constrains and deludes us, so we live a life where our existence resonates with the purest form of our creation.

Our creation overflows past every false idea our irrelevantly molded personas attach to.

## A. Living Freely

We made our way down from Karsha Monastery to the village below, where a local family agreed to host us for lunch. In no time, we were seated in a compact dining space inside their traditional mud-brick home. One of them had invited us when he saw us pass by his little grocery shop. He was happy to welcome us and offer a simple meal of rice and *dal*.

The day ran its course, and after our highly satisfying meal with the family, we made our way back to Padum. As we continued on our way, we came across another school where we could see a few people near a vehicle parked outside the closed school. We approached and asked if they were going to Padum. They said they were and gladly took us with them. We rode back to Padum with some schoolteachers, who were highly interactive and told us all about Zanskar and their village.

They dropped us at the Padum market, from where we walked back to our guesthouse to finish that electrifying day. There were still on-going celebrations in the home of the bride from the previous night's wedding. Quite an upbeat atmosphere surrounded where we were staying.

Later that night, Dan, Shira, and I were sitting in our room, having a pleasant chat when the guesthouse owner came to offer us some *chang* again.

I asked Dan and Shira if they wanted some. Dan replied, "Nahh ... I'm good." While Shira replied with a teasing smile on her face, "I'll try a glass." I smiled back and asked the guesthouse owner to get a glass of *chang* for her.

Shira contentedly sat on the floor, relishing the glass of *chang* while Dan and I sat on the bed facing her and talked about how stunning Zanskar was. We had been blown away by its rapturous beauty. "There's no place like Zanskar," Dan said, and both Shira and I agreed.

Shortly, an enthusiastic local woman who had somehow found out about us barged into our room uninvited and asked us if we wanted to ride with her to the village of Anmo the next day. She entered like a tornado and sat on the bed next to Dan and me. She started throwing all this information at me in Hindi about what we could do and where we could stay, while I translated for Dan and Shira, who could not understand her.

The guesthouse owner who brought her to our room stood by the door while she carried on like a maniac.

Anmo was the last village in Zanskar, where vehicles could reach. I told Dan and Shira that she was offering us a ride to Anmo the next day.

Shira responded chirpily, "Guys, we could trek to Phuktal Monastery from there."

I asked the woman if that was possible. She replied in a hassling tone, "*Haan, haan.*" The only way to get to Phuktal Monastery was by trekking as no roads went there.

Dan and I looked at one another and said, "Yeah, let's do it."

Some sort of shrewdness was attached to that woman. All three of us had sensed it as soon as she'd barged in and started trying to convince us to go with her.

I let her speak with Dan and Shira for a second to go outside the room and quietly ask the guesthouse owner by the door if she was trustworthy. As we surreptitiously walked away from the room, he whispered in my ear, "Be careful of her. She always wants to rip off foreigners."

That was difficult to believe as the Zanskari locals were so friendly and welcoming. But I guess there's always a black sheep in the crowd, the first one to be infected by the disease of greed before it spreads rapidly to everybody else.

We were a bit wary of her intentions, but we ignored her frantic behavior and decided to go with her anyway. We said we would go with her the next morning, and later told Jean Louis. He was willing to join us along with another trekker from Italy, who had arrived at the guesthouse that day.

The coming days would be the most inspiring days of my life. Everything I had done until that moment would start making some sense and provide me with the fuel I needed internally to keep going forward on whatever hell of a nameless quest I was on.

The quest was taking me away from everything and everyone, but simultaneously bringing me closer to my true self. A self that was learning not to attach itself to my ego nor incline itself toward being part of any system. A self that was cutting away the strings to stand independently of all possible distractions.

Those distractions may seem like the most important thing at the time as they keep our minds in their comfortable, usual position tuned into an idea that seems to temporarily support our welfare.

But anything we think we know and convince ourselves to become a part of in the name of the greater good or our everyday survival, is no better than anything else. No matter how highly we think of ourselves as a species, at some future point, we will perish.

This may seem like a harsh reality, but it is true of everything in the natural world as we know it. Nothing lasts forever and history is a clear indicator of that. Many species have come and gone, and humans will go too. A time will come where we will not exist. That is not depressing or sad, however. We condition ourselves to think of it that way because we attach ourselves to the idea of extinction.

But the key is to let go of our attachment with our bodies and the obsession we have with humanity's continuous survival. Only then can we learn to break past our survival matrix and see beyond what confines us so we cannot actualize the truth of what passes by us.

It is the ego that blinds us. It is the ego that forces us to keep projecting our self onto the world outside. If we cannot do it ourselves, we do it through our children – by turning them into further projections of our egos. Ego is so extensive in the human world today that everything we have built for ourselves externally is dependent on it to thrive.

If the ego feels threatened, we feel threatened. If the ego does not thrive, we are unsuccessful in the capitalist world – the self-centered "I" needs to flourish so others will deem it successful.

And if a person tries to break away from this self-obsessed "I" and adopt the possibility of an egoless "I," we view them as unworthy. We break their spirit to tarnish their souls and force them to forfeit themselves and follow our enslaving process of emphasizing and growing our egos.

## B. By the River

The next morning, we were up and ready to go before the sun could kick in and vaporize our skin. A vehicle used for transporting construction material was waiting outside the guesthouse. A young man was seated in the drivers' seat, and the woman from the previous night sat next to him. A few other locals were seated on the row behind them. Jean

Louis and the Italian man stuffed themselves into that row, leaving no space to insert more bodies into the vehicle.

Consequently, Dan, Shira, and I happily sat over its back end, which had no roof over it and was bursting with construction material and other junk. There was no flat surface at all, so we sat on top of the construction material, covered by a ragged, torn sheet.

*What else could we ask for?* I thought to myself. We had a three-sixty-degree view of an enticing landscape flowing past us for the ride.

The only challenge was that because the road was not paved and was stubbornly bumpy, we were left with sore buttocks by the end of the ride.

The vehicle's sides had metal rods poking out, so we tightly clenched them to balance our bodies for the ride up and down that outrageous route to the village of Anmo. Many a time, it felt as if the vehicle was going to fall off the road and into the Tsarap River at the valley bottom. It separated one side of the alpine peaks from the other and left its imprint on passersby's ears.

The Tsarap River was curving in the opposite direction toward Padum, where it eventually merged with the Stod River to form the Zanskar River. That river was famous for the Chaddar Trek available in the winter season when the river froze and mutated into a white blanket of ice.

Over that entire ride of a few hours, none of us could take a breather, and we didn't want to either, as it was one of the most stirring rides we would ever be on. We didn't come across any other vehicle, which in itself was quite astonishing. However, we did come by construction workers laying the foundations for the new road.

They always gleefully screamed and waved at us – especially when they got to see Shira, an Israeli goddess.

In a few years from then, Zanskar would open up to the world. We were lucky to have been able to see it in its bare setting with hardly anyone around.

Locals always approached me first because they thought I was a tour guide. They would talk to me in their broken Hindi wherever we went. We always found it somewhat amusing because no name categorized our relationship – it was a pure connection among three people on their discrete solo paths seeking something more in life than its usual charade.

That "something more" cannot be defined in words. It can only adhere to the underlying meaning of freedom.

Freedom from everything and everyone.
Freedom from ourselves and this world.
Freedom from every idea and each thought.
Freedom from the mind and the body.
Freedom from the soul and the heart.
Freedom from the past and the future.
Freedom from the sun and the moon.
Sky and sand.
Trees and rivers.
Mines and mirrors.
Roads and sewers.
Divine and sinners.
Wars and accords.
Self and service.
Right and wrong.
Black and white.
Him and her.
You and I.

When we arrived in Anmo, we were freed from the ride but not the woman. She acted the way the guesthouse owner had implied and started asking us for plenty of cash for finding us the ride.

What she asked from us made no sense, and then she lied by saying she had told me the amount she was asking for and that I had agreed. She blamed me and started making a scene at the small *chai* shop, where we were eating our breakfast of Maggi noodles before setting out on the trek to Phuktal Monastery.

All three of us knew she was lying. We didn't react but decided to get some cash out of our pockets to collect a sum to satisfy her greedy desire. We paid her more than the ride should have cost, but not as much as she was asking for – settling somewhere in the middle to stop her from screaming and making a scene. She was purposely trying to get attention as somebody who had been victimized by the outsiders.

It was a rare occurrence during my time in Ladakh, but none of us flinched and were able to tackle the situation. After all, we had been warned by the guesthouse owner the previous night, and we still took the chance.

Somehow greed spreads like a virus. Once a person is infected by it, he or she can't act outside what it does to their mind. Greed corrodes so much that a person cannot see beyond it and is consumed by the spreading of it. Greed is a virus as malicious as any other and has already spread across the world. We do not see how it assiduously kills us and the world around us when we continue to let it be the decisive force operating our world today.

Her theatrical performance in that small *chai* shop above the heavily flowing Tsarap River was a vivid indicator of how greed had found its way even into the secluded region of Zanskar.

# XI. BLANKET OF STARS

*A*FTER BREAKFAST, WE QUICKLY* set off to toddle down the mountain away from Anmo Village toward the Tsarap River flowing in the valley bottom. A footbridge was loosely hanging across it, which we carefully crossed to get to the other side of the valley and begin our trek for Phuktal Monastery.

I didn't care much about where we were heading, so long as we kept walking surrounded by the drunken valley's silence.

There were five of us, an older Italian man being a recent addition to our troop. And even though we were walking together toward a common destination, we were each occupied in our separate world.

Jean Louis and the Italian guy were leading the way as they wanted to get to the Monastery as quickly as possible, but Dan, Shira, and I were in no rush. We were not so concerned about reaching, but merely walking, happen what may.

It was a breathtaking valley with mountains as vigorous as I had ever seen before. Their changing colors, along with their 3D formation, vividly captured my eye and transported my mind into another world – leaving my body flooded with my ecstatic senses.

In turn, my senses delivered an astonishing experience to my mind, leaving it blown away by the mighty spirit visible in those tenacious rocks. They made my physical presence seem entirely insignificant. More importantly, they made my spirit feel more alive than ever before.

It was a brief but transitory time of walking at such a high altitude with mountains as old as they could be and a roaring river running below the edge for the entire way. My ears were never left alone by the erupting water's gushing rumble.

Several hours into the trek, we arrived at a small village called Zamstzang. Calling it a village was not a fair call, as the flat land on the mountain top contained two houses, only one of which was occupied.

An elderly *Zanskari* man came out of the house as soon as we arrived. He affectionately welcomed us to his home and offered us some water. As we were in no rush, we decided to stay there for the night because it had a beautiful farm behind it, and more irresistibly, it encompassed an unbroken view of the valley.

An open field lay in front of his home, and as we walked away from it, a large area of boulders revealed itself. Sitting or laying on top of those boulders, I could plunge myself into the mystical illusion evoked by that enchanting valley and be guided by my mute inner voice to drift somewhere below my false layers.

The elderly *Zanskari* man's grandchildren were also in the house. They were only young, and we became their amusement for the day. Their parents were not around. They'd left the house and the children in the care of the grandfather, a gentle and quiet man.

He gave the five of us the floor of his living room to rest on. It was a cramped space with an old-school burning stove fixed to the floor. Whenever he cooked for us, the room would got chock-full of smoke that had a pungent smell, which interacted with the muddy walls in that dungeon-like space to create a dynamic atmosphere.

Moving around in that old house built by traditional *Ladakhi* methods was like going back in time and finding ourselves in minute darkened spaces. It almost felt like the house was inside a hidden cave.

The grandchildren were a thunderbolt of energy, and they found friends in Dan, Shira, and me, as soon as their eyes glimpsed upon us. They did not leave our company for the remainder of the daylight. We played with them in the open field, carrying them on our shoulders and throwing them up into the sky only to tightly hold them again as they hurriedly fell back. Eventually, we lay down on the large boulders looking over the valley while the kids fondled Dan's and my beards.

Hardly any dialogue happened that day; there seemed no need for it. The elderly *Zanskari* man joined us in the boulder field to tell us about drawings that had been engraved on the rocks thousands of years ago.

He told us that anthropologists from the west had come to study them. We were astonished and captivated to see those prehistoric carvings on those massive stones. They were unique, so none of us had seen anything like them before.

They were in all forms, communicating messages with some underlying meaning we could not interpret, but they sure got our attention and had us strolling around the area investigating them.

We could not believe what we saw, as it was highly unexpected and extremely riveting.

He slowly cut the vegetables while we sat in the confined space, silently observing him. There was a sense of calm about the way he was preparing the meal. It was almost meditative watching him. The vegetables were grown on his farm, and he made a warm soup for us that helped in combating the temperature drop initiated by the sun's drowning.

Only when we thought that our day could not be any more magical were we proved wrong when we went back out into the natural world's vastness after eating our dinner in the house.

We went out after our senses had savored the elderly man's warm soup and were amazed by the sky. A million twinkling stars crowded it, complemented by countless strokes from falling stars. I had never seen a sky like that in my entire life before ... and neither had Dan and Shira.

The sky and the earth were not separated.

We weren't just watching the stars – we were a part of them. The chill in the air did not matter because the myriads of falling stars staggered us as we lay on the rocks. We forgot everything, lost in something as simple as gazing at the stars.

In today's highly efficient and artificial world, that sort of activity is considered unworthy of our time, but it was an inspirational moment for me.

If someone had asked me a year before where I saw myself in a year's time, my answer would never have been, "Ahhhhhh ... I see myself lying under the open night sky far away in the Himalayas ... utterly lost with nothing in my pockets and no plan for the future ... not knowing what I'm going to do next, or what's going to happen, but somehow feeling entirely in sync with myself and the natural world around me in an enlivening moment ...

"Ahhhhhh ... and not living in the future or the past ... but virtuously mesmerized in the present with no artificial constructions or noise ...

"Ahhhhhh ... and summoned by nature's gods into dethroning my empirical values and adopting a newly discovered way of looking at the world with fewer layers creating an illusionary perspective – different from the forged version of reality I used to hold so dear, without knowing it was just a falsified creation by my mind."

My old vision for the future vanished somewhere in proximity with those falling stars, which reflected a canvas where I was painting away my spirit by using imaginary strokes of my hands that mirrored the lights streaming down the glowing sky.

## A. Cha Cha Cha

The night faded. The stars asserted themselves over our feet and left us frozen after experiencing the sky's dominance of our tiny bodies.

Separation occurred between the old and the young in the morning – Jean Louis and the Italian man left early to continue their prime intention of getting to the Phuktal Monastery as quickly as possible.

Without thinking about what we were going to do next, Dan, Shira, and I had a leisurely start to the day with the elderly *Zanskari* man. We had embraced his slow pace and had a light morning meal with him before setting off on the path toward Phuktal after saying goodbye to the kids.

There were two ways to Phuktal – one along the same side of the mountain range that we were on and one along the other side of the valley, where far up in the mountain we could see another village. The elderly man had told us the day before, pointing his fingers at that village, "That is Cha."

For some reason, we decided to go through Cha Village. That meant we had to make our way down the mountain to cross the boisterous river by cautiously walking on another suspension bridge.

Walking on one of those loose bridges always made me feel it was going to break apart any moment, and if it ever did, after dropping down into the rapidly flowing river's full-bodied current, I would not make it out alive.

The village did not seem that far but descending one mountain and climbing another required a solid effort.

Cha was an outstanding village, more than land with a few houses. It was the home to many people spread throughout with large fields of green. We felt as if we had entered an unabridged, old world, which had been hidden until then.

After crossing the stream of crystal-clear water flowing down the mountainside toward the village, we entered alongside the tenderly established white-colored Buddhist *stupas* at the village entrance. Sweeping fields of barley, the prime crop the Zanskari people harvested, saluted us. The scenery hypnotized us.

A young *Zanskari* man saw us passing by the green barley fields. He was standing higher than the fields, and on seeing us, waved at us, and signalled us to follow him. We complied without any hesitation and started walking in his direction and soon met him.

He was dressed in jeans and a shirt and wore a baseball hat. He smiled at us and then asked us to follow him, and we did.

He took us to his house, where his mother, along with his brothers and sisters, lived. They invited us for lunch inside their traditionally styled *Ladakhi* house, which we had gotten quite accustomed to, by then. However, this one was a little bigger than the others we had been inside before. The young man was one of many, brothers and sisters – there were over ten of them in total, including the girls.

We discovered later that he was a monk and lived in a monastery in Southern India. He told us about his journey to monkhood while we were sitting inside their house having lunch. It was not an unusual thing to hear in the Buddhist world. Many Buddhist families sent one or two of their children to live and study in monasteries when very young.

The young monk had come to visit his family after several years at the monastery. They got few opportunities to do such a thing. Having lunch with that family while getting to hear about his experience of growing up in a monastery made for an awesome afternoon.

Our lunch was a simple meal of vegetable curry and rice. The vegetables were all grown locally on their farm, and they kept a substantial stock of rice inside their kitchen.

We weren't quite sure if we were going to continue walking to Phuktal that day, but after lunch, our bellies gave us a definite answer – we weren't going anywhere. We decided to stay in that house for the night, where the family accommodated us in one of their rooms.

By then, I had gotten very used to Dan and Shira's company; trekking with them in such a remote part of the world only brought us closer together. A deep sense of trust and respect for one another had developed among us. We embraced our unique personalities, gave one another the necessary space, and simply devoted our time to engage with the hypnotic surroundings while conversing over time.

It was another one of those magical days where time disappeared, and my decision to leave Leh, not knowing where I was heading, was overflowing gently in the present moment.

In the evening, we went for a wander around the village. These Zanskari villages were far-flung from everything, so the villagers had to rely solely on their surrounding natural resources for all their basic needs.

Their water requirements were fulfilled by the stream flowing down from the glaciers. They had solar panels installed on their housetops for electricity. The toilets were built in traditional *Ladakhi* style, based on a composting system that did not waste any water.

For cooking, most villagers used an old-school burning stove or brought in a gas cylinder from Padum, which was tough, as somebody had to physically carry it on their shoulders by foot or on horses from Anmo.

There was no phone reception for calling or the internet. If somebody wanted to get in touch with the outside world, they had to use the village's one satellite phone. Cha was as secluded as it could be.

We used the satellite phone service later in the evening to connect with our respective families to let them know that we were alive. I could not remember the last time I had spoken to my family, and they weren't aware of my whereabouts, so I thought it would bring them some peace to hear that I was ok.

One of the houses at the topmost part of the village offered this satellite phone service, and we had to go into a small room inside it to access the phone. For some illogical reason, the phone could only connect for a few minutes per call, so we had to be streamlined.

My parents couldn't believe where I was – and I had to tell them, "It's ok ... I am fine ... don't worry about me ...." These were the usual phrases I used to reassure them so they would feel secure about my whereabouts.

They'd seen me vanish before and go on solo adventures to many different parts of the world and were used to my exploratory character by then ... but this time, something was significantly different. And they could sense that as well.

I was no longer just traveling and had not just gone on an adventure for a few months. I made a conscious choice to leave behind the original life path that is forced down our throats from a young age to inculcate answers into us for, "How we are supposed to live in society?" and "What we are supposed to do to fit in?"

It's an outrageous path. It slowly drains the life from us, even if it doesn't bring us to the tipping point where we ask ourselves, "Why the hell are we doing this?" or, "To achieve what?" or, "To prove what?"

I was entering another stream of living, which could not be labeled by the external world. And with time, I was willing to go to any extremes to uncover the depths of my existence, and more significantly, I could not see any other way to live life anymore.

## B. Israelis in India

The three of us went and sat down on a colossal rock further up from the house after making our calls with a fat phone set. From there, the valley and the village were within our panoramic field of vision.

We were sitting and simply gazing at the view when at some point, Dan began humorously imitating young Israelis who come to India traveling in big groups after finishing their mandatory military service.

It was hysterical seeing these big groups follow a route named the Hummus Trail, which took in all the famous spots for Israelis in the country ... hummus obviously representing the exquisite culinary delicacy that Israel is very well known for.

The Hummus Trail followed many villages in the State of Himachal Pradesh, where the plant of cannabis was widely grown for making hashish or *charas* from its resins. *Charas* was an undeniable attraction for many young Israeli travelers who'd just finished their military service.

When I was in Leh, I discovered that Leh was also part of the Hummus Trail, and Changspa Road was the central stop for Israelis traveling together, who smoked *charas* all day in their big groups. This is a very generalized statement, and it stereotypes specific human beings as having a single identity. Still, it was a trend that was difficult not to notice.

I was in company with Dan and Shira, both from Israel but much older than the young ones traveling in groups. Dan and Shira had a lot more experience in life, along with having finished their military service a long time ago. They had not come to India as part of this trend.

It was funny noticing these young Israelis saying and doing similar things. As Dan was an excellent actor, he could imitate his countrymen in a humorously cynical manner. He would mimic the various Israeli personality types in India by putting on a thick Israeli accent and meticulous facial expressions while pronouncing phrases such as "Brother ... Israel is the best country in the world ... we have the best hummus ... best army ... best everything. Israel is the best ..." and so on.

His imitation was so accurate that we could not hold our laughter. Shira and I would burst into tears whenever Dan started doing his comical mimicry of what he termed "Israelis in India."

Sitting at the topmost part of the village looking down at the mammoth valley was one such occasion. Dan gave us one of his best performances. Both Shira and I began laughing uncontrollably. It was the most I had laughed in recent times. We told Dan he should be a comedian, as his timing and delivery were impeccable.

After coming down from our endless laughter, we talked about India as a whole and how incredible a place it was. It was an ancient civilization where every region generated its own history, culture, language, belief, and value system. But beyond all the cultures and ancient stuff, I was realizing over time that it was the land India was positioned on, that mattered the most.

There's a deep sense of mysticism attached to being in the land of India. As a seeker, you wonder if the land itself caused the evolution of the human mind from its primitive form into a higher level of consciousness, back in the day. This land has given birth to countless enlightened sages and saints through human history. How can that just be a mere coincidence?

India has forgotten about this currently. Along with the rest of the eastern world, India has blindly adopted western capitalist values without really thinking in depth.

Capitalism assumed full force in the west in the last several centuries. The greed inflamed by it has carried the human mind away from operating multi-dimensionally to being uni-dimensional. Materialism then unleashed its full force on us and made us ignorant of everything else, including the mystical workings of the natural world around us.

The deep sense of mysticism you can experience as a wanderer moving through India is something beyond the one-dimensional way of living. It is truly transcendental in nature, which most who are currently residing here have forgotten about, as they are no longer in tune with what holds us to this sacred land.

I had not been completely in sync with this natural phenomenon until I came back to India and felt its energetic explosion surfacing through my veins.

A depth comes from simply being in parts of the land, such as the Himalayas, where the mountains themselves can carry you deep into the abysm of that unseen explosion.

The land can certainly trigger expansion through the self and allow us to see past it all and be truly amazed by the spectacular life we have been born into.

# XII. THE PHUKTAL WAY

*T*HE SUN WAS REFLECTING through the bleached glass window of the room we slept in. It was hinting to our eyes that it was time to wake up and unveil the day by looking out the window at the remarkable barley fields. It was the sun's natural wake-up call. Dan and I began the day with our shared customary meditation session, while Shira went out on her morning stroll around the village.

In a while, we had our light breakfast. Along with some *chai* prepared with yak milk, we were also offered a sweet powder called *sattu*[12]. Locals mixed *sattu* with *chang* to make a paste and worked in the fields all day while binging on it – to remain energized throughout the day, the young monk said. I tried some of the paste, which did not have much taste to it.

Soon after our meal, we thanked the family for taking care of us, and in no time, fused again with the silence of the towering mountains while we gradually trekked toward the time-worn monastery of Phuktal.

It was a gloomy day with the sun cloaked behind thickened clouds and mist masking the mountains, so it seemed we were walking among clouds. The mountains around us appeared unreal. We could see that this land must have been beneath the ocean in eons past, as we stumbled upon imprints of fossils and seashells.

It seemed implausible to envision a time when these mountains could have been underwater, but that's the kind of climatic change the

---

12  *Sattu* is *tsampa*, roasted barley that is ground to a flour.

earth in its natural formative cycles must have gone through to bring us where we are now. It won't be surprising to see future changes in our planet's natural formation, either. Oceans may take over more of the land, while the climate with its rapidly changing patterns could affect our natural surroundings in ways we cannot imagine. However, thinking about the possibility of these gigantic mountains being beneath the ocean in the past was preposterous. My mind could not deal with such a possibility.

The mountains we were walking on emitted a sense of power I had not experienced before. I could always sense their supremacy and felt they were communicating with me. The energy in them was so robust it was difficult for anybody not to feel affected by their vigor.

At some point on our way, I decided to stay with the mountains at a spot where I could easily sit and be. I told Dan and Shira to continue and that I would meet them at Phuktal.

They solemnly agreed and went on their way, while I sat in the heart of the valley with no soul meandering around me. The only thing I could hear was the gregarious sound of the river from the valley bottom. I was all alone in that endless moment feeling truly alive because of the expansive surroundings encircling my physical being. Every part of me was fueled with the abundant cosmic energy flowing through me, enabling my mind to integrate with the universe. My physicality felt negligible in that moment of complete assimilation.

None of the trivial worldly things mattered anymore that I used to think mattered so much. It was not because I realized they were unreal and part of the grand illusion in which we all cease to coexist. Rather, it was because all the things we think are so critical to our lives and deserve so much of our attention are just pieces of an obscure puzzle, which will eventually perish.

The sky was roaring at my feet as I stood in that valley's heart with closed eyes and an open mind. Droplets of water started to fall from the sky and brought my awareness back to the space around me and got me moving again. I had no idea how much time had passed since I had separated from Dan and Shira. The water began trickling down my face more actively. I had to increase my pace not to be drenched by the time I reached Phuktal.

No one could be seen around me, and I was sure that plenty of time had elapsed since I took that moment to close my eyes and be with the mountains. At some point, I was running while cutting through those energized mountains with beads of water chiseling my face.

I ran up the mountains in the hope of glimpsing the ancient monastery I had come from far to see, without knowing that this was where I was heading. The unforeseen destination had chosen me as its companion. I just followed through with whatever was taking control of me, guiding me, holding me, and ultimately teaching me.

A frameless entity beyond my imagination held me together through a time where everything I thought I knew had dispersed into the darkness. That was all I could see and be with while those vulnerable moments streamed by, and life was being rekindled in me. By conjoining with my unyielding desire not to be defeated by my innate fears, I was letting go of my past and continually trying to embrace the unknown.

Essentially, an endless battle not to be governed by fear got me to leave my original path in New York and travel to Peru, where I was introduced to this depth within myself in the Amazon Jungle. At the time, I did not know that such a momentary encounter would grow into something that would take me further into the causality of our existence.

It returned me to India and triggered my urge to break myself apart piece by piece – and slowly brought out the rage concealed deep inside the crevices of my system. I was compelled to acknowledge the burning fire nestled in my bloodstream, which provoked me into disengaging myself from our deceptive world's caricatures.

No more could my mind accept the false story it had been brainwashed into believing all my life. By deliberately untying itself from this story, my entire being was being prepared to welcome this rage. When fully unleashed, it would take me over and push me to the ground, demanding that I endure it while I let go of everything there was to let go of.

From a distance, my eyes caught sight of the Phuktal Monastery. Its core was concealed inside a cave but the rest of the white-colored fortress was cinematically spread across the mountain. At the valley bottom, I could also see the river flowing alongside the landscape on which the monastery had been delicately planted.

A much smaller building came my way, as I was closing in on the monastery. I entered, thinking it would provide me a roof to cover my head from the rain. It was a decent-sized space with a long, wooden table placed at the far end closer to the monastery. Dan and Shira were sitting at the table.

"There you guys are!" I said to them as I hastily entered.

They smiled and replied, "Yes, this is the guesthouse where the monastery accommodates its visitors." *It could not be any better than that*, I thought.

On seeing me come in with drenched clothes, a monk in red robes grinned in my direction and asked if I wanted some *garam chai*. I gladly answered, "Yes!" only to find out later that he was the guesthouse caretaker.

Two white women were seated on the floor next to the table where Dan and Shira were. They greeted me as I went past them and sat next to Dan. They were Americans who had arrived in Phuktal earlier that day on a long trek originating in Manali in Himachal Pradesh.

As we talked with them, we discovered they had been traveling around India on their bicycles. My initial response was, "You mean motorcycles?" to which they replied, "No. We mean bicycles. We began riding from Kanyakumari about a year ago."

All three of us were stunned.

I asked in astonishment, "The two of you have come all this way from Kanyakumari on bicycles?!"

They replied in humble voices, "Yes, more or less."

They began riding their bicycles from Kanyakumari, which is the southernmost point of India, a year before, cycling from there along the south-western coastal belt of India to the State of Rajasthan. They told us that as women, they were wary of riding through the States of Haryana, Delhi, and Uttar Pradesh, so they had taken a train from Rajasthan to the State of Uttarakhand. From there, they hopped onto their bicycles again and rode up to Manali to begin their trek to Zanskar.

Dan, Shira, and I were speechless. They were just in their early 20s and had covered so much of India on bicycles! I couldn't believe their story when I first heard it.

Not only is India a vast country. It is also a difficult place to get around. Even more so, if you are women on bicycles – in addition to being white-skinned, which automatically attracts more attention from people. I thought what they had accomplished was phenomenal.

Ladakh being a melting pot for adventurers, I frequently crossed paths with inimitable people attempting all kinds of wild challenges. Cyclists, climbers, runners, trekkers – you name it – and I had met somebody or the other undertaking some sort of daring feat. Meeting such enthusiastic, determined, action-driven characters was fascinating, but what I liked most about these two women was that they were not trying to achieve anything.

They were simply drifting along on their bicycles, riding past the country's changing scenery and scenarios to learn more about themselves and the whole country. There was a sense of humility in them, which was so refreshing to come across.

I could relate to them at that point in my life for not having a goal or mission because at the time I was operating in that sort of space as well. It was a space of lostness with no purpose in absolute terms and no meaning to find.

My space was a mere tangent of nothingness, where my mind stood aside from ongoing worldly delusions and was learning not to be bothered by what other people thought about me, or what society wanted me to be, or how much I needed to grow, or where I wanted to be in ten years' time, or whether I would be able to blah blah ....

A never-ending list of petty worries comes with being born as a human in today's highly fractured world, but these mentally draining worries do not solve anything for us. They do succeed, though, in keeping us away from rejoicing in the present moment, the moment we fail to exult in, the moment that will never return. Instead, we are seasoned occupiers of our minds. We either constantly think about how we used to live - or how we are going to live. In the meantime, we forget to live.

## A. Stuck in Hell

The rain grew in so much volume in the following hours that we agreed - without having to discuss it - that we would visit the pristine site of the Phukal Monastery the next morning. There was something special about that spot without a doubt. Just by being there, I could feel a sense of completion within myself. I passed that night and the subsequent day savoring the end of a phase.

Stationed away from everything and listening to the raindrops within sight of the ancient monastery next to us made us feel part of a lucid dream that our minds could not fully comprehend. I felt as if I was operating beyond a logical state and breathing in a surreal version of this new-found reality.

The next day only further enhanced our time there. Most of the monks from the monastery had gone to attend the large gathering of monks near Padum. As a result, we got the whole monastery to ourselves for that day with no one in sight, except for a few young monks, who were taking care of the place while everyone else was gone.

The monastery's main temple was delicately constructed inside a thundering cave and acted as the monastery's foundation.

I always liked visiting old monasteries, temples, mosques, churches, or other such divine places, where people could let go of their sham guards and surrender themselves to something much bigger and mightier than themselves.

We can call it God, or the universe – or any other name – but these places can inspire a sense of surrender in people. That allows them to recognize the storm wreckage they might be going through and somehow cultivates the internal strength to deal with it.

I had realized one thing from visiting such divine sites. Even though they hold a lot of power within them, it is ultimately up to each person to recognize the power they have within themselves for dealing with life's challenges, no matter how strenuous they seem.

We may occupy ourselves by fighting about the name of the god we believe in or what our religion is, but it is all an internal battle at the end of the day. No matter where we go in the world, if we cannot look within ourselves and realize that all the tools for ending our suffering and overcoming our fears reside within us, we are indisputably missing the point.

Visiting an abundance of sacred sites in the world is useless if we cannot accept this one simple truth that may hold the key to unlocking all our hidden doors. Nothing external can provide us with the answers or the realizations that may spur us to transcend our current situation.

Some external elements may work as a trigger, but the rest of the path is for us to walk alone. We can do this by taking an internal approach that helps set us free from all our fears, doubts, anxieties, and our being's other limiting aspects – the things that hinder us from accessing our full potential.

---

It was a night in disguise. I was disconnected from the world beyond the mountains with no thoughts or emotions flowing through me. My mind in a state of complete emptiness was further distanced from the grumbles of worldly delusion.

From the moment I shut my eyes and let my body become horizontal, I was unsure if I would wake up again in contact with my core with a similar framework as before. The change was so rapid that only my mind entering the state of nothingness prevented it from crashing.

An untouched longing was growing on the surface and taking a toll of my mind by speedily relegating it to a dark place where return seemed implausible.

A prison erected by the unseen materialized around me. It was not the first time I had experienced such a thing – I'd been stuck in a similar hell-like place during my time in the Amazon Jungle.

Over months of dwelling deeper within my depths, I was purposely trying to excavate my grim fears, but from time to time, they would haul me off to this hell-like inescapable prison. It left my body paralyzed, with my fears dominating my every cell and banishing me to a state of complete helplessness, where nothing could come to my rescue.

It was a state of sheer torture, but I had gradually started coexisting with it by trying to detach myself and observe its darkness that still conquered my constant attempts at negating my fears and breaking away.

Somewhere deep inside myself, a reassuring light flickered to help me breathe through this entrapment. In it, the only thing I experienced was a state of unbroken agony, disrupting my mind and traumatizing my body by shaping it into a living corpse.

# XIII. BOND AMONG STRANGERS

*T*HE MORNING WAS A daze where life seemed to be happening in dream-like flashes, with no discrepancy between the real and dream worlds. They had combined into a single entity, leaving my mind consumed by over-spilling, boundless phenomena.

The day began with softness in my eyes from simply beholding the changing beauty of that beloved land. We missed out on saying goodbye to the two American women as they departed early in the morning. Only Dan, Shira, and I remained at the monastery guesthouse, along with its joyful caretaker.

It was one of those days when it was impossible to conjecture when it began and when it ended.

We roamed around the temporarily uninhabited monastery all morning, braising time into nothingness. We passed through the walls of a forbidden kingdom with no souls alongside our bodies, but the sole immensity of a limitless sky hanging over our heads. We forfeited ourselves within the exuberance of that space's creation.

A profound change had been transpiring in me since I landed in Ladakh, but it was only in these last few days that I had started realizing just how pivotal its effect on me was. Every day was like a new day in its creation. My mind was not only learning to make sense of the world around me in its rarified form; it was also being sculpted by continuously having to process events from my untold past and nonexistent future.

The land around us was speaking to me while we walked past the monastery's creaky walls and eventually found ourselves sitting inside the solitude of the main temple. There, I let my unfurling depths take

over to uncover the mystery of what was holding me together when nothing seemed to matter anymore.

My mind struggled periodically to keep up with the emerging changes since I had left New York for this unknown quest. It was too much to handle sometimes when my emotions inexplicably intensified. Presumably, my entire life was roused all at once, and I had no control over anything. The only thing I could do was surrender myself to what was shaking me apart from my core's roots.

With darkness making a dome over the day's light and leaving our eyes sunk by the windows, I felt a ray of glimmering hope as I sat inside the buried doors of an edifice resting in the distant mountains.

On that night in the company of two glinting waves, I gravitated into the absoluteness of the world that extended far into the sky. Almost nonexistent in myself, I was somehow unable to distinguish myself from everything in front of my eyes.

Hours after our exploration of the Phuktal Monastery and return to the monastery guesthouse, we were sitting on a wooden-framed bed inside our tiny room. The room had plain white walls and a shaded window overseeing the mountains on the other side of the valley. I was reciting to Dan and Shira the stories I had been writing from my travels in Peru.

Never in a million years did I conceive that I would be writing. It was not something a boy growing up in an Indian business family was trained to do – or learned to aspire for, in life. Nobody in my family could understand the choices I had made since my exit from New York – traveling to the Amazon Jungle in Peru or wandering through the Himalayas. Nothing seemed to be proceeding as per the usual plan enculturated into humans worldwide, especially in India.

In the beginning, my mind struggled to accept these changes of direction away from the familiar, human-made fabrications. But with time and space, I became familiar with hatching out of the survival mindset into an expanding framework, where no external human fabrications could brace my mind. Only truthful traits of our creation were able to grip my mind and stir it to see things beyond our limited understanding of the world.

So, even though nothing I was doing made any logical sense to the people in my life or for the survival matrix implanted in my mind by social conditioning, I could not control any of it. It was all coming from a source beyond me. I couldn't control my actions anymore and had given into the mystical powers of the nameless phenomenon, which was carrying me along from one place to another capriciously – and untying my being from the entanglements that prevented us from experiencing the true essence of life.

While I was sharing some of my writings with Dan and Shira amidst the enfolding quiet, they were intently listening to what I was reading – it was a deep moment of honest sharing.

When I finished reading a lengthy passage and looked away from the laptop screen and into their eyes, Shira sighed, "I could really feel the emotions behind those words ...."

Dan stayed quiet for a moment and smiled at me from a distance saying, "I want a signed copy from you once you publish the book."

I smiled at both their comments, and our night continued to sail along with the crusader's ship on a no-man's-land held forever by the continuity of that moment.

## A. Running for Life

The next morning, I woke up with a surging current blazing through my spine. Somehow, I knew I had to get back to Leh as quickly as possible. Though not sure where that thought came from, I was convinced that I had to.

I hastily woke up Dan and Shira, who were a bit startled by my energetic presence so early in the morning – as was I.

I was tremendously raging with fire that morning. I was unsure about what had happened during the night when I was disconnected from everything, but something had altered in me. I felt the presence of an overpowering surge in my heart, which had to be released.

They sensed it too and were onboard for leaving Phuktal that day. We were quick to get to our feet as I was not the only one feeling the spill in my bones that morning, and soon after our senses had awakened, we were on our way to Anmo Village.

Rather than trekking back through Cha, we cut across the river and through the other side of the valley, where the village of Purne soon greeted us.

The three of us were walking at our own paces distant from one another, fully synching with the surges streaming through our bodies. I was having a difficult time stopping myself, as my body wanted to fly between the mountains, not walk.

The sun was overly harsh that day, so walking was a bit demanding, considering we were at a high altitude. But the generation of the current in our systems was extraordinarily fierce and furnished our legs with immense potency – they had to move continually to keep discharging the energy.

We had a stopover in Purne for lunch situated closer to the bottom of the valley next to the Tsarap River with an enticing 360-degree scenic view of the whole valley.

We found a *Zanskari* family in the village of Purne who fed our hungry souls. Dan and I were sitting next to one another, conversing about Shira – she was standing in the distance trying to tune into a bunch of cows tied outside one of the village homes.

"She's special ... isn't she?" I said.

"Yeah, man ... she's just on another level."

"I agree. I don't think I've met anyone like her before. Someone so pure."

"Yes ...." Dan nodded in agreement and continued. "She only just sees good in people. Shira –"

"and she doesn't judge anybody whatsoever," I interrupted. "It's amazing."

We did not halt for long for lunch as the currents in our bodies were flowing too effusively to be restrained at one spot. They had to be let loose.

After our meal, I told Dan and Shira that I would see them at the next village, Tzamsang, where we had stayed for the night watching the starry sky.

I quickly went ahead on my own, diligently picking up the pace so the current flaming guided my feet through my bones.

The sun was vibrating aloft, and the desert-like mountains responded to its charm by producing a scorching atmosphere for my body. The heat boring through my skin into my veins warmed my blood so it could support my provocatively charged muscles.

I was propelled expeditiously by the flowing current and in no time, I arrived in Tzamtzang, where the elderly *Zanskari* man was thrilled to see me. The children came running out the door to hug me, expecting I would play with them as I had the last time. And so I did.

Afterward, I took a breather from that pounding release by sitting in the shade of the elderly man's house for my body to recuperate before I continued on the last stretch to Anmo after waiting for Dan and Shira to arrive – it was going to be a thundering stretch.

They maintained a decent pace, though their bodies were not as charged as mine was. I left them far behind, not knowing how fast I was going as I was consumed by my body's need to disperse energy. The discharge from every cell in my body carried it, and at some point, my feet couldn't stop themselves from going even faster – I ran through the mountains.

While going up and down those massive mountains, my body notched every single rock reliably with my toes as if my feet were not separate from the ground. I was integrated with the land beneath me, breathing heavily along with all life around me as I ran fiercely, not dressed in layers of fear but drenched in the colors of freedom.

I ran the whole way back to Anmo Village with intermittent breathing stops to feed my overworking lungs with oxygen so they would not collapse from having to accommodate my body's selfish desire to run on those altitudinous mountains.

I went far ahead of Dan and Shira and arrived in Anmo before sunset to end the day's trek. My run came to a halt as I entered the pathway leading to the outskirts of the village. I found a lovely family who could host us for the night. It was a sizable house with blushing trees planted alongside its boundary walls reaching for the skies and linking it to its dreamy farm.

Anmo was more spread out and home to more people than the villages we had stayed in for the last few days. To make it easier for Dan and Shira, I sat down on the house's roof, where I could see the village entrance. That way, I could signal them when they approached the village, so they wouldn't have to search the entire village for me.

Fields of green were spread through the village, endowing my eyes with a tranquil view while unending tears were raining down from them. It was a release triggered by my wholehearted submission to that liberating run through the mountains.

My whole being had dissolved in that surging current, which had me flying through those felicitous mountains and ultimately bringing me to peace.

A culmination of congruence – with a pinch of gratitude – between everything in my life had brought me to that moment. I was absolutely uplifted and overjoyed from continuously experiencing the realism of life's parabolic curves that boot you through the ups and downs of being born as a human.

Every step toward the unknown swells with the possibility of evolving beyond our unwillingness to let go of everything we think matters and accepting the ever-changing onset of a life, which has no meaning or purpose attached to it.

Every step toward the unknown breathes independently of everything we think we know and unfolds solely as a momentary eventuality.

———— ∞ ————

Just when the darkness was spreading onto the ground, I saw two familiar figures walking toward the village. I screamed, waving my hand at them, "Shira! Dan!"

They acknowledged my call by raising their arms, and soon I had them sitting by my side on the kitchen floor inside the mud house. A young *Zanskari* girl was preparing a meal for us while we slowly sipped a cup of hot *chai* to ease our throats from the chill following the sun's disappearance.

I still had a surging wave filling my eyes with water as I expressed myself to Dan and Shira in words pouring out of my heart. Their eyes could not resist tears either. Dan's eyes relinquished a trickle as he steadily used his index finger to swish it away from the skin below his eyes.

During the entire course of the unbroken dialogue between the three of us, the most powerful exchanges occurred when no words were spoken, and our eyes communicated our heart's will. Whenever such a profound exchange takes place, it always generates a surreal sensation in my body.

———— ∞ ————

My time in Zanskar Valley was crucial for distancing myself from the commotion of our modern-day civilization.

Zanskar was still somehow protected from the creed of evils surrounding today's deceptively globalized world, and I was not sure how long it would stay protected from them. Once those evils infiltrated a land, it sucked the soul out of every single person, leaving them enchained by a triumphant, illusionary picture that tarnished their minds and imprisoned them in a world of human-devised cages.

Tibetan Buddhism's influence was preserved within locals' lives in several villages and could be felt primarily revolving around the values of happiness, compassion, and liberation.

Without a mindset governed by greed and ego-driven wealth creation, *Zanskari* wealth was still associated with happiness – not by how much cash and real estate a person owned.

I was not convinced, though, that it would stay the same in the approaching years.

It was warmly refreshing to come across a place like Zanskar in 21st century India, where most of the country was heading toward completely losing itself in the vanity of making money while undermining the importance of this human life.

It is crucial to secure our species' physical survival and encourage our fellow humans to question our existence on this planet. Blindly accepting the notion of mounting, material wealth can be self-sabotaging; it does not consider issues like the natural world, the socially deprived, and the mentally challenged.

Depending on the capital we secure, we are stamped with approval for our actions. This mechanism sits very well with escalating the world's economies and continuing to expand the material wealth of the super-wealthy sitting on top of the food chain – who do not need this extra wealth anyway. Our planet's limited resources can not fulfill the greedy desires of all the humans currently residing on it.

That system forges more inequality and incites anger, frustration, and desperation among those shown the glorious possibility of accessing material luxuries – if they work hard enough to accumulate loads of capital.

In reality, most of the world's population cannot realize the possibilities advertisers repetitively display. To make matters worse, they are termed "failures" by society because of the uni-dimensional approach endorsed for measuring personal success and failure.

In the olden days in a vast country such as India, those who renounced everything in life to seek liberation were highly revered. Now, many consider them worthless, because they are not striving to achieve a goal that allows them to be labeled *successful* in worldly terms. For this label, life is condensed into a balance sheet with assets and liabilities determining a person's net worth. It ignores other variables that relate to actual personal well-being.

Who is to say what really defines a person's true well-being?

But that sure was an interesting thought that revisited me time and again as I walked through what remained of Zanskar Valley.

---

We found a local man the next day who could give us a ride back to Padum. Fortunately, his vehicle was parked not far away from the house we were staying in, so it all worked out smoothly.

Soon after another one of those roller-coaster rides through the valley, we were back in Padum at the same guesthouse as before. The owner was away, so we were received by his younger brother, who was managing the place in the meantime.

In the afternoon, we went to Padum's market to find a shared taxi for the three of us to go to the Suru Valley the following day.

Suru Valley was the valley closer to Kargil – further away from Zanskar – with the famous peaks of Nun and Kun stretching to almost 23,000 ft (7,000 m). We had seen both peaks on our way to Padum and had been astounded by their beauty and strength. As a result, none of us wanted to miss the chance of spending a night next to them.

Suru Valley was influenced by Islamic culture, so it would be a refreshing change from the predominantly Buddhist Zanskar Valley.

After reserving our ride for Suru Valley early the next morning, we sat in a casual eatery by Padum's main chowk[13].

Across the dusty road, we saw the two American women we had met in Phuktal Monastery. We enthusiastically screamed in their direction while simultaneously waving our hands. They recognized us right away and came over. They invited us to a house where they'd been hosted by a few locals. The older woman, Caroline, told us they had found some polite locals who had offered them the use of their roof for their tents for the night. "He also has rooms for visitors, so you guys could stay there as well," she added.

We liked her proposal and decided to move from our previous guesthouse, located a bit too far away from the main chowk in Padum. At the new residence, the owner was happy to host us and gave the

---

13  A chowk is an intersection of roads.

three of us a room for the night, along with a complimentary container full of *Chang*.

That night the five of us treated our senses by swigging that lucid drink on the rooftop of our temporary new home while talking about our crazy experiences traveling around India as mere seekers. All of us had cut our strings from the tumult of our previous lives and were now trailing down indefinite paths not knowing where they were taking us. Trusting in the power of the unknown, we were moving past our fears and learning to embrace new lives.

In the light shade of the moon with blackness covering our faces and stars glittering through our eyes, we dwelled in the calm of that night with vigor in our hearts, sharing a moment of integrity. We were strangers from foreign lands who had somehow been brought together in that twinkling to put down our shields and obliterate our guards.

The wind was becoming more robust, and the thumping night brought us to the end of that unnamed gathering. We said goodbye to the two Americans wishing them the best for their strenuous journey ahead with loving embraces to shower them with our admiration for all they had been doing.

## A MAGICAL WORLD

I see a world beyond my eyes.
If only we could live in it.
If only we could breathe in it.
It is a world full of magic.
It is a world full of possibilities.
Love for all.
And all for love is what rests in this world.
This world sees no boundaries.
It sees no color. No ramifications.
It is a world where the light meets the dark.
The yin complements the yang.
And we live beyond ourselves.
It is a world where I see nothing.
And nothing sees me.

# XIV. BACK TO LEH

**W**ITH OPEN SPIRITS, WE were driving away from Padum toward Suru Valley. The land of Zanskar continued raining its grace on us. The vehicle encased a space where my body felt trapped by the crush of people; my mind sensed expansion from beholding the fluctuating scenery passing by.

A long ride awaited us; the vehicle's tires kept rolling all day. We moved out of a Buddhist land and entered an Islamic one. Swapping between mosques and monasteries, and green and white houses always meant it was easy to see what religion dominated the region we were driving through.

Nun and Kun's sky-piercing peaks became visible from a distance, telling us we were soon to become a part of Suru Valley.

It was a tiny village where we were dropped. We couldn't see many people, and we were not sure where we could stay. With our backpacks strapped on our shoulders, we started strolling through the little alleyways secured between walls of mud-brick and dense stone.

On seeing us, an affable young man came inquiring soon enough, *"Aapko rehne ki jagah chahiye?"* to which I replied, *"Haan."*

We followed the young man who slipped us through narrow lanes, with houses pressing in on both sides until we reached a guesthouse on the hilltop positioned explicitly for tourists visiting the village.

It was very silent; we were the only outsiders there. There was no commercial activity in the village either. The young man helped us get a room for the night. It was laid at an angle cultivating a clear view of the gigantic peaks rearing up on the other side of the valley, Nun, and

Kun. It was surreal, that view. It felt like we had entered a screensaver on a laptop screen.

The shift from Buddhism to Islam was dramatic in terms of religious influence. What didn't change, though, was people's receptivity and hospitality. Whe, later, the three of us were walking around the village at sunset, the villagers we came across were so excited to see us and greeted us with a lot of warmth. It was almost too invigorating at times.

This experience always made me realize how religious identities can be used to set up a desired perception in our minds based on extreme content targeting a group of people based on the religion they practice. In fact, at ground-level, people are people. The religious propaganda and biases that accompany brainwashing people to promote division are intended for organizing people on the relative level. It does not define people on an absolute level.

On an absolute level, there is goodness in all people.

It does not matter which religious identity people label themselves with - or were forced or born into - because religion is not the root cause of any problem. Humans are.

Humans in power have been using religion as a weapon to divide us for centuries. Putting people in specific boxes sanctions those in power, so they can rule over us, manipulate us, make one box fight another in the name of a given god or ideology - all ultimately to promote their powerful vested interests.

What we fail to see is that none of it matters at the end of the day. Nobody is born with an identity. And nobody dies with one.

It is only in our life that we adhere to a single identity based on where we were born, what we studied, or what became of us when we grew up. All these factors are imaginary creations of our minds. They may harbor in us a strong sense of identity - especially if we devote ourselves to studying and believing the historical and religious texts, cultural implications, commanding literature, and other things that go along with this imaginary creation. However, at the end of the day, it's all irrelevant if we realize it is only part of an impression we have been born into.

When we die, we won't take any of these externalities with us.

It is only real because we make it real in our minds and then take part in a grand drama – playing our specific roles as actors, conscious or unconscious, and abiding by the rules of a game that nobody can win or lose. Still, once we recognize that, we might have a delicate insight and accept that we are all puppets in a world made of theatrical performances.

———— ✺ ————

It was my last night of going to bed alongside my travel companions, Dan and Shira. In just twenty-four hours from that instant, we would be back in Leh and separate from one another to resume the next phases of our respective lives. They were not staying in Leh for much longer after our return, so a "see you later" with them would soon be in order.

I would continue to dwell in the abyss of my being to unveil more of the hidden layers of darkness encircling me and continuing to hold me back from experiencing life in its pure form without any superficial layers attached to its distillation.

I struggled within myself every day, trying to let go of my fears that were consuming and exhausting me. I was acting like a zombie as I couldn't keep up with the alterations my mind and body were going through.

A touch of fervor in my spirit kept me contained through those times of change. Everything I previously thought I knew was hastily breaking apart. It baffled my mind in every possible way and continually shook my internal system. I was going through hell inaudibly and inconspicuously.

———— ✺ ————

We were up early on that last day together as wandering seekers. Our guesthouse caretaker had suggested we get on a bus departing for Kargil from the village main street in the morning.

Only the three of us were on that street in the morning, though it was less of a road and more of a dusty pathway with a few houses and a tiny shop with closed shutters. We were unsure if a bus was coming, but luckily some young students in school uniforms appeared and shyly confirmed that one for Kargil would be arriving soon.

We waited for about half an hour for the bus, which looked as old as possible when it parked in front of us. Again, it looked like it would be one of those rides, where the number of people would be double or triple the seating capacity, and everyone would ride along unintentionally crunching one another. We were used to rides by then where the conductor tried to squeeze every single person into the bus, so it operated beyond maximum capacity.

Luckily, this bus was not packed, and we were able to find seats on it. It got seriously crammed, though, the closer we got to Kargil because it stopped at many places to pick up heaps of people, mostly students in school uniforms. The boys getting aboard were excited to see us – well, Shira, in particular.

It was a quick ride, and soon we were finding our way through the Kargil market to get food from a local joint where Shira could ease her craving for jalebi[14]. For the entire bus ride, that was all she'd been asking for, so as soon as we got there, we had to find somewhere that made it.

It was a colorful eatery, which offered all sorts of Indian sweets and food options. The owner was a bulky guy whose belly was sticking out toward the floor. He invited us into his eatery in the most loving manner possible and started feeding us as if he wanted to make us look like him by the time we left. After imbibing all that fried food and sugar, the adrenaline rush from being on the street teeming with people and vehicles overcame us while moving briskly to the bus station to catch a ride to Leh.

We could not find any buses going to Leh, so we decided to hitchhike instead. Seeing us walking Kargil's streets with our bags strapped on our shoulders, a local guy took us in his car and dropped us at the Leh-Srinagar Highway.

We were in a bypass area in the company of many trucks parked next to the dhabas. As the Line of Control[15] was not far away, military regiments were stationed in that region.

---

14 Jalebi are ball-shaped Indian sweets made of fried batter and a sugary syrup.
15 The Line of Control (commonly referred to as the LOC) is a disputed territory separating the Indian and Pakistani controlled parts of Jammu and Kashmir

It was about noon, and the sun was shining at its peak, and there we were – stranded on a highway in the middle of nowhere, raising our hands for the vehicles passing by to give us a ride to Leh.

The wind was in our favor, and our adrenaline rush was transmitted to the road. We displayed our enthusiasm for the passing vehicles. A young *Ladakhi* driver going to Leh while pumping hip-hop in his car stopped and took us along with him.

He was up for an adventurous ride, and so were we. Throughout the whole journey, we jammed to his music – and stopped at random spots to explore hidden sights. That included sneaking inside somebody's sweeping apricot orchard spread out in profusion on the land to pick plenty of fresh apricots that were lying in countless numbers on a grassy field with nobody at the scene.

It was an open invitation from the land. Even though unplanned, everything was rippling in a synchronized manner and we simply responded accordingly. We weren't thinking about doing anything. We were just playing along with everything that was happening, not thinking about the whats or hows, simply being in the flow while letting go of controlling our every move.

What was amazing was that the three of us were on the same page. None of us were worried about anything. We'd surrendered ourselves to whatever was naturally occurring, without trying to tweak it – just letting it be as it was meant to be.

Our bodies were thoroughly charged by the adrenaline induced by surrendering ourselves to the road.

We were the observers and the actors of the show shaping itself on its own, until we arrived in Leh, which seemed to present itself in an instant as if the whole day had never happened.

The car dropped us close to Leh's main bazaar, where we left for our previous guesthouses as our loyalties rested with the families who had taken care of us beforehand. I was to keep seeing Dan and Shira for the next few days before they left for the State of Himachal Pradesh, so it was not a bye yet.

I rambled along the alleyways wrapped around within Leh, spreading their maze-like network in between the houses separated by the never-ending mud-brick walls. It was the first time in many days that I knew my destination. I was headed to Chow Guesthouse to settle back into living my simple life.

That was a life I had certainly had a break from, in the preceding days. The ancient land of Zanskar had sent me back in time to help me broaden my mind's horizons and make me realize that the resources for dealing with all the darkness that was consuming me over the preceding months were within myself.

Over half a year had gone by since I'd abruptly left New York following the emergence of a mystical inner voice. I left my old self behind to travel through Peru, where, in the depths of the Amazon Jungle, my whole being had shuddered apart in the tantalizing Ayahuasca[16] ceremonies guided by a powerful Shaman from an Amazonian tribe.

Somehow, I survived those tormenting ceremonies, which paved a nameless path for me when I left the jungle – the one I was now on. It was leading me through unexpected and unforeseen life situations, bestowing a lifetime of teachings on me, that came from surrendering my being to this world's mercy.

This world opens endless possibilities when we leave behind our comfortable lives stuck inside the caged, human-made palaces that domesticate our wild animal-selves. Those domesticated selves then compel us to act as sophisticated, well-dressed, well-versed, efficient robots, living according to the rules of pretentious institutions requiring that we act in certain ways so we can fit on an assembly line – keep breathing ... survive ... but not actualize.

## A. Pain is an Old Friend

"*Aa gaye wapas,*" said Aunty merrily, on seeing me enter the door of her house. She was standing in her garden. I smiled at her and said, "*Jullay, Aunty. Aap kaise ho?*"

She replied, "*Ek dum badiya. maine aapka room tayyar rakha huya hai,*" to which I replied, "Thank you, Aunty!"

---

16 Ayahuasca is a vine, native to the Amazon region, which is considered sacred by the indigenous communities there and is used to conduct healing ceremonies.

"*Kaha kaha gaye aap?*" she asked with curiosity sparkling in her eyes. "I ended up going all the way to Phuktal Monastery!"

Her excitement showed in her face, and she reiterated, "Phuktal!!" before continuing, "*Bohat khubsoorat hai waha par.*"

"I have never visited a place like Zanskar before. It is magical!"

She continued, "*Woh to hai!*" and escorted me to my room, which was the same as I had left it before I followed my sudden urge to get out of Leh into the wild unknown.

But now that I had done that and come back, I felt at ease from having followed that itch. It had taken me all the way to Phuktal Monastery, united me with Dan and Shira, and brought such incredible experiences to a wanderer, who had somehow found love in himself, though he was still lost in his quest.

The subsequent week went by with my easing back into my life in Leh. I started writing again and spent some evenings with Dan and Shira before they left for Manali a few days later.

On our last night together, we gathered at our meeting place – the Original Ladakh Café. Tani and Rigzen blessed Dan and Shira using a courteous Buddhist ritual of placing a *khatag*[17] around their necks to show their respect and bid them farewell for their upcoming travels. The *khatag* represented the unconditional bond that Tani and Rigzen had developed with those two beautiful souls.

Saying bye to Dan and Shira was heartwarming, but as they went to board their bus, I told them, "I'm sure we will meet again very soon." They agreed with slight nods and the most genuine smiles and then vanished into the night's darkness.

———— ∞∞∞ ————

During the following weeks, I submerged myself into the vivid world of depicting what my heart was experiencing with the words flowing through me.

After my heart's recent expansion in conjunction with my vigilant attempts to deconstruct the self-image I had adopted for engaging with our society, a dazzling shift was smoking in its raptures.

---

17  A *khatag* is a delicate piece of white cloth.

I was back in the rhythm of writing whatever was coming. And when not writing, I was interacting with whoever came along as a passerby in my day-to-day.

We were now in August, and I was beginning to discover fresh new spaces around Leh as I mindlessly wandered. One fine afternoon I was strolling away from the main bazaar through some empty fields, which captured a full view of the mountains encircling Leh.

I was going toward my guesthouse when I saw a place with an extended mud wall and a small wooden door fixed to its side. The door was painted in yellow up to my waist height. A timber board hooked on the wall above the door had "Soul Curry" engraved on it.

I wondered if it was a restaurant, but it did not look like one and was located well away from the busy street of Changspa where all the eateries and cafés were.

I was curious about what it was as it stood on its own in the quietness of the land away from everything. I walked through the wooden door and along the pathway inside. Poplar trees were planted on my right with thick and tall white trunks.

After a few steps, the space started to broaden out. I was soon received by an amiable *Ladakhi* man with a glistening face. He looked as if he was in his late 30s and approached without hesitation. He stared deep into my eyes when he said, "Hello ... how are you?"

I responded with, "I'm great! What about you?"

He shook my hands while smiling directly at me and said, "I'm good too. My name is Rigzen. I am the owner of this place. Come on in."

"Hi, Rigzen. I am Kartikeya. Nice to meet you," I said as we shook hands.

His hospitality and sincerity stirred me, so I decided to follow through. Rigzen then gave me a tour of his newly nurtured space. It had an open seating arrangement replicating a village format with an unobstructed vision of the mountain range in the far distance.

I asked Rigzen when he'd opened the space. "Just a few weeks ago. It's very new," he replied enthusiastically.

There were rows of poplar trees planted across from the seating area, just inside the extended boundary walls. A hall named the "Buddha Hall" was next to the seating area past the walkway. It was a simple box-like construction, with a cone-shaped top. The hall was empty. Its floor had a smooth, brownish carpet, and its walls were painted in a light purple.

"This is so minimalist," I said as we entered the hall.

"That's the idea," he replied. "I want to keep it simple and use this place for film screenings and artist gatherings."

"That's very interesting ... how come film screening?"

"Because I'm a filmmaker and want to dedicate a space in Leh to appreciating this specific art form."

"Ahhh ... that makes a lot of sense."

His eyes were suffused with kindness alongside a deep sadness buried in them. I did not know the reasons for the sadness, but all I cared about initially was that he was a very genuine and kind-hearted person. Later, I would find out about his creative pursuits and what a phenomenal artist he was.

Going through a deeply introspective and vulnerable time in myself, I had become sensitive to other people's emotions. Everything they felt, I could feel through them, as I no longer held onto my guards and was becoming more and more connected to all life around me. It was overwhelming, but I was growing in empathy for others – especially those who were dealing with pain in their lives. I now understood what it meant to suffer and go through pain myself.

I could not help being taken by the sorrows of others but felt they could feel more at ease when they received genuine consideration from my unspoken words that:

*I understand what you're going through now because I myself am dealing with my inner devils – but trust me, it's going to be OK. We will come out of this together.*

*We only have to avoid giving in to our fears and doubts, which are not real anyway. They're just creations of the mind, and once we realize that, we can learn to detach ourselves from them. And slowly, with time, those fears will pass, the same as everything in life passes away.*

*We only have to observe this pain of ours. Embrace it for what it is and know that it is temporary, and with time it will melt away like everything else.*

# XV. TIME TO SERVE

*T*HE EVENING IN SOUL Curry went by in conversation with Rigzen. It was like a spontaneous meeting of old friends – we were reconvening from where we had left off previously. Maybe that was in some other life form before this one, as the Hindus or Buddhists suggest.

A deep sense of familiarity pervaded our candid exchange. My mind almost felt as if it had already been a part of those conversations before.

I knew I had found another place in Leh where I could be when my mind was unoccupied by the congruence of words, or I was not aimlessly wandering around the ageless land of *lamas*[18].

Letting go of my heart's, heavy compulsion to express every little facet of the change it was undergoing went on for weeks. Then, when my heart was finally accommodating to its inner explosion, my mind decided to go back to the Vipassana Meditation Center situated in nearby Saboo Village. This time I would not go as a student but as a server for the students in return for free accommodation, food, and a daily, designated meditation time.

It would be another ten-day silent retreat, where students devote all their time to looking inward and meditating for ten to eleven hours a day with no external distractions whatsoever.

Even eye contact with fellow meditators was not permitted. The students were in an environment where they could completely disconnect from everything to re-connect with themselves.

---

18 *Lama* is the title for a teacher in Buddhist monasteries.

I told Aunty a few days before I was going to serve. She was thrilled and said to me, "*Seva dene main bohat powerful experience hota hai. Isme tumhari khud ki bohat growth hoti hai.*"

To which I replied, "Hmmmmm," and thought to myself, *probably because it could help me let go of a lot of the ego so heavily ingrained in my system.* I was not sure if my ego could be thoroughly eradicated, but at least, with consistent effort, I could lessen it as much as possible.

I could then diminish my attachment to my self-image, which used to be critical for my material progress in the capitalist world. My ego's attachment to that self-immage was my most significant obstacle to genuine realizations relating to the truth of our existence beyond our human-contrived illusions.

My odyssey with ego had been the most interesting one of all the human parameters that define our actions.

The ego provides the fuel most of the time for our success in today's money-driven, I-centric world. We consistently try to prove ourselves while trying to establish this "I" in worldly terms by gaining money, influence, or recognition.

The "I" craves what can keep our ego secure and mind satisfied. Those cravings tirelessly drive us to earn merits and rewards from the human world, that might be in the form of capital, respect, recognition, or perhaps appreciation.

But really, it is the ego providing solace while we thoughtlessly work toward establishing this "I," and set it up for so-called success.

When working in New York or studying at university in Boston, I was taken over by ego, which wanted to prove itself and be on the top in everything to feel satisfied, secure, and proud of itself. What was I trying to prove or achieve? Something that would satisfy my parents' or society's endless expectations of me? Something that would help me reach a place where I could only look down and not go up any further?

Assuming I had arrived at that place, where nothing in the world was inaccessible anymore – power, money, fame, or influence (you name it) – would this ego be satisfied?

"What would fully satisfy the ego?" I began to wonder repeatedly.

I did not know whose ego it was! Was it mine or somebody else's? Was the ego real or just shaped by my mind based on the competitive environment I grew up in – where if you weren't ranked at the top of your class, you weren't worthy? Or was the ego derived later in life when, if you weren't placed high in an organization, you hadn't worked hard enough? Or alternatively – if you weren't high-paid, you weren't being rewarded well enough?

*What could satisfy this ego?* This question kept weighing on me as I settled into giving this ego away on a platter in service to others while distant from the illusionary creations of humanity.

—⚭—

A few months of traveling, writing, meditating, practicing yoga, reading, meeting, and connecting with all kinds of people from differing backgrounds had passed while I stayed put in Ladakh. However, I didn't know what I was trying to accomplish.

All I knew was that something in me kept changing every single day and making me go through deep realizations. At the same time, I was watching the disintegration of all the hidden constructs within me, which had previously held me back from experiencing life in its full gutsiness.

The day of leaving for the meditation center was on the horizon. Several travelers I met in those last few weeks in Leh decided to come along with me. They were going to sit in the course as students while I would be serving.

It was fascinating to observe so many travelers who had been long interested in doing a course like this. They had incidentally met me somewhere around Leh and discovered during our brief conversations that I was soon to leave to serve in a ten-day silent meditation course. That piqued interest for many, so they joined me the day I was leaving for Saboo Village.

Instinctive acts such as these derive from a way of life entailing a seeker's mind. It is a way of life in which your every day is a new day, and you do not live by a structured itinerary. Instead, you surrender to whatever colludes with you as you move along in correspondence with the thundering, irregular waves.

You welcome the teachings from life as they come to you in their subtle forms, receiving them with an open heart. You perceive the power that derives from surrendering to the universal source of energy flowing through you, which reaches its full force when you can align yourself with it and truly resonate with its purity.

## A. Questions to Ask Ourselves

I had been writing extensively in the week before I was to begin serving in the ten-day day Vipassana course. I was so immersed in the act of writing that I didn't know where my days went.

Tani would comment things like, *"Itna kya likh rahe ho aap?"* as hours disappeared while my fingers were busy pumping blood.

Later in the night, when darkness enclosed Leh, I would make my way to Soul Curry to sit under the presence of the open sky and wildly stare at the moon until there seemed no distinction between the moon and the heavens.

What a sacred time it was for a seeker's soul – getting to express itself by day beneath the shade of the burning sun and rest itself by night beneath the respite of the blushing moon.

And when my being could not feel any more connected to the natural world around me, the time came to devote myself in service of others for the upcoming ten days.

A group of us left for Saboo Village in an old van one morning with me seated in the front seat next to the driver. The seats behind were filled with people from all around the world. Most of them were going to a silent meditation course for the first time in their lives.

A sense of nervousness was obvious in the eyes of those who would be sitting alone in silence away from everything for ten days. They would become familiar with their inner worlds – the most ignored of all worlds today.

Many presume that being in silence on your own is overwhelming. Staying silent turns out to be the easiest task in such a course! When the madness of our monkey mind takes over, we can see how much junk we carry within ourselves – for no good reason. A mad monkey mind is far more challenging to deal with.

Throughout the conscious and deep layers of our subconscious mind, everything we have done in our lives becomes a pile of junk that corrodes and obliterates us, makes us ignorant and sluggish in our actions, and deteriorates our mind.

We do not live in our day-to-day. We merely mark time by keeping ourselves busy – busy doing things we are unconsciously driven to do, that we might not even really like doing.

Above all, we succeed in falsely convincing ourselves that the delusion of the so-called happy life we're so busy "living" is real.

We go through our whole lives without once seriously questioning the "why" behind our existence ...

"Why are we here?"

"Why are we born in the body of a conscious being?"

"Are we just here to survive and then eventually die? That is what all other animals do."

"What makes us unlike the other animals? ... Is there a difference? If so, what is it? How do we find out?"

"What makes us human?"

"What makes our species capable of creating artworks ... inventing machines ... constructing outstanding buildings ... accessing a higher means of consciousness?"

"What makes us different?"

Do we ever wonder that? Do we ever have such questions in our minds? Or are we OK with blindly following a planned regimen molded to keep us in check ... in line ... in the system ... to support its benefactors, who are themselves caged by it?

All we are doing is surviving; we do not know why we do what we do.

We just do what we've been told to do. We are caricatures in a devious play, unaware of the roles we are playing.

## B. Life of a Server

The van dropped us at the meditation center, where nothing had changed since I had last been there. It was still as barren as before with the renowned peak of Stok Kangri visible far in the distance, enfolded by mountains.

The course was to begin later in the evening when the clock instated Noble Silence. From that moment forward, all you would hear was nothing. Noble Silence extended beyond no talking to no eye contact, no physical contact – no anything.

You are basically on your own in what could be considered a prison, though one you voluntarily choose to imprison yourself in. You willingly give away all your belongings, including your cash and phone. Your life is no different from that of a monk or a nun for the days of imprisonment. You live in isolation by yourself, meditated in silence all day. You learn to accept the law of impermanence as you experienced the rising and passing away of all human sensations, such as pain, joy, bliss, lust, and so on.

Lucid sensations arose and passed while I determinedly sat down in a lotus posture to observe them without reacting to them. In the process, I championed the creation of a space within yourself for shedding the layers of despair.

Being a server for the course was an exotic experience. I was with two other servers, a young man from West Bengal and an older man from Delhi. Because of the older server's age-based limitations, the other guy, Pulkit, and I did most of the work.

Arjun, the center's manager, who was strict and rigorous in his attitude, instructed us about what to do and how to do it.

We solemnly complied with most of his demands, even though some were a little out-of-line. As I had decided to serve to let go of my ego and pride, I did not question anything and conformed with every rule.

The course was full beyond capacity; the men's dormitory was accommodating more people than it was designed for. We had to lay extra mattresses on the hallway floor outside the rooms, and I had to sleep on one of them alongside the students because no other space was available.

Due to the lack of resources and help, I was involved in almost all everyday operations ensuring the course ran smoothly.

I had to wake up by 3.45 every morning to ring the wake-up gong for students at 4 am. They struggled to get out of their beds at such an early hour – I was the devil who had to make sure everyone was awake and in the meditation hall by 4.30 am.

Other than being the timekeeper, I also assisted the cooks with meal preparation in the kitchen. I was responsible for cleaning the bathrooms and toilets in the men's dormitory, which was beyond the female dormitory toward the mountains behind the center.

The men's and women's dormitories were segregated by the creation of an imaginary thick wall. That was consistent with the strict rule of fully separating the sexes for the duration of the course. I was also told by Arjun to make sure that all students complied with that rule.

The students were only allowed to speak to the servers – but only when they really needed something. No communication of any other sort was permitted. We were given strict instructions not to indulge in any communication with students unless it was extremely urgent or something that could not be handled without talking.

Even though the course was full beyond capacity and understaffed, I still managed to take four to five hours every day for my own practice. Somehow, it all worked flawlessly even though both Pulkit and I ran around all day to complete our daily chores.

I was operating on such a pure level of dedication and desire to serve others that I was always filled with energy. That made me appreciate that when people are genuinely occupied in serving other people without wanting anything in return, they are fueled by this wanting to give from a pure space.

That space is not driven by their need to accomplish something for themselves, but by wanting to make sure that the other people face no obstacles in doing what they are there to do. Servers are there to facilitate while a person carries on through his or her journey.

It was such a refreshing way to be. I was learning that it was not about the self but the selfless. The more I leaned toward the selfless, the more enthused and contented I felt in myself.

The days of service went by in no time. By the end of the ten days, I grew more in compassion and understanding of why it's imperative we take some time out of our busy lives and fully dedicate ourselves to serving others without wanting anything in return or thinking about our interests. It is imperative to make a wholesome effort to put the others' needs first and willingly choose to dedicate ourselves to their service.

I found it difficult to practice because of my many years in the competitive worlds of business and education. I had been coddled into not thinking about anyone but myself because that is what allows people to become successful in worldly terms. It made me so self-centered and self-focussed that I failed to see things beyond myself.

Consistently putting the needs of this "I" before everyone else to fulfill the ego's desires can be very self-destructive. We may not be able to relinquish the ego's rewards derived from our self-promoting and self-indulging modern systems. Ultimately, by doing that, we only become hollower in ourselves. We have no care or sense of sharing with others, no love – we kill our humanity.

Built on the ideals of survival of the fittest, the external systems of the 21st century are piloted by our primeval instincts, which do not promote the ideals of unification, solidarity, and oneness. They are, instead, driven by the influence of division, jealousy, and power.

As a result, the world of today can be easily divided and ruled.

Conflicts are made more readily than resolutions are formed.
Violence is more promoted than regretted.
Peace comes at a cost.
Wars cause profits.
Power is always in the hands of the corrupt, which we have all become.
We willingly tie our wrists to the hands of those who seek to rule and not to serve.

———— ∞∞ ————

When the ten-day Vipassana course came to an end, and the students could communicate again, it was like the explosion of many Jacks-in-a-box. Many could not stop talking; they were so excited to speak again and share their insights with fellow students.

Their faces were glistening at the course's end, whereas they had seemed to struggle acutely with their internal battles throughout it. The changes in their faces were quite extreme from beginning to end. Having seen that change as an observer, as a selfless server, I felt extremely gratified.

I was glad that I had decided to do such a thing, which taught me that it is not about me, but something much bigger than myself.

We start recognizing that a lot goes on in this world hidden from the human eye – things that are unfathomable, illogical, and way beyond our understanding. It goes against today's popular notion – flaunted by many – that "I know it all." The truth is, however, that we do not know it all – and in knowing that lies our redemption.

Then a familiar scene repeated itself – I was again sitting in the front seat of an old van next to the driver with a bunch of people from various parts of the world sitting behind me. The only difference was that no nervousness was attached to them anymore; they were more centered.

Integrating back into civilization would take them a few days. Stories and insights were being shared among people on the seats behind me while I talked with the driver who came to pick us up to take us to the Chow Guesthouse.

Returning to Leh and swirling in among the movement of vehicles and people thoroughly involved in the tasks of living day to day set off a sudden shift in my nervous system. It came alive again in response to the stimulation from the external world, which had not changed whatsoever. Neither would you expect it to change in a mere ten days! Being in complete silence on your own in isolation and dealing with the mayhem of the mind can make ten days feel like an eternity at times.

The van stopped outside the gate of Chow Guesthouse. All of us dispersed into the surrounding barren land to go on our separate paths while lingering with the changing tides of our unique stories.

# PART TWO
# A TIME OF ANONYMITY

# I. REUNITING WITH THE ELDERS

*I*T WAS TIME FOR me to say goodbye to Ladakh; I had received a message from my father asking me to return to Delhi.

On my grandmother's request, my father had organized an eight-day *Bhagawad Katha* in a city called Gwalior in the central state of India, Madhya Pradesh. That state is commonly referred to as the nation's Hindi Heartland. On my return to Delhi, we were to leave straightaway for Gwalior, the city where I was born.

In the *Bhagawad Katha*, essentially a story-telling event, an esteemed *swami*[19] was to narrate one of the most revered scriptures in Hinduism, *Srimad Bhagavatam*, considered to be one of the great *puranas*[20] in Hinduism.

A cascade of traditions and philosophies that shape the Hindu religion stem from the *Srimad Bhagavatam*, which depicts the glorious stories of *Lord Vishnu* and his ten major avatars. The most prominent are *Lord Rama* and *Lord Krishna*, who are significantly celebrated in India by most of the Hindu population. Still, today, many practice Hinduism in its different forms and identify themselves as proud Hindus.

My grandmother who I refer to as *dadi* while growing up in Gwalior, had been diagnosed with Parkinson's earlier that year. It slowed down her body radically and animated her emotions out of her control.

---

19  A *swami* is a senior member of a religious order in Hinduism. It is also used as a title.

20  The *puranas* are ancient Indian epic poems written in Sanskrit. *Purana* itself means ancient.

Growing up in a city like Gwalior, I barely had any exposure to the world outside our house, locality, and the school I attended. Phones did not exist then, and television came into the picture much later. So, I think I was lucky enough to have been able to grow up in a generation running around outside the four walls of our house, able to do what children are supposed to do. That's unlike what happens in today's digital world, where children grow up consumed by technology and wholly disconnected from the natural world around them.

The arrival of Parkinson's in my grandmothers' body was something none in our family had ever anticipated.

Everyone knew her as a fierce and active woman who had devoted her whole life to serving others while focusing on women's empowerment in India. Women in most parts of the country are still perceived as objects of possession. My grandmother was becoming increasingly dependent on others for even simple acts, such as getting out of her bed.

It was a shock for my grandfather and father, who were strangely unable to comprehend the situation or grasp the need of the hour, especially my grandfather, that I referred to as *dadu*. He is a kind-hearted, soft man on the inside but tough on the outside, who had been utterly devastated by this situation. He had been dependent on my grandmother all his life for emotional and mental support, and now, unexpectedly, the tables had turned. Even if she wanted, my grandmother could not be of much assistance to him and had become altogether dependent on him for everything.

All that was left was her burning spirit. It was keeping her alive and giving her strength to fight Parkinson's, which was seizing control of her motor neurons and making them inactive and unresponsive to the commands from her central nervous system.

I saw my father's message asking me to come to Delhi on returning to Leh after serving at the Vipassana course. The *Bhagwatha Katha* was to begin in roughly a week in Gwalior, so I immediately booked a flight for Delhi and informed Aunty after booking it, "I'll be leaving Leh in a few days."

She replied with solemnity in her eyes, "*Jaa rahe ho? Apna dhyan rakhna.*"

She was used to people coming and going by then. But having spent close to three months in Ladakh, she and I had formed a special bond. She did not think of me as a guest any longer, but as part of the family. And so, she treated me like one as well.

It was time for me to move forward and see what life outside Ladakh had in store for me. I knew it was not a goodbye with her as I was certain I would return to Ladakh one day. There was no doubt about that. When? I did not know, but it was going to happen as these three months in Ladakh had left a lasting impression on me, which I knew would not fritter away over time but only increase in potency.

It had been a time of deep change within me when I had let go of my past and hordes of inner demons. I was ready to embark on a fresh chapter. I would continue embracing the unknown in life – ready to go further in-depth by overcoming my fears and abolishing the roots of darkness, which had hindered me from welcoming the ever-blazing light of sovereignty in my heart.

I told Tani and Rigzen in the Ladakh Café after finishing up some writing for the last time. "You guys have been like brothers to me, taking care of me these months, when I was processing a lot of stuff. I can't thank you both enough." I had tears rolling down my eyes, and so did they while they were giving me a tight hug and saying, "*Aap bhi kya bol rahe ho. Yeh toh humara farz tha.*"

I left the doors of Ladakh Café to wander around Leh for one last time and take in everything I could and say goodbye to the many familiar faces who were used to seeing me around and sharing a sincere human-to-human connection.

---

It was September of 2017 when I left Leh in the morning after a final glimpse of the memorable sunrise from behind the mountains encircling Leh.

While flying above the luminous Himalayas on the way to Delhi, I felt immense gratitude in my throbbing chest for everything that had occurred in the last few months during my complete relinquishment in the hands of a power more vigorous than myself.

I was being shown a path that was unwinding itself as I trailed along it, accepting its anonymity, not knowing anything about what was forthcoming.

In Delhi, I landed back among the footsteps of millions of people running around, chasing I don't know what.

Feeling untouched by the city's intensity, I got myself a ride to Noida, where my parents lived.

My mother, Sunita, welcomed me with happiness radiating through her eyes and with hope in her heart that this time her son might not leave again and would stay at home forever. This is a mother's customary wish – particularly Indian mothers – who are generally a bit more affectionate and possessive toward their children.

It could also be a cultural thing. In India, after turning eighteen, most youngsters are labeled as "adults" but stay with their parents. Many are part of joint families with uncles and aunts and their respective children living in the same household.

India has been incorporating the western world's nuclear family living arrangement over the last many decades – more so in big cities than in smaller ones and villages – nevertheless, communal living is still primarily rooted in the country's culture. It is a predominant factor in the country's chaotic operation, which depends on people cooperating to make things work.

You can always find a guy for anything, and somehow somebody always knows somebody who knows somebody who you know.

It is probably the most intricately networked country outside the effect of social media. With over a billion people, you would expect the odds of strangers having a mutual connection would be relatively low, but somehow, you are proven wrong most of the time. A mutual connection can always be found. It is a spectacle I can never understand.

On seeing me again after a while, the first words from my mother were usually "*Kitna patla ho gaya hai,*" and the first ones from my father, Atul, were, "*Aa gaye bhatak ke.*"

This time though, I had lost a lot of weight from being so immersed in trying to find answers to life's quests. I had stopped caring about what I was eating, or if I was eating at all. There were many days where not a single grain entered my mouth, and just water sufficed.

Wandering like a nomad without any cause or purpose fitted well in describing my time in Ladakh. I hadn't cared about my whereabouts or anything else for that matter.

My parents didn't say it at that time, but I could see on their faces that they were starting to get really worried about me during those days when they got to spend some time with me.

Worrying thoughts such as *Is he going to become a monk or a sanyasi?* Or *What is he doing in life?* Or *When is he going to stop this? And come back here? Work in the family business?* etc., etc., could be plainly seen on their faces.

My mother – who I refer to as *mummy* – is a wonderful woman who always carries herself with a lot of grace. Very elegant, she is a simple woman in a world built around her house, husband, and children. Her body is small, but her heart compensated by being so enormous with intuitive attributes of kindness and generosity dictating her existence.

Her face is round, featuring shiny, whitish skin to go along with her supple lips, dark eyes inside slender sockets, and thin black hair that dropped to her middle back.

"She is all heart, and I am all mind," my father – who I refer to as *papa* – would always say. He is not a very tall man and doesn't have a dominating physical body, but his presence created an intimidating experience for people meeting him the first time.

A workaholic and determined businessman, he had scaled up his business enormously by working vigorously from a young age. His face is much more oval in its curvature with big, round, black eyes, a subtle mustache above his broadened lips accompanied by a clean haircut, and a dark skin that he'd inherited from my grandfather.

My parents are at the opposite ends of the personality spectrum, with one being extremely gentle in her ways and the other being fairly obstinate in his. What brought them together was their core value of wanting to do good and be good, which both my sister and I received from them as we were being raised.

This time the sense of worry on their faces could be seen beyond their eyes and led me to see further into their minds.

I chose not to respond to any of their questions because I honestly did not know how to, as I didn't know what I was going for in life. How do you say things like, "I want to find the reason for our existence," or

"I want to find the truth," or "I want to be free?" These phrases almost sound too ridiculous when said out loud - if not naïve - in today's highly condescending world.

So, I kept it all to myself. All my fears. My self-encompassing darkness. My doubts. My misery. I kept it all to myself - not sharing anything with anybody while trying my best not to give in to life's unnecessary distractions either.

I played the role of being their son - or whatever else people wanted to perceive me as - without explaining myself or talking about the things I had been doing. I stayed in my shell, as nothing I could say to anyone would change anything. All that mattered was that a profound shift was occurring in me, making me feel everything there was to feel. The breaking of the layers in me was so incandescent that there were no words in the dictionary to express the fire-storm wreckage blazing through me.

I adopted this way of being during my days of visiting Gwalior and attending the *Bhagwath Katha*, which went on all day long for eight days. On the eighth day, a free feast - a *Bhandara* - was organized for the unprivileged sections of society.

A revered *swami*, an eminent scholar of the *Vedas*[21], and someone who also taught Vedanta[22] in his several *ashrams*[23] across India in cities such as Ujjain and Haridwar, narrated the *Bhagwatha Puranas*. Every day a large group gathered for his ongoing narration in a sizable meeting room in a Gwalior hotel, owned by family friends.

The swami was dressed in yellow attire, covering only the lower part of his body, while the upper part was left bare-skinned. The space between his eyebrows had a bright *tilak*[24], which complemented his outfit well. His head was clean-shaven, and so was his face; they appeared to glow in the reflection of the ceiling lights on his skin.

---

21  The *Vedas* are a group of the oldest religious texts inscribed in Sanskrit that originated from ancient India.

22  *Vedanta* is an ancient spiritual philosophy associated with Hinduism.

23  An *ashram* is like a monastery where you can retreat from the busyness of the outer world and delve deep into your spiritual practices.

24  A *tilak* is a colorful mark devoted Hindus put on their foreheads.

Every day for hours, he would sit on a decorated chair on a stage. His *chellas*[25] and an ensemble sat beside him. During the day's tale, they would sing Hindi *bhajans*[26] along with some musical accompaniment to add depth to the *Puranas'* narration. It generated a vivid atmosphere for the listeners in the hall.

## A. Indian Family Dynamics

I had not been to Gwalior in a long time, and only in my very early days had I spent time in the city. I had moved to a private boys-only boarding school built on top of the historical city fort at the age of ten. It was an old school built by the Scindias, the city's royal family, who used to rule the town back in the day.

The school was strict, and my father thought it would be a suitable place for me to attend as it would make me more disciplined in life. He also thought this was the best of Gwalior's educational options, so it made sense for my parents to send me there. I did not object or question my fathers' decision.

Going to a boarding school didn't worry me because as a young boy, I was quite detached in many ways and didn't get affected by having to move away from family and live on my own in the company of other young boys from different parts of the country.

The school had strict rules against parents visiting unannounced to see their children. So, although I was living in Gwalior, in a way, I was not. The school was organized to keep the students detached from the world outside and engaged in the world inside those old fort walls, assembled over a century previously during the British Raj. British traditions greatly influenced the school.

I lived and studied there for five years before moving to Noida with my parents. They had left Gwalior as my father's work demanded a great deal of travel while I was in the boarding school.

Most days in a month, he was away from Gwalior anyway, so it made logical sense for the family to move to Delhi, the Capital City of India. It was much easier to get around the country from there. Being one of

---

25 *Chellas* are disciples.
26 *Bhajans* are devotional songs and hymns.

Delhi's sister cities with affordable housing, Noida seemed the perfect fit to allow my father to fulfill his business ambitions.

He had always been an ambitious man, my father. At the age of twenty-four, he started his own business with the small amount of $1500, which he had received from my grandfather Gopal Das Ladha, who had established his chartered accountancy firm at a young age.

My grandfather's father, my great-grandfather, Har Govind Das Ladha had also established his own business, selling garments at a young age. He got money from selling all kinds of stuff by going around the City of Gwalior on his bicycle as a teenager. He was not educated at all and did not want my grandfather to study either. On marrying my grandmother, my grandfather decided to get an education, which his father strenuously opposed.

My grandmother, Manorama Ladha, came from a family of well-educated people, lawyers, doctors, and engineers – the most revered professions in Indian society. Classic stereotypical Indians in the western world, especially in America, are doctors and engineers.

My great-grandfather had two marriages. He had three children from the first marriage, one of whom died. The remaining two were my grandfather, the eldest, and his younger brother, Jagdish Kumar Ladha. Their mother, my great-grandmother, Geeta Devi Ladha, died not long after giving birth to Jagdish.

With his second marriage, my great-grandfather had many girls and boys. He also had a brother who died at a young age from a heart attack and left behind plenty of other children for my great-grandfather to take care of.

So, my great-grandfather and grandfather, the eldest of all the children, were responsible for taking care of the entire young family. They lived together in one house in the main market area of Gwalior, known as Lashkar.

This is a typical Indian family arrangement that has been followed for many years. It provides the communal structure and living that India is still known for.

This is just my father's side of the story. There was a similar tale on my mother's and my grandmother's side.

As a result, I grew up knowing all the families on all sides, except for my mother's mother's side. Still, there are a lot of people in what we would term as "family" in India.

If I were to start counting the exact number as of today, there would be hundreds considering that everyone had children, who had their children – and the drill goes on. The family is a virtual village on its own.

This brief depiction of the family tree is critical because when I got to Gwalior – after a long time – to attend the *Bhagwath Katha*, almost everyone from my father's and grandmother's sides of the family were there. Not all the people from my mother's side were there, but more than enough to keep the dice rolling.

So, I was doing more than going back to Gwalior to rekindle my relationship with my grandparents, who were already in a state of shock from having to deal with my grandmother's fight with Parkinson's. This would also be a reunion for the whole family, including distant relatives who had arrived for the occasion.

## B. Religion vs. Spirituality

As I was not religious in my beliefs and did not operate under the guidance of any holy scriptures, I never really participated in the rituals and actions decreed by numerous religious texts.

Even though I grew up in a Hindu merchant-caste family, where everyone in the household diligently followed the many guidelines governing the day-to-day lives of most Hindu families across India, I never really understood the significance of all the rituals and traditions.

Besides, even though my values in life were strong because of my good upbringing, I moved to America before I turned eighteen and found myself more distanced from religion.

Ironically, I would get closer to spirituality over time not because I wanted to, but because that's what life had in store for me.

I figured out for myself that religion and spirituality, as we know them, are two antithetic aspects of life – even though they might have a lot of intertwining elements. All religions were born because singular individuals were highly connected to their spirits and the divine within themselves. But over thousands of years of human history, religion in most scenarios has not stayed true to its probable original intention -to end human suffering and liberate people from this illusional life.

Instead, religion became a weapon for organizing people in the name of God, miscellaneous symbols, and contradictory ideas. Empires have been built and destroyed in the name of religion, and still today, politicians across the globe use religion as a tool to divide and rule us.

In India, before a child has a name, his or her religion, caste, social status, and other such labels have already been decided by society.

Instead of letting our children grow up without any social conditioning, we start brainwashing them in the name of religion or god, and other such aspects of life, to provide them with an identity based on a history they can feel proud of. And if under any circumstance, that identity is threatened, we are willing to fight for it till death do us apart.

But do we ever ask ourselves, what for? Because it says so in the scriptures? Or, because this is what God wants us to do? Or, because this is what our religious or political leaders tell us to do? Or is it a matter of the survival of our identity? Of our faith? Of our religion?

All of this makes me wonder – how can we be so scared of losing something that can't be destroyed by any external means?

Just because we are born in a family, which identifies itself with a distinct religion or a way of life doesn't necessarily mean we have to follow it. The only thing we need to follow is what's truly inside us. And what's inside us doesn't come in any form, symbol, name, or identity. It is nameless, pure, and simply divine. It has no identity, no symbol, no one way of being. It is oneness in its absolute entirety.

It has no name or religion or rules attached to it. It is free of everything and stands with nothingness, perfectly secure, not needing any external affirmation from the so-called preachers of god.

True spirituality is imperative for the growth of our spirit, which is eternal and cannot be destroyed by anyone. It stands beyond our understanding of the world, sincerely reflecting the sublime nature of our existence. It is what holds us together in times of darkness and fuels our fire for getting up every morning and living our lives how we want. Spirituality expands and levitates our being, so it becomes joyful and accepting of the world around us. We can connect to it fearlessly with no black shade covering our eyes and only the lightness of the sky flowing through all our vitality.

Somehow, we have managed to take this pure nature of divinity and corrupt it in the name of religion to spawn a distorted version of spirituality. From something wholly internal and personal, it has been turned into an external mechanism for brainwashing and organizing people. They can then be easily controlled and manipulated by those sitting at the top of the food chain to fabricate propaganda on behalf of their vested interests.

# II. SWAMIS, BHAJANS, AND DADIS

*W*HEN THEY SAW MY *dadi* physically struggle daily during the Katha, there was sadness in people's eyes, especially amongst her family members.

To avoid being noticed by others, *dadi* sat all day on a chair, barely moving an inch and listening intently to the *swami's* remarkable narration of the *Bhagwatha Puranas*. He was a master storyteller, able to grab hold of his audience intensely. He studied and read the audience very well and adjusted his narration accordingly, which helped him connect with his listeners personally. It was a great form of storytelling.

The whole time, I sat at the back of the hall listening to the *swami* narrate the various depictions and tales about the many Hindu gods and observing people's constant entering and leaving the hall while the *Katha* proceeded.

I was still in my own world even when listening to the *swami* narrate the *Katha*. All the dialogues and depictions of the god Vishnu in his various avatars mentioned in the *Puranas* were not merely sources of teachings and messages for spreading via storytelling. Many also considered them to be real events from back in ancient India. He was telling the Purana's mythological stories in the pure belief that they had really happened.

Who's to know if it all happened? But rather than critically thinking about what he was saying, I simply sat there taking in whatever came.

Layers of darkness were still uncovering within me, which I was trying my best to hide from the outside world. I learned from my *dadi*, who was doing the same thing while fighting her own private battle. An admirable woman, internally and externally, my *dadi* had a small body with an oval-shaped face that carried a pair of kind eyes. Her hair was dark, curly, and always combed backward and held in a clip. She always wore a simple *sari*[27], but rarely any jewelry on her body, which correlated with her groundedness.

She had always been good at hiding her emotions. Therefore, she was the diplomatic one in the family, the go-to-person for everyone when a crisis deepened in any dispute among family members.

Family drama and politics are a core part of Indian society. If you have so many people as part of your family, there tend to be a few crazy ones in the herd always trying to concoct a drama or be part of one. It helps feed their hungry souls and destructive minds, which can only be satisfied when a drama is going on.

In some ways, I think it is an essential part of experiencing life, so you learn to recognize those people who love feeding on drama. With time you can grow in wisdom to remove yourself from them; being with them and feeding their toxicity or unnecessary theatricals is such a waste of energy.

Not many knew that my *dadi* had been diagnosed with Parkinson's, and whenever anybody asked the family members, who knew what was going on, they would blame aging. My *dadi* did not want people to find out she had Parkinson's, because she was still processing that herself and didn't want other people feeling sorry for her.

She despised being felt sorry for. Her deep spirit as a fighter and a strong woman had not yet accepted that her body was not the same anymore, and her deteriorating physicality related to her age didn't help either.

Though seeing the way she was now, I could not spend any one-on-one time with her, as she was always with someone in my grandparents' house because of the *Katha*.

This is the house I grew up in with my sister, Shivangi. My grandfather decided to get this house when my father married my

---

27 A *sari* is a garment commonly worn by women in India.

mother, so we would not have to grow up living alongside other family members in our ancestral home's communal arrangements.

The house was built on two floors with several rooms and a large hall on the upstairs floor. It was full beyond capacity for the *Katha*. Many of our relatives were staying there, as well.

The ones staying in the hotel where the *Katha* was being performed visited the house early in the morning onward. It was like an extended family reunion along with a *Katha*; there was constant socialization throughout the nights and days.

I had not seen most of my relatives for years, so obviously, I was bombarded by questions about all sorts of topics. Some were about the U.S. Some were about my recent travels to Peru and Ladakh. Mostly, they were: "When are you joining your father in his business?" I was so used to hearing this usual charade of so-called practical questions that I could dodge the bullets without getting into any trouble.

Along with the unending questions, I was also receiving all sorts of advice because that's just how India is. People are great at giving advice and preaching about the right way to be in life – their way being the only way and no other truly sufficing.

At first, it was a bit overwhelming for my system, which had been operating in such an internal mode for the last several months in Ladakh, distanced from everything and everyone, that it took me a few days to get into the groove of interrogation and advice sessions.

My appearance in the traditional Indian attire of *kurta pajama*, along with long hair, automatically affirmed for people that I had entered the crazy world of spirituality and figuring out life. Generally speaking, that world doesn't have a negative connotation attached to it in India. In many ways the country's history developed around that. Nevertheless, based on their explicit outlooks on life, the way people's perceptions varied was not close to the space I was actually in.

I was not trying to be spiritual or dress in a manner that called for unwanted attention from other people based on their perceptions of who they thought I was. I was not trying to be anything or anybody – I was only trying to figure out how I could be true to myself beyond the social expectations of being the only son in a business family.

As such, I was automatically presumed to be living and acting within a certain, socially generated and socially approved framework. But how could I be true to myself if I dared to deviate from that? I would not be acting responsibly if I did, and I could well cause misery to my parents, who conceived me to fulfill my duties as their son by doing what was expected of me – not what was desired by me.

It was a dilemma. I could not understand why my decision to deviate from the customary path was causing so much reaction from others. My not being able to answer questions such as: "What's your plan for the future?" or "What's going on these days?" or "What do you want to do in life?" etc., induced grave concern in the minds of others.

Although these people were my well-wishers, and I wanted to provide them with some justification for my actions, I sincerely did not have answers to their questions. So, I chose not to answer most of the time or stayed silent and just listened to whatever they had to say without responding because I didn't know what to say or how to, for that matter.

The "I am writing a book" explanation came in handy the most. Even though I was unsure what I was writing, I was just rushing along with the flow of the words pouring out of me describing my time in Peru.

I wasn't thinking much about what would be made of it. "Maybe a book?" But I was not ruminating about anything more than that, and sure as hell, my mind was in complete chaos from having to process all the internal change going on in me. With the added externalities relating to Indian family dynamics, I was in total upheaval.

I ceaselessly watched my breath and let go of all the crazy thoughts passing through my mind, and still somehow rejoiced in the uproar of those moments. It was preposterous how people had so much expectation based on whatever image they carried of me in their minds. Being born into a family of high achievers always generates more expectations in the minds of others.

When I was in the system working my way up, devouring myself in the madness of making money and climbing up the broken ladder, people felt so satisfied with my actions because they matched their expectations of me.

But then something changed. An unexpected life decision was made solely by me without consulting anybody. It was based on a powerful feeling that invigorated me and urged me to leave the original path I had been set onto and follow an unknown one. Somehow, it straight away called for rejection and opposition from the immediate society around me. They might have been unable to say it to my face, but I could sense it through their very vocal eyes.

All I had done was to follow what felt genuinely right for the first time in my life. It took an immense amount of internal effort to build up the courage to walk on this nameless path, willing to lose everything in the process.

Except that, from having to break away from everything that binds us, contains us, or holds us from experiencing life in its true colors, I gained something so precious that could be neither bought nor sold, but only earned.

## A. An Evening with the Swami

I was sitting in the *swami's* company in his room after the day's installment of the *Katha* one night. When not a storyteller, he was also an astrologer and a counselor, among other things.

People used to visit him in person in the evenings to share their life problems, hoping he could provide them with solutions that would help end or lessen their misery. Their issues ranged from anything relating to personal relationships to business complications to health issues – literally anything and everything.

Immensely learned and experienced in life, he did provide the answers many were looking for. So, I tried to open myself to him as well, thinking maybe he could stimulate me with insights or realizations that would help me overcome the darkness consuming me. I was continuing to go further into it and losing control of my mind and myself.

Nothing could describe this darkness; I could not pinpoint anything about it. It was entirely abstract and had a strong sense of heaviness about it, which overpowered me.

I was sharing about my time in the Amazon Jungle and Ladakh with him.

"I don't see a point in being a part of any of this. I want to go further in-depth in myself to figure out what this life is about. I feel disconnected from everything and everyone. I don't want to be a part of this jangle, where people think they're getting somewhere and doing something, but really at the end of the day, it won't matter, and our lives will end just like that. So, what's the point?"

He had a certain depth in his voice when he said to me, "Where you are now can be a dangerous crossroad. And I might have to stop you here."

After a moment, he continued. "You need to think about your *dadi*. Her condition is deteriorating. You should spend some time with her."

"I will spend time with her, but I can't right now because I need to see through the book that I'm writing. And the space I'm in currently means I won't be of any help to her."

He said, "Hmm–" and just in that instance, there was a knock on the door, and some of my father's friends came in to meet with him to discuss their business troubles.

Demonetization had taken place in the country only a while before this. Overnight, Prime Minister Narendra Modi announced his government was going to disbar rs 500 and 1000 notes – supposedly in his fight against corruption.

That had happened when I was still in New York, so I did not get to see the madness and trouble at the time. Even months after the new currency was introduced, the country's cash flow notes were interrupted by a severe cash shortage. Many businesses, especially small- and medium-sized ones, had suffered harshly.

Demonetization had severely slowed down the economy and caused an overhaul of the country's cash flow, as most of the country was running on a disorganized, cash-based transactional cycle.

The men who had just walked into the room started discussing demonetization and the economy's troubles with the *swami*. At the same time, I sat in a corner listening to what they had to say as the night faded away, leaving me stranded by the door and alone in myself.

———— ∞ ————

The days of the *Katha* went by, and just before it was about to end, I decided to continue moving around the country aimlessly.

It was difficult for me to see my *dadi* the way she was, and I told myself I would at one point come back to Gwalior and spend some time with her, but now was not the time. Having spent several days in Gwalior in the company of so many relatives and family members, I was ready for solitude on my own.

It had nothing to do with anyone else. But with the kind of depth I was dealing with, I needed space both physically and mentally to process everything bursting through me.

Being simple and streamlined in their ways, my parents and grandparents were struggling in themselves with their thoughts of me. I could clearly see it on their faces. My *dadi* was the least worried, and my *dadu* admired my guts the most, while my mother and father were excruciatingly troubled by thoughts of *What is he doing?*

The gravity of that question was taking a more substantial toll on their minds. A million of our relatives and acquaintances were asking them the same question. And they were expecting a predictable answer such as: "He is going to start working with his father in business," or "He is going to start something of his own," or "He is preparing for higher studies," or "He is thinking about sitting for a competitive exam." These are the usual scripts you hear everywhere in the country when interacting with people.

It was tough for them to see their bloodline, who would eventually be responsible for the genome's further growth, becoming a goalless seeker. Their bloodline was not fitting into Indian society's usual survival matrix by following a set pattern based on age, gender, and apparent capacity.

After the *Katha*'s conclusion, the *swami* was to leave for the City of Rishikesh to lead another *Katha*. There he would be narrating the same *Bhagwatha Puranas* to a large group of *Bengali*[28] traders, who were visiting Rishikesh specifically for it.

"These *Kathas* are for crowdfunding," the swami told me one day. "They help me run my *ashrams*."

---

28 *Bengalis* are people from the State of West Bengal.

"I understand. We all have to do what we are here to do, and if this helps you run your *ashrams*, I get it."

Even though I was seeking through my own efforts in India's ancient land, I was clear in my head that I was not going to blindly follow a *guru* – or anyone else for that matter. I knew the whole time from surrendering myself to the world that nothing external, nobody outside of myself – no matter how knowledgeable and charming – could provide me with the answers to my life's quest. No god, no religion, no human, no place could lead to the ultimate realization.

Meeting somebody could work as a trigger. Listening to their experiences could provide some intriguing insights and ideas that I could later pursue and test for myself and adopt if they worked for me, but it would be nothing more than that. I could respect people who found their solace in devoting themselves to a symbolic figure – human or a statue – but that was not the path for me.

My path was to deconstruct all the layers while listening to the absolute voice within me, which kept igniting the burning, eternal fire that kept on strengthening me and nurturing me with the courage to stay true to myself.

I had not told anyone yet, but I had decided to go to Rishikesh after Gwalior and stay with the *swami* and his *chellas* in his *ashram*.

I was not going to attend another *Katha*. That would be too overbearing for my mind after having already sat through one. By day, in the Holy City of Rishikesh, I could go out and be part of the tapestry of the sacred land. By night, I could hopefully spend some time with the *swami* – possibly pick his brains. It sounded like a good deal to an accidental writer seeking more in life than its usual gimmicks.

We were riding back to Delhi from Gwalior after a sublime conclusion to the *Katha* with a *havan*[29] staged in the front garden of my grandparent's house.

Led by the *swami* himself, the chanting of mantras was musically accompanied by his *chellas* surrounded by the night's dimness. Many

---

29  In the Hindu tradition, offerings are made in a *havan* in the name of god inside a consecrated fire pit, while the priests read a set of mantras from venerable scriptures in Sanskrit.

people gathered around the fire to be a part of the holy termination of what turned out to have been a lively congregation of people, related to our immediate family by blood or other forms of human relationship.

## B. An Unending Silence

I traveled with my father and mother for the four-hour car ride from Gwalior to Delhi.

The City of Agra, with its world-famous historical monument of the Taj Mahal, was at the halfway mark. Renowned worldwide as a symbol of love, it was built by the Mughal Emperor Shahjahan in the memory of his beloved wife, Mumtaaz. An influx of thousands of tourists from around the globe came each year to soak up the presence of the stunning shrine.

Having passed the Taj Mahal, I was sitting in silence in the front seat as the car raced on the Yamuna Expressway that coupled Agra and Noida directly. That was when my father said to me, "You need to start working now. You need to start earning money again."

I had spent all the savings I had earned from my job in New York. I was back to ground zero financially after my lengthy traveling time in Peru and then in Ladakh. I was now dependent on my family to afford as little as a one-course meal.

I didn't know how to respond, not because I didn't want to work, but more because I didn't know how to tell them that I didn't see any point in working anymore.

An uncomfortable silence filled the car when he reiterated the words, "*Kuch bol ...*" with a hint of frustration in his voice. My mother was quietly seated next to my father in the backseat of the car. Both were expecting me to say something in return. They hadn't been able to get a single reaction out of me since my return from Ladakh, and I could see on their faces that it was starting to bother them.

I thought it was now time to tell them briefly about what I had been going through. So, I sketchily narrated why I decided to leave my job in New York and ended up in Peru. Having spent such a deeply introspective time in Ladakh, I was not yet ready to start working again.

I didn't quite tell them that I didn't see any point in doing a typical job or following a set pattern in life. Still, I conveyed the message that I was not just traveling but in this deep elusive phase of trying to make sense of my life and life as a whole.

The existence and the truth of what held us together were the kinds of things I had sunk myself into, and it was not something I had any control over either. It was just happening.

That is not the usual activity for a young man today. In their 20s, most people aspire to the life I had already attained in New York - a good job, friends, women, partying - all of which I consciously chose to leave behind. I sought something more in life, which could not be expressed in words, but only felt in my chest so achingly I could consider no other option.

Moved by what I had said, my parents were unable to respond. Complete silence remained in the car until the tires ceased moving, a silence permeated by solemnity, angst, confusion, and uncertainty.

## UNSPOKEN WORDS

The times were getting tough.
The weight of the world was starting to be felt.
Eyes were rolling away.
Mind was unsure.
Heart was overthrown.
Spirit was fading away.
Nerves were feeling grey.
Bones were losing hope.
Time was feeding away.

# III. DIP IN THE GANGES

*RIFTING AWAY FROM THE* set pattern of living, we are "supposed to" follow sires numerous challenges. There were times when I struggled while walking on a path with no confirmed life security.

*Is it ok to be dependent on my parents and other people so I can do what I need to do?* That was one of the many questions surfacing through my mind.

I had lived a financially independent life right after college during my days of working in New York at a job that I loved. It was difficult for me to accept that I was now at the complete mercy of my parents and the world. I could always go back to doing another job or supporting my father in his business, so I would be financially secure day to day. But knowing it would not provide me with the answers I was looking for stopped me from returning to that life.

Taking this alternative path in a country such as India, where countless people worked to secure their physical survival day-to-day, was a privilege.

All I needed money for were the basics of food, water, and shelter. Then I could focus my energy in congruence with my spirit, as it guided me to adopt a more wholesome and complete way of living – and simultaneously inspire others to do the same.

None of the peers whom I grew up or attended college in Boston with were doing what I was currently doing. All of them were braided into a similar competitive environment to what mine used to be. They were busy pursuing their ambitions to work in a high-profile job or build a company – or some other such reputable career – for which the financial rewards and high social status were peak life priorities along with the security that came with that.

Security means money because that is the means for procuring even the basic amenities of food, water, and shelter in today's capitalist world. These three assure our species' physical survival, which is something that our world – even though it has more wealthy people than ever before – still has not been able to secure.

Or maybe we have chosen not to – if people were not living in survival mode, how would our capitalist systems work?

Capitalism on paper doesn't sound too bad. But when you tie it with greed and systematic framework that is controlled by a market that doesn't value human life, or any life for that matter, as much as it values capital. Then it sparks for a creation of a space that wants people to feel insecure and anxious about the future, to trap them in a survival mindset.

Our systems today, when put in practice want people to live in fear so they can be controlled and manipulated. Inequality – in all senses – and class division – based on where you fall along the food chain – decides where you stand in the world.

It's a model of infinite economic growth based on the exploitation of finite resources and people. Economies keep on growing in trillions of dollars alongside inequality of wealth distribution. Greed driven capitalism continuously amplifies anger and frustration in the minds of those who see what's possible in the idealized "success" stories shown by marketers – but those people are somehow not ever able to get there.

We readily describe them as failures without realizing that no one in this world gets where they are today without many direct and indirect factors playing their parts in getting them there.

There is no doubt that immense amounts of effort and hard work may have been put in by those we term as "successful individuals." And the virtues of hardwork and competence should always be rewarded if we are to evolve as a society. The materialization of anything can not happen without physical action, but that is not all there is in a generalized roadmap for "success."

There is no general recipe. Everybody is different, and so are their circumstances at every stage of life.

We continue to build our foundations on an extreme sense of individualism while ignoring the need for us to work together to empower and support one another – especially the weaker sections of society. Thus, we never acknowledge how compassion and a sense of community are equally important in life if we are to create a harmonious world in the long run.

We need to find a balance between the individual and the community. For us to live joyously, we need to incorporate the desires of both the individual expression and the communal bondings.

We should not keep on breeding most of the world's population to be a very mechanical and robot-like labor force to support a short-sighted system that is massively destructive of our planet.

That system also minimizes the human side of things and leaves us working like robots. The human workforce will soon be replaced by AI machines anyway, as there's no way humans will be able to compete with intelligent robots working 24/7/365 and performing their jobs more efficiently than humans.

This is a significant period in our history. In the coming decades, we will see the formation of a new world order. Everything in the external world will change as dramatically as possible concerning the global economy, technology, and climate.

These changing times allow us to realize that our strength does not come from being robot-like but more human-like.

Being born in the body of a conscious being, we can transcend ourselves and realize the illusion we are living, and become truly free in ourselves from all the ongoing external charades. Doing that, at this moment, may seem trivial, but in the long run, it is not.

As much as anything else, the importance we place on everything is based on how others around us think and what they consider unimportant.

Realizing that things are always ending is where the beauty of life rests. Only then can we genuinely understand the importance of the moment we are in. Only then can we sincerely appreciate the importance of being alive in the body of a being that can evolve – which is itself, is a blessing.

If we continue failing to promote this primary reason for which we live on this planet, we are really missing the point.

―――∞∞∞――――

Having left the job and spent all the money I made on my travels, I was now penniless but still wanting to move around India as a nobody while writing my book and figuring out more of whatever it was I was trying to figure out.

With no intention of starting a company or doing something that would provide a lucrative form of income, a battle frequently raged between my biology and my ego. I was not working toward securing my future survival or thinking about having a wife or children. I was now in a state where to do what I needed to do – which I couldn't convey to people in the present-day, money-driven world – I had to let go of my ego and my feeling of guilt or shame to ask for money from my parents in the form of a donation.

It was not for doing something that would generate money or for spending on unnecessary luxury, but the basics. I did not care what I ate, or where I slept, or what I wore, or what means I used to travel.

Comfort or luxury meant nothing to me any longer, so long as I could use the approaching days to keep on understanding the depth in me and exercise the craft of writing to paint a vivid picture of the world as I saw it. This was based on the many different experiences I was gaining from wandering around different places. I was observing how people from differing backgrounds lived and thought. I was viewing with my own eyes the beauty in our natural world. Simultaneously, my thought process was being challenged to understand unaccustomed ways of living. All this was an attempt to get to the root of things, so I could exclude myself from my conditioning and perceive the world in its pure form.

I could do nothing but ask my parents for money, which would allow me to keep doing the things I needed to do.

I looked at the money I would receive from them not as something I was entitled to because I was their son, but as a form of donation, because of some untold and mystic reason that I was in the situation I was now in. For me to keep going further in my nameless pursuits, they would be the donors who provided me with the tools. Those tools would primarily help me fulfill my spirit's burning desire to overcome my internal darkness, walk away from the outside world's judgment and criticism, and devote myself purely to the pursuit of true happiness.

∽∾∾∽

I was again leaving my parents' house, a ritual that had become too familiar for them. They were used to me going a million times over the last many years.

This time, they were apprehensive. Even though they knew I had pure intentions and were willing to help out, deep inside, they were struggling to accept my ways. They probably wondered why I could not be like a normal Indian man – like the ones they saw around them.

I was more certain than ever that the ride I was now on was more than just a rough one for me – it was also a testing one for my parents. They had been forced to be introspective because of my unpredictable actions, but their minds were also in deadlock from trying to accept that things were not playing out the way they had initially envisioned.

Their son didn't fit into the image they had fancied for him based on what their lives had led them to believe. Now, they were going through a tough time accepting the capricious nature of reality.

I could see how their minds were relentlessly fighting against it all, not willing to give in to the reality of what was happening and wanting to keep following their fantasy of a fictional future.

This is one thing that not only my parents but most of humanity – including myself – struggle with. We construct fantasies and projections for our careers and our future, depending on the expectations we have from our loved ones. They govern us today, so we can work to achieve those perfect ideals we have for our imaginary future.

But when the future does not fit the image we've sculpted, our mind struggles to accept it because of its attachment to the projected future. It feels dissatisfied and discouraged when things do not fit with its vision of the future.

During these few months of going through such an unexpected ride, I learned that we could have all the images and ideas we want based on how our future might look, but at the end of the day, nobody really knows what's going to happen. If we can accept this day-to-day, going through life becomes relatively easier.

## A. By the Window

This time my destination was Rishikesh. Considered to be the birthplace of yoga, Rishikesh was a holy city in the Himalayas. I arrived after a train ride from Delhi's Hazrat Nizammudin Railway Station to Haridwar, another sacred city situated in the foothills near Rishikesh.

Both cities were major destinations for Hindu pilgrims and devotees, attracting people from all walks of life to receive divine blessings and be healed by the electric charge flowing through the sizzling water of the River Ganges. That river is called the *ganga ma* in Hindi – Mother Ganga – by many Hindu devotees. They have a strong belief that dipping in its waters can aid a person in being free of their sins.

They were situated in the small and alluring State of Uttarakhand and its extraordinary natural environment of the Himalayan mountain range, sacred temples, and divine Hindu sites. Both cities had always been prime draws for travelers and tourists alike.

Train rides in India are probably the best way to get around the country. You are always surrounded by interesting people and witty characters, who are extremely inquisitive about your life and somehow always interfere, so you can't ever maintain any physical space.

The concept of "physical space" is alien to the land of India. With a billion people, it is hard to be in a spot with no other people, especially on public transport overwhelmed by large crowds.

On a train, you can sit by the window and watch the country's changing landscape. It halts at many stations. *Chai walas* and other vendors offering all kinds of snacks get on and off the train quickly to tempt your belly with their treats. Your senses work at their prime when mixtures of pungent smells float in the air; you feel you are part of some 4D movie.

As one of the world's largest employers, the Indian railway is one hell of an organization.

From the minute you set your foot inside a railway station in India, you feel like you have entered a microcosm established within the cortex of this massive country. It is a whole new world operating within its own footprint. Striding through antique platforms inaugurated during British rule of India delivers you into a parallel reality, where history can be sensed and seen through the shades of the old walls.

I reached Haridwar and then went to the *swami's ashram*. It was the same *swami* from Gwalior. He had several *ashrams* situated across the country, and I was to spend the night at the one in Haridwar before heading to Rishikesh early the next morning with him and his *chellas*.

It was an old *ashram*, commanded by a much older *swami*, who belonged to the same lineage as the *swami* I met in Gwalior. Their school of thought founded on Vedantic principles had several *ashrams* across India, with a discrete *swami* living in each one like its head monarch.

The *swami* from the *Katha* in Gwalior had his main *ashram* – the one where he lived and taught *Vedanta*[30] – in a city called Ujjain. He was only visiting the Haridwar Ashram on his way to Rishikesh, where he had been invited by a large group of Bengali traders to run another one of his *Kathas* on the *Bhagwatha Purana*.

I arrived late in the night at a large complex on the periphery of which the *ashram* was built. The *swami* himself was to arrive even later, and he came shortly with his main *chella*, a young Hindu priest named Mukut, who accompanied him everywhere and had been his disciple for many years.

I was taken to a simple room for the night, and it seemed like I was the only visitor in the *ashram*. It was tranquil, other than the muttering chatter from the student dormitories in the background.

I used to refer to the *swami* as Swami ji. The word *ji* at the end of somebody's name or title is used in spoken Hindi to indicate a sense of respect when addressing that person. Usually, I addressed the *swami* and most people I met in India by adding the *"ji"* to the ends of their names. It was a more dignified way of interacting with them.

---

30 *Vedanta*, a Hindu philosophy, is one of the world's most ancient spiritual philosophies.

After *Swami ji* arrived along with his *chella,* Mukut - who was always very excited to see me - and his routine night time conversation with the *ashram*'s older *swami,* I went to bed. I wanted to be ready to begin my days of tagging along with the *Swami ji* and his entourage of Hindu priests.

It was all like a vivid dream.

I had no idea what was happening or what I was doing.

I had stopped thinking about anything.

---

The next morning, I woke up early to accompany *Swami ji* for his dip in *ganga ma.* He'd asked me the night before if I wanted to come along, and I had readily agreed. The river was close to the *ashram,* and we could get there on foot.

It was raining that morning, but we didn't let that hinder our plans. We embraced the water dropping onto our skin and made our way to the River Ganges.

I had last dipped in the Ganges when I was much younger and had not known what I was doing. It was along with my family. I had done it as part of what all children from Hindu families did when visiting Haridwar and Rishikesh - imitate their parents to do what they did. Many Indians refer to it as "an act of washing their sins" - "*Haridware jayenge paap dhone.*"

It felt quite refreshing to be getting into bristling cold water where you could wash away your evils - I sure had many to be washed away. You kept on plunging beneath the water while holding your breath and then emerging to breathe again. The cycle was repeated for as long as you wished.

We went to a part of the river where no tourists came. It was known only to the *swamis* and locals, so it was desolate all around as I dipped in *ganga ma* to wash away my sins.

Soon afterward, we were on our way to Rishikesh. More of *Swami ji's chellas* joined us on the car ride. It was almost like touring with a rock band, but a religious one. They performed *bhajans* while *Swami ji* narrated the stories from the *puranans* for set audiences, who were trying to gain some insights and noble values from the ageless Hindu texts.

For many, it was a way of cultivating community, socializing, and spending time with their relatives and friends while being involved in an activity that called for devotion and introspection.

It was almost unbelievable seeing myself as part of that religious crew. I had never imagined that I would be in such a situation. But I thought to myself at that moment, *that is what life and traveling are all about*. It is a matter of welcoming any possibilities that let you have a unique view of the world, which can eventually broaden your perspective on life. It enables you to understand why people do the things they do and act the way they act.

In comparison to the life I led in the western world previously, this was on another spectrum.

⸺ ❧ ⸺

We arrived in Rishikesh at the Vanprastha Ashram after driving for about an hour through the region's wilderness. It was a huge *ashram*, situated next to the gaily flowing Ganges River close to *Rama Jhula*, one out of Rishikesh's two famous bridges over the Ganges River. The other was *Laxman Jhula*.

Both bridges were majestic in their construction and named after the two famous brothers from the *Ramayan*, a major Sanskrit epic tale from ancient India. It is a flawless piece of Indian literature, in which *Rama* is the incarnation of *Lord Vishnu* and is born as a prince in the Kingdom of Ayodhya. *Laxman* is *Rama's* younger brother.

Vanprastha was not the kind of *ashram* that any traveler would go to. You could not live there for a long time doing your practice alongside a teacher in the company of a set community.

It was more like a low-key resort whose rooms weren't luxurious. Still, they were very affordable, so large groups of Indian communities from middle-class families could visit the place for a week or so to attend a *Katha* or any such religious proceedings. At the same time, they also get the opportunity to be in Rishikesh. It was a vacation spot for big groups, whose members fall more on the older side of the age profile.

I had no idea how I had ended up in a place like that, but was happy, nevertheless. I was getting to see another side of the coin while staying with a *swami* and his *chellas*.

The house had two floors with a kitchen, living area, and several rooms. In the vicinity were similar houses. It didn't feel like an *ashram* but more like a community with many separate dwellings in the same architectural style.

Somehow, I was just an observer of the whole show. I let myself be taken entirely by whatever or whoever came into the picture. Without trying to judge anything or make any predictions, I was there purely as a nonexistent being. I was least bothered by the happenings in the outside world; I was thoroughly attuned to the inside world.

## LIGHT OF DARKNESS

There can be no light without the darkness.
Darkness is what provides us with the ability to recognize the light.
We are made of both – darkness and light.
They live in us, and we in them.
To understand us, we need to understand each of them.
Light without darkness is no light at all.
Darkness without light is no darkness at all.
Life without understanding the light of darkness is no life at all.

# IV. REMEMBERING THE BEATLES

*S*WAMI *JI* *LET* *ME* have one of the rooms on the upstairs floor of the house we would be living in during the *Katha.* A temporary prayer zone was set up in the living space on the ground floor. A small statue of one of the Hindu gods that *Swami ji* carried with him was placed there.

All *Swami ji's chellas* were *pundits*[31], and each of them had a specific responsibility for the event. One carried out the morning prayers; one was the chef, and so on. The team of priests made sure that all arrangements were conducive to *Swami ji's Katha* running without any hassles. They were also responsible for handling the inflow of infinite visitors who came by the house daily to meet with him.

For many, he was a god-like figure, and they treated him that way as well. Prostrating themselves at his feet, people would ask him for his blessings and advice hoping that they could be freed of their distress and misery.

While growing up in India, I had always seen people devoting themselves in that manner to such god-like humans. There are many of them in India. It felt a bit odd sometimes when I saw people performing such an act. I had always thought that on an absolute level, all humans were equal regardless of how highly knowledgeable and realized someone might be.

Possibly, it invoked a sense of surrender and devotion in people when they relinquished their upright posture at the feet of the other

---

31 A *pundit* is a Hindu priest.

and simultaneously diminished their egos. However, where do you draw a line? Is it just a ritual that you perform when you come across such a person – because that's what you have been culturally conditioned to do – or do you consciously choose to bow down only when you feel respect for the person in front of you?

I figured that I would not give in to the ritual aspect by blindly following what others around me were doing. In modern India, that is something that I feel we need to move away from. If we are not conscious of our selves and not working toward realizing the illusion involved in all human creations, it doesn't matter what activity we shadow.

We can entrust ourselves to a god, or a human – or any symbol – and with pure devotion, we can cultivate surrender because that is what devotion in its correct aspect teaches us.

Unless we make a genuine effort to take responsibility for our lives by recognizing that nothing external can end our suffering, all that devotion might be of no use. It might stop us from perceiving that nothing external can provide our redemption.

Redemption comes from within. We can label it any way we want to help our minds make sense of it. However, I felt in those moments of being in Rishikesh with *Swami ji's* crew for the *Katha*, where I saw heaps of people bowing down to *Swami ji* or praying to a symbolic statue of a god, that devotion in its purity must impel some release within us. It seems to come from surrendering to an external object representing the pinnacle of what we can attain by being at one with the divine.

Devotion without any willingness to combat our inner devils, so we can break away from shielding fear and dogmatism, is not devotion at all. We might adhere to the rules instituted by the external world most handsomely and be acknowledged by the people around us for diligently following rituals supposedly derived from specific scriptures. However, it is possible to do that without letting ourselves surpass our physical selves and witness the actuality of life.

We need to ask ourselves why we are blindly following what we are told to do.

Blind faith can be detrimental to humanity's uplifting, as it merely paves the path to a herd mentality – to not questioning anything. We must ask, so we eventually realize what allows us to be free from our fears and defilements. Only without them can we live without being held back by anything or anyone. Only without them can we delicately resonate with our true selves.

## A. House of Priests

In the mornings, I attended the *aarti*[32] in the house I was living in. Following that, all the priests and *Swami j,* left for the *ashram's* large hall where the *Katha* was taking place. I made my way outside the walls of Vanprastha Ashram. As the *Katha* carried on until the evening, I got the entire day to myself for wandering around Rishikesh.

Rishikesh was swarmed with *babas* [33], which was unsurprising as Rishikesh is a holy city. The word *baba* is used as a mark of respect. Nowadays, unfortunately, many people busily roam around posing as *babas* or *gurus* and misusing the power inherent in those labels to mislead people.

Rishikesh is crowded with fraudulent babas. Many are trying to woo westerners, especially women, for money or physical pleasure by pitching deceitful healing practices to them.

I initially thought I had entered a marketplace whose best sellers were yoga and spirituality. It was almost surreal to observe.

It was relatively calmer and seemed more authentic around *Rama Jhula* in comparison to *Laxman Jhula,* which could almost be seen as a spirituality and religion supermarket.

"One day at a time," was the motto I was breathing by. Without paying much attention to what others were doing around me, I did my best to absorb myself in enjoying the scenic views while engaging with the land's divinity. I sat by the speedily flowing Ganges to write and let time's fluidity take over my days.

In the evenings, my eyes could shimmer along with the burning flames on the banks of the Ganges, where the Hindu priests chanted prayers followed by an *aarti.* Huge number of people joined in to sing

---

32  An *aarti* is a Hindu ritual of worship using fire.
33  A baba is a Hindu ascetic.

along with the prayers whilst feasting their devoted eyes on the powerful reflection of the fire floating on the Ganges.

The *Ganga aartis*[34] took place at numerous spots, some more well known than others.

I went in and out of many *ashrams* and temples while wandering around Rishikesh, not following a set pattern or a plan. Sometimes I would sit in the shade of stupendous large trees or in front of some pristine idols of Hindu gods. I would be in the company of nobody but myself with my eyes open and my mind not busy contemplating anything but learning to be while my body was gradually melting away.

One day, I was sitting inside a *chai* shop, situated close to Vanprastha Ashram on the walkway that divided all the buildings – a string of *ashrams*– from the *ghats*[35] along the Ganges. I was writing on my laptop when one of the two women sitting next to me asked what I was writing about. Her hair was golden in color, her eyes green, and her skin was clear and snow-like.

"I'm writing about my travels in Peru."

"Wow! Peru ... my name's Lindsay," she said, and pointing her index finger at the woman in front of her, "This is Meagan."

"My name's a bit harder than both of yours ... I am Kartikeya, but you can call me Kart if that's easier. Nice to meet you both. What brings you to Rishikesh?

"Yes, Kart is definitely much easier!" Lindsay said while laughing. "Well, we are both yoga practitioners. Megan was planning to come to India, and she asked me if I wanted to join her. So, I said, 'Why not' – and here we are."

We talked for some time. They told me about their experience of traveling around India. "We were in Delhi with a group of women from other parts of the world to support a local organization that teaches kids in the slums of Delhi," Meagan said. Her hair was darkish brown, while her skin was more tanned, and her eyes hazel.

---

34  A *Ganga aarti* is an act of praying to the holy Ganges River.
35  A *ghat* is a flattened embankment with a staircase leading down to the river.

They were both from California and very friendly. They were staying in a hotel on the other side of the river just next to the *Rama Jhula*, and would be in Rishikesh for few more days before making their way back to Delhi to board their flight for the U.S.

"It's been tough traveling in India as women," Lindsay said. "I've been glad to have had Meagan with me. India can be an overwhelming place."

"Yeah. I know. I mean, I don't face the same challenges as women traveling here, but I know it's an intense country to get around."

We conversed for a bit while familiarizing ourselves, then Lindsay said to me, "We're planning to go to the Beatles Ashram tomorrow. Do you want to join us?" Without any hesitation, I said, "Yes!" The word "Beatles" was enough to get me hooked.

"So, is this like a proper *ashram*?" I asked.

Meagan replied, "No, it's closed now. It's more like an abandoned *ashram*, I guess."

"Well, we'll find out tomorrow then," I said.

They left soon after that. I stayed to watch the sun go down by the Ganges. And just when I could see the flames from the evening *aartis* striking the river and catch the prayers being sung by the priests, it was time for me to get back to the Vanprastha Ashram for dinner with the priests.

We all sat together on the floor of our house, where the priest who prepared food, a fella named Shyam, fed us immense amounts of rice and *dal*, mixed with *ghee*[36].

Heavily plump in my belly with all the food, I later sat with *Swami ji* inside his room. I listened to the problems of the many people who came to see him, hoping his advice could help them lessen their troubles. The nights went by in interactions with people coming and going. All of them had similar concerns, business or family/relationships/children related. It was somewhat like listening to the same words emerging from the mouths of a variety of faces.

*Swami ji* would look through their respective astrological charts and recommend remedies to help them ease their way back into life. The

---

36  *Ghee* is clarified butter made from buffalo or cow milk.

solutions always involved donating something to someone or carrying out rituals cited in a timeworn book.

I was not always sure how much the solutions he suggested would help. I felt that whatever was happening in the world outside our perceived jurisdiction was not in our control. The only thing that could be somewhat within our power was how we chose to react to any life situation.

While we can carry out the many rituals and various assignments based on people's suggestions, I felt they do not necessarily reveal a problem's root cause.

Some things are in our control, and some are not, and if we keep worrying about the things that are not, we are not helping ourselves in any way. We are using our energy ineffectively.

Instead of focusing on what's not in our control, we should strive to work on things that are – starting from our daily habits, to the people we choose to spend our time with, to the decisions we make regularly, and other such daily activities. Suppose we can train ourselves to stop focusing on things that are ultimately out of our hands and start investing more energy into what we may have some control over. In that case, we can get ourselves out of the victim mindset and into an empowered one.

It is essential to develop a mindset where we do not just depend on others' guidance but learn to become secure and confident in our abilities. We can then keep listening to our inner voice, which in its untainted form already knows what we need to be doing.

This way of thinking can help us gain a fresh perspective, so we realize that most of our problems are not problems at all. A problem only exists because we perceive an issue as a problem.

If we can learn to distance ourselves from a problem and merely observe it, it can be deliberately extinguished over time. This furnishes us with the needed mental space for coming up with practical solutions to implement to help solve our issues – instead of performing a ritual of some sort that has no connection whatsoever with the root of our problem.

Hearing the problems of so many people night after another sometimes made me feel sad, not because of what they were going through, but because they weren't willing to face their root causes and quickly gave in to the web of fear. They let their fear decide what they were going to do.

I felt deeply compassionate for them, as they could not see that they were entirely driven by fear and were its victims.

It was evident that fear was holding them back. As I had been trying to overcome my fears – which had taken me through hell for as long as I could remember – I understood that when fear takes hold of us, we give away our internal power to others.

Fear is the most potent weapon humans in power have for controlling other humans, and they have been using it for centuries. When we are fearful, we can be easily persuaded.

Can you imagine a world where every single human being is utterly fearless? What would that look like? It is almost impossible for us to imagine such a possibility, as we are all busy living with fear intact within our being.

> Fear over our hearts.
> Our minds.
> Our spirits.
> Our everything.
> We are products of fear.
> Fear is all we have.
> Fear is all we have become.

## B. Letting It Go

The next morning, I reunited with Lindsay and Meagan at the local *chai* shop where we had met the day before. From there, we walked to the Beatles Ashram, which was situated further south from the Vanprastha Ashram. Away from Rishikesh's busyness, the Beatles Ashram was now part of a wild reserve and had become a tourist destination.

The place was almost empty when we got there. We conversed along the way. Lindsay, especially, was curious about what I was writing. So, I told her about my time in the Amazon Jungle and Peru, why I had decided to leave New York, and what I was now doing here.

There was a sense of connection between her and me as we could easily relate to each other's stories. She was going through a big change in her life as well and told me how yoga had made a considerable impact on her in dealing with the intense emotions that she had carried around for years.

Meagan, too, was going through a shift. She had been contemplating starting a new venture to support people in need. She thought it was essential for us to give back to the world and not be consumed by greed.

It was a meeting of strangers in which I could express myself at a vulnerable level, and so could they. It reminded me of the beauty that human associations can entail.

Being in the Beatles Ashram was like being in an abandoned village hidden inside a jungle. It was as if we had been secreted into a magical kingdom with mammoth trees whose voluptuous roots spread everywhere, even through hobbit-like structures where the ashram people used to live.

These free-standing two-floored constructions were dome-shaped. When we were inside them, we almost expected a hobbit to pop up at any second. Insects, mainly spiders with outsized drooping webs, were everywhere, so we had to be continuously aware of our surroundings.

A man at the entrance of the *ashram* also warned us, "Keep your eyes out for tigers. They come here sometimes." The *ashram* was part of a National Park, which was also a Tiger Reserve.

It was an interminably extensive *ashram*. Structures erupted from nowhere, and as part of a tribute to the Beatles, breathtaking artworks were spread everywhere from one end of the place to the other. Most of them were accompanied by the lyrics of famous Beatles songs carved on the walls.

It brought a sense of nostalgia in combination with inspiration to our hearts.

They were the first mainstream celebrities from the west to visit India in the 20th. Century who had been seeking something more than the usual. This led to India's opening to the world's artists and seekers, who come here to resonate and bring out their effervescent, burning creative spirits.

Somehow, the three of us, in our separate ways, were part of that trend.

The trees and the wildly multiplying roots were so evocative that in some moments, I felt I had been teleported back in time and could visualize the life of the people who used to live there. We moved apart to explore the place, each at our own pace, quaintly tuning our ears into the messages conveyed by the long-standing trees.

My feet slowed down as my every inhalation became deeper. After exploring for some time, we ended up in a sizeable but open hall. It seemed ideal for yoga and meditation classes, which was probably how it had been used back in the day.

It was architecturally sited so you could watch the sun setting by *ganga ma* in the far distance. Its walls were worn away; layers of paint were cracking and peeling off in an almost-transient fashion. It was a space ideally suited for a Beatles concert.

The artworks around the disintegrating walls were almost unreal. We sat on the abandoned building's floor at a distance from each other, quietly absorbed in our private worlds when Meagan turned on a Beatles soundtrack on her phone. Sitting amidst the broken walls with trees covering the site and the song "Let it be" floating in the background, the twilight began to arch out while our eyes soaked in the sun.

# IF ONLY WE COULD LET IT BE

The world could take a pause.
Pause from human madness.
Madness derived from an illusion of reality.

Reality we fail to see.
We only see what we are shown.
What we are told.
What we have deceptively become.
We don't see beyond those layers.
Beyond us.
Beyond self.
Beyond time.
If only we could let it be.

# V. ADIOS RISHIKESH

**W**E SOLEMNLY FILED BY the River Ganges away from the Beatles Ashram toward *Rama Jhula* as the sun was dipping down, and the choruses of evening prayers started being captured by our ears.

On our way back, we saw many *babas* who lived in the open by the river. They wore simple pieces of orange-tinted cloth while holding wooden sticks in their hands. *Babas* were known for their esoteric and occult spiritual practices, in their quest for liberation from the human body.

India is a land of many lineages of *babas*. Each one lives and carries out a defined set of practices and traditions – some of which are very extreme and almost unimaginable for typical human beings – but remain within the rules of their lineage.

As we passed some empty fields on our way to *Rama Jhula*, we saw some *Aghori Babas*, one lineage that adopts an extreme way of living. As part of detaching themselves from their physicality, they go as far as having sex with corpses to realize the illusion of it all and free their minds from indulging in any sort of human, bodily pleasure. Theirs is an extreme practice, and when I heard about it, I felt it was not essential for realizing the illusion of the world we live in. Though, it makes you recognize the extent some people are willing to go to so they can realize the truth for themselves.

Their version of the truth may differ from yours. Ultimately though, all that matters is that we realize on an absolute level, that our existence calls for oneness amongst. In a real sense, there is no difference between any of us.

We have invented all the differences on the relative level. We continuously function with an "us" versus "them" mentality, which allows such divisions to occur. Unfortunately, we do not see how the illusion we live in relates to all our humanly twisted, destructive mechanisms, which regularly succeed in dividing us, not uniting us.

I parted from Meaghan and Lindsay outside the gates of Vanprastha Ashram. We said goodbye to one another and continued on our separate paths. I was going to see them once more the next day, their last day in Rishikesh. They had invited me to have dinner with them at a restaurant near *Laxman Jhula*, a livelier part of Rishikesh, where many travelers stayed.

The *Katha* was due to end in a few days as well, and *Swami ji* and his *chellas* would leave Rishikesh just after its conclusion.

I had spent more than a week with the Hindu priests and *Swami ji*, while living in the same house as them and experiencing their way of life – while naturalizing with the world's unplanned eventualities outside the *ashram* walls by day. I was feeling ready to move away from Rishikesh; it was time for me to be on my own again in a relaxed atmosphere where I would be least bothered by anything and anyone.

Dharamsala seemed like the appropriate place at the time. I had no idea what I could expect from it, but I had spoken to some travelers in Rishikesh who'd just been there. They told me that it was peaceful up there as it was almost October, and not many people were around – which is all I needed to hear to decide that was where I would go next.

I would make my way up from the State of Uttarakhand to the State of Himachal Pradesh and eventually end up in Dharamsala.

A famous destination for Buddhist devotees and travelers, Dharamsala is a home away from home for His Holiness, the Fourteenth Dalai Lama, whose residence is in a large monastery built in Mcleodganj, a small town near Dharamsala.

The Dalai Lama has been living in India in exile since 1959 when China invaded Tibet. He was forced to leave his own country, and since then, has been fighting a non-violent battle to preserve Tibetan culture and Buddhism. He has been trying to bring the world's attention to the Chinese government's wrongdoings: they have been maltreating and molesting the Tibetan people for decades.

I found out all about this a long time ago when I first visited Mcleodganj as a student. I had just started college in America and was visiting my family in India for the summer with an American friend, Benjamin.

He and I visited Mcleodganj for a few weeks. We stayed with a host family and devoted our time to teaching English and Math to students in a Tibetan school. That is when I first heard the story of Tibet and Buddhism.

I was still relatively young and unable to grasp the whole thing back then, but it triggered something in my spirit for the Tibetan people's cause. So, going back to Mcleodganj this time several years later when I had become a devoted seeker intuitively wandering around India looking for answers – and simultaneously undermining everyone's expectations of me – would be a new experience.

———— ✤ ————

*Swami ji's chellas* always used to good-naturedly tease me in the mornings, saying things like, *"Kaha jate ho aap?"* or *"Kisse milte ho aap?"* or *"Kya likhte ho aap?"* We had developed a playful relationship – they laughed, whatever I did. It was apparent they expressed their fondness of me by teasing me.

It was heartening to share those laughable moments with the *pundits* over food every day while they tried to feed me comprehensively to have me gain big bellies like them. *"Aap bohat patle ho,"* many of them would say, especially the chef, Shyam, who had the most superb smile of them all. I never saw him not smiling.

Shyam was always farting and was a prime target for the other priests who just made fun of him the whole time and sometimes bullied him too. It was almost like being in a group of childlike priests. They were so naïve and innocent in their ways, but full of life and flatteringly devoted to their god and *Swami ji*, which I thought was very admirable.

As decided, I met with Lindsay and Meagan the next evening at a restaurant just by the Ganges near *Laxman Jhula*. I left the *ashram* early in the morning, heading in that direction and stopping at many random spots on the way. I was exploring unknown spaces while also taking some time to write and absorb the last bits of what Rishikesh had to offer before leaving in a few days. I occupied my whole day by moving at a gradual pace until it was time to reconvene with Lindsay and Meaghan one last time.

We had an enjoyable dinner by the Ganges after the disappearance of the sun. We welcomed the full moon and our emotions flowing in congruence with *ganga ma*, which was glowing to its utmost in the shimmering moon. We blazed after being awakened by our senses and felt ready to embark on the next phases of our lives.

Post dinner, we slowly toddled along the busy street next to *Laxman Jhula* and eventually crossed over the river to get to the other side, where we took a taxi for *Rama Jhula*. It was one of those old, white Ambassadors, which reminded me of my childhood. Lindsay really wanted to ride in one, and both Meagan and I were unanimously on board with that.

Sitting in that Ambassador took me back to my early days when Ambassadors were the only cars in India. A large shift stick was next to the big steering wheel. Prominent colors twinkled inside the speedometer. The engine made its voice heard – it was a car that reverberated like a truck.

We got off on the mountain above the *Rama Jhula* and descended the staircase to visit a local shopkeeper who dealt in Indian handicrafts. Meagan had to buy a stock of *malas*[37], the ones made up of idiosyncratic, colorful beads. We saw them worn by many *babas* and travelers around Rishikesh. They were used for chanting purposes or, in today's world, as a fashion statement.

Meagan was going to start selling the *malas* in the US as part of her fresh venture. An equitable portion of profit would go to supporting organizations from around the globe working toward uplifting lower sections of society.

I told her this was incredible and that I could not wait to see what came of it. She was buying the *malas* from a modest, young, local man, who operated a little boutique shop close to *Rama Jhula* next to the Sivananda Ashram.

Hours had gone by when I recalled it was nearing the time when I could last get into Vanprastha Ashram. "I have to get going, or else I won't be able to enter the *ashram* as they close the doors at a certain hour," I told them.

Meagan still had to work some things out with the mala guy, so we hugged and parted ways while Lindsay accompanied me to *Rama Jhula*. We wished our best to each other while continuing to embrace whatever the world had in store for us.

"It was incredible meeting you two," I said to Lindsay, "and I hope you continue doing great things in the world."

She replied, "You too! Keep on following your heart. It can never lead you in the wrong direction."

We turned around, fully smiling at one another before going on our independent paths.

I walked across *Rama Jhula* with the River Ganges spiritedly flowing beneath my body. A current was ecstatically thumping through me as I kept lowering my guards and I felt more and more enthused by everything that had been happening within me.

I went to bed that night not able to sleep – as on many a previous night –within the confines of my mind's vastness. Its spectrum was

---

37  A *mala* is a string of often 108 prayer beads.

getting broader every day from processing the changes, learnings, and new experiences it was persistently being captivated by.

Visions of my travels until then, in combination with everything held in my mind's deep subconscious layers, unfolded uncontrollably every single night.

I would do my best to observe all the lucid imagery and not be hijacked by it, as it gripped every part of my brain cells and stimulated my entire body into a state of constant wakefulness. I did not know what it was like to sleep anymore. I did not sleep the whole night – a regularity my mind had almost gotten too used to by then.

<hr />

With the sun's light slipping through the gaps between the curtains of my colorless room's window, I knew it was time to get up and join the *aarti* downstairs with the priests for one last time. It was the last day of the Katha. *Swami ji*, along with his *chellas* were to leave for Haridwar that night.

I had been practicing yoga with an Indian yogi who was supposedly 105 years old and taught yoga in the garden at the front of the house for free. He had been teaching yoga for god knows how many years in that *ashram* and was known to others as somebody who could not die. It was unimaginable to think he was 105 years old, as he looked more like 65.

Not letting my skepticism rule my actions, I just learned from him whatever I could.

I had been adopting non-judgmental and non-skeptical ways of being, as I was trying to give myself more room to listen to what other people had to say without thinking of it as true or false, right or wrong. I was learning to accept the words as they came, without any appraisal attached to them.

The Katha concluded grandly that night outside the *ashram*. An all-embracing *aarti* took place by the River Ganges. All the *Bengali* traders and their families soaked in *ganga ma* during the proceedings.

I watched the flames of the *aarti* blazing by the Ganga and observed the devotion in people's eyes.

Shortly after the *aarti*, everyone rushed inside the *ashram* to get their things together and be on their way. Many, as well as *Swami ji* and his priests, were leaving that very night. My stay with them had come to an end; I planned to get on an overnight bus to Dharamsala the following day.

So, for that night, I had to move out of the house and Vanprastha Ashram after saying goodbye to *Swami ji* and his *chellas*. I touched his feet as he was leaving along with his crew. Touching someone's feet is a commonplace ritual in India and performed by many. It can be perceived as a symbol of respect for the elder. And even though I was moving away from the country's ritual aspects, I would still, in some instances, find myself bowing down to specific individuals to pay my due respect.

This was one such occasion. *Swami ji* said to me, "*Apna dhyan rakhna,*" as he rode away in his vehicle, and I continued walking down the *ashram's* lengthy pathways for the last time. Passing by the communal houses, lush gardens, and large temple at the front of it, I floated out of the *ashram* to stand on the walkway dividing it from the *ghats* on the riverbank.

Several *ashrams* were nearby, so I decided to walk around to find a room for the night. I first went to Parmarth Niketan, the *ashram* right next door, but it was booked out as a large gathering was happening there. After that, I went to Ved Niketan, another *ashram* located further south from Vanprastha.

Ved Niketan was much quieter but ironically a bit racist against Indians. The Indian clerks at the reception said, "No," to me just because I was Indian.

*They only want westerners?* I wondered to myself. Then one of the two men confirmed my thought by saying up front, "We usually don't give rooms to Indian men. You know how they are."

I did not react to their racist attitude, which was crazy because they were Indians themselves. This was my first such encounter, and I did not want to think about why they did not want to give me a room, but I didn't want to go looking for another spot. So, I gently said to them, "Look, I have been staying next door in Vanprastha Ashram for over a week with a *swami*, and now I just need a room for the night. I will be leaving early morning. I won't be any trouble. I just need somewhere quiet to stay."

The two men looked at one another in a peculiar manner and then offered me a room for the night. It was possibly the worst room I stayed in since I had started traveling around India. However, I didn't care because I just needed somewhere to spend the night, and at about rs 200 ($3), the room barely cost anything.

There was something weird about that *ashram*, though. It did not feel as relaxed as Vanprastha or as enlivening as Parmartha Niketan. Right from the beginning, when I had the racist encounter with the receptionists and later inside the *ashram*, it felt strange. I could not understand why and did not want to think about it either.

So, I just told myself it didn't matter and spent the night in that prison-like cell they gave me where the paint was peeling off the walls, the ceiling had spider webs all over it, and the bedsheet smelled like dust. I spent the night there, not able to sleep.

The next morning, I swiftly left the *ashram* to get a bite at a trendy food joint in the small market near Parmartha Niketan. I also spent my afternoon in Parmartha Niketan sitting under the shade of an enormous tree observing the swarm of people incessantly moving past me before getting a shared car ride down the hilly roadways of Uttarakhand toward Haridwar to board a bus for Dharamsala.

―――∞∞∞―――

It was a busy bus station with loads of local buses filled beyond their maximum – a sight I had gotten very used to by then. When a bus was not bursting at the seams, my mind would become intrigued wondering what was wrong!

I found an HRTC (Himachal Road Transport Corporation) bus leaving for Dharamsala. It was a government-operated bus recently started by the State of Himachal Pradesh to boost tourism. It was relatively more comfortable and spacious than the other transport options I had used until then. Because it was a new service and not many people knew about it, they were handing out tickets at a highly discounted price.

I took the deal, and my body traveled through India's mountains not propped up by other people's bodies for a change. Instead, it had the luxury to breathe through its skin for the whole ride.

It was another one of those rollercoaster bus-rides, where I was unsure what the driver was on to keep himself acutely alert while driving ferociously through a zig-zagged highway built alongside precipitously-edged mountains. On one side of the road was the continuous hardened surface of a mountain, and on the other, a bottomless darkened valley.

Even though being on these rides in India was an adventure, I somehow always felt confident in the bus drivers' ability.

It felt like they were induced by the properties of some chemical drugs to keep themselves forever alert. At the same time, they drove for countless hours without interruption; their eyes stuck on the road without blinking for even a fraction of a second.

The bus had a few more travelers on it and some locals from Dharamsala itself. It was almost a passenger-less ride, which I had not seen during my whole time back in India. I took the liberty of lying down in the back row where all the seats were unoccupied and used that as a bed for the whole night.

A German traveler was seated in the row in front of me. She and I talked for a bit, sharing our experiences about getting around India. I always found it fascinating how western women managed to get around the country, as they attracted unpleasant interactions. They were perceived as sexual objects by countless Indian men simply because of their skin color. Because they were traveling alone as women, they were assumed to be easy targets.

Women in general – regardless of their skin color, what they wear, and what they look like – can face a hard time getting around India. Unfortunately, with the way society is set up, women and girls are inevitably beneath men on the stairs.

This applies to the whole world, but in the context of India, men and women are raised differently. This is based on pre-existing biases about the sexes which have indisputably shaped modern Indian society. The two sexes are not able to coexist harmoniously.

The disempowerment of women and girls is a sad reality in India. There are many variables – the suppression of sexuality, unnatural segregation of both sexes from childhood, no sex education or awareness in the schooling systems or at home, and false beliefs in most parts of the country that sons are somehow better than daughters.

Many other factors inevitably distance the two sexes. All this produces an environment where men in India grow up seeing unfortunate biases against women every day.

Beliefs such as: "Men can do anything they want and get away with it." And "Men are better than women." And "Men don't need to be questioned because they are men." And "The rules that apply to women don't necessarily apply to men, because they are men." And "It's ok for men to be with many women, but it's not ok for one woman to be with any man other than the one she is forcibly married off to." And "Women don't know what they are talking about." And "Women are weak." And "Women are always questioned about anything they do, but men are never questioned." And "Women are objects of possession." Daughters being married off in return for dowry is a prime example of this.

These beliefs are only some of a huge bunch that make a displeasing reality in India, and many of them are deeply ingrained in people's minds. All these biases have erected walls between men and women. Without us working together to break these walls and let men and women come together to coexist as one, regardless of the sex someone is born as, we as a society can never progress in our way of being.

Single women traveling around India have to keep up their guard. I had hoped it was not the case. However, I felt and saw how men and women were treated differently in most scenarios, more so in some regions than others. But the difference prevailed throughout the country.

Obviously, this is a very generalized way of looking at a notably complex issue, but nobody can deny the existence of an uncomfortable atmosphere in India specifically targeted at women. It can be noticed easily even by a man when you move around the country.

The German traveler and I conversed for a bit. I gathered some insights into her experiences while getting around the country, and then my eyes started to resist staying open. My body then lay down for my mind to fall asleep, but, at the same time, it continued to be aware of the constant movement of the bus drifting along the pitch-black highway.

My eyes only uncovered themselves when the bus finally stopped in Dharamsala the next morning. Everyone got off the bus in a zombie-like fashion, their bodies feeling worn-out from the journey.

A taxi driver approached me as soon as I got off. I told him I needed to go to Bhagsu, where a friend of mine from Israel, Ori, whom I had met in Leh, had suggested I go. She got me a cheap room for a few days in a local family guesthouse in the upper part of Bhagsu.

Bhagsu is a tiny village further up from the main town of Mcleodganj. As I was not familiar with Dharamsala, I'd decided to follow her lead.

*I can always move somewhere else after scouting the area,* I thought, as the drive to Bhagsu started.

# VI. TIME FOR SOME COMMON GROUND

*I WAS IN A SMALL* Maruti Alto for the drive up Jogiwara Road from the City of Dharamsala toward its adjacent town of Mcleodganj. This town is designated as "Little Lhasa," seeing as it is home to His Holiness the Dalai Lama and many Tibetans. It was all more compact than Rishikesh.

Since it was early morning, we luckily missed out on the traffic. I was to find out later that because of the limited physical space in Mcleodganj, the roads got congested quickly, and you could be stuck on them for hours without moving whatsoever.

Fortuitously, it was also the month of October; the prime tourist season for Mcleodganj had already ended along with the summer months of May and June. That opened up space as the influx of tourists to Dharamsala had lessened.

It did not take us long before we passed an intersection where the road split in two - one for driving up to Mcleodganj and the other for driving down from it - primarily to manage the traffic by having two one-way streams. The vehicles going up to Mcleodganj took the protracted Jogiwara Road, also referred to as Khara Danda. The vehicles driving down from Mcleodganj used Temple Road.

Below the intersection, Jogiwara Road and Temple Road merge into a single, relatively broader road with a two-way flow of vehicles, which continues to Dharamsala another 5 km below Mcleodganj.

As we drove up on the one-way section of Jogiwara Road, I missed out on seeing His Holiness the Dalai Lama's main temple, which is also a monastery. It is next to Temple Road, just where the downward vehicles are routed away from Mcleodganj toward Jogiwara Road's eventual two-way traffic.

On the one-way section of Jogiwara Road, we passed an indefinite number of closed shops on both sides of the road and then arrived at the Main Square, where we turned right on Bhagsunag Road for the village of Bhagsu.

From the Main Square, there were another three possible directions. One of them was Mcleodganj Road, which made its way down toward Dharamsala. If you took an aerial view of Mcleodganj, you would see it was carved into a mountain that you could climb up from opposite sides – Jogiwara Road on one side and Mcleodganj Road on the other. It meant that there were two entry and exit points for the town of Mcleodganj.

The other two roads from the Main Square led to the village of Dharamkot. The broader one was Dharamkot Road, adjacent to the narrower Bhagsunag Road. It went upward toward the village of Dharamkot and downhill toward the village of Bhagsu.

Another deviation – referred to as the Trail to Triund Hill – also led to the village of Dharamkot, but it was much thinner and steeper. Multiple entry points and exit points applied to the village of Dharamkot as they did to Mcleodganj. The Trail to Triund Hill started at an adjoining curve on Mcleodganj Road, and it went downhill from Mcleodganj toward Dharamsala.

The Main Square was at the convergence of these various ways. When the traffic peaks, Main Square in Mcleodganj is the last place, you want to be. It is a nightmare with traffic congregating in a cramped zone, with no space whatsoever.

There were tons of hotels and guesthouses along Jogiwara Road and then on Bhagsunag Road, which got its name from the famous Hindu temple of Bhasgu Nag dedicated to Lord Shiva. *Nag* translates to *"snake"* in English, as that is what Lord Shiva is known for – he has one draped around his neck.

We drove on Bhagsunag Road, which eventually curved inward toward the Bhagsu village while missing out on Bhagsu Nag Temple at the end of a narrow diversion off it. The temple was a tourist destination for Indians and flooded by heaps of people every day. Its prime attraction was a waterfall.

My ride continued along Bhagsunag Road to its end, where my friend, Ori, had come to pick me up. She was from Israel, a skinny girl with long brown curls that stretched down to her upper back. She had green eyes, an oval face, and ivory skin that integrated well with her confident features. She and I had met at the end of my time in Leh, just before I went to serve at the Vipassana course. She was one of the students who had sat in that course and departed for Dharamsala afterward.

Dharamsala is a frequent stop for travelers to India. It is home to the Dalai Lama and has its roots tied with what is left of Tibet after the Chinese government invaded it and destroyed its culture and heritage.

Over the years, Dharamsala's whole economy and its surrounding region have been built around the Dalai Lama. According to Tibetan traditions, he is the reincarnation of Buddha, "the enlightened one."

Also denoted as "the Living Buddha," the Fourteenth Dalai Lama is revered across the world by countless admirers. He is widely known for his message of peace, endless devotion toward his people, and his intention to inspire humanity to take the path of freedom and non-violence by practicing compassion and love for all sentient beings.

When I decided to come to Dharamsala, I messaged Ori asking her where I could stay. She recommended I stay in her guesthouse, situated in Upper Bhagsu. It offered cheap rooms along with a scenic view of the Himalayas.

I saw Ori standing by the road just as the driver said to me, "I cannot go any further."

"This is perfect. My friend is here," I replied.

I was happy to see Ori. It was an unforeseen meeting with a friend from Israel. "*Shalom* and welcome!" she said to me.

I replied in a jesting tone of voice, "It's funny that you're the one welcoming me! It should be the other way around, as I'm the one from India."

We laughed, and then I followed her up the stairs built at the end of the road where the vehicles had to stop. You could get to Upper Bhagsu only by foot, so I followed Ori up the concrete stairs. On one side, there were guesthouses, eateries, little stores, etc. – the usual mix of tourist entertainments – and the other side had an open view of green mountains corresponding to the one we were walking on. It was so green everywhere, the very opposite of Ladakh, which was very desert-like.

From the top of those stairs, the whole valley down to the Kangra District was visible. It almost felt too close, as if we were connected with everything. We were not just looking at the mountain range from a distance – we were part of it.

We did not climb all the way up the mountain, even though the whole of Upper Bhagsu looked so enticing. Several of its buildings were visible from where we stood.

Ori was staying in a guesthouse built on a plateau with a farm next to it. The family who owned the farm ran the guesthouse as well, which had no name. It was a very non-commercial setup operated by a local *Himachali*[38] family. Ori introduced me to the young woman who

---

38 *Himachali* denotes the people from Himachal Pradesh

managed it. She was the wife of the man who owned the house, but he was only there in the evenings.

I could communicate with the young wife in Hindi. She wore the traditional Indian attire of *salwar kameez* and always kept her head covered with a *dupatta* (a light piece of cloth) that went around her neck to keep it firmly retained over the crown of her head.

She was happy to receive me and called me *"bhaiya"* (brother). I reciprocated by calling her *"didi"* (sister).

She showed me a simple room, which had a window with a direct view down the valley. I was happy to have that room and thanked Ori for helping me out.

Ori was enrolled in a yoga teacher training course in Bhagsu, like many women travelers who came to India to learn yoga. Many yoga schools operated in Bhagsu, not as many as in Rishikesh, but enough to get attention. It was interesting to see how these schools made certified yoga teachers out of beginners in a month. Yoga is a practice that requires years of dedication and utmost conviction before you can think about teaching it to others, but I guess today, nobody has years to devote to it before sharing it with others. Everything has to be quick, and we need to see the results even before the seed has been sowed.

I did think the yoga courses should have been marketed differently, not as "teacher training." That would have allowed the students to come with the clear intention of learning more about yoga, its philosophy, and improving their practice in the process. That would be better than thinking about becoming a yoga teacher just after a month of starting yoga, which seems naïvely early. But that is not my place – I was merely an observer.

Hopefully, the courses helped people and got them on the path of higher realization about the truth of their existence. That is what yoga was originally designed for, and that's what mattered.

Today, yoga has become a billion-dollar industry as it has been heavily marketed for its benefits for the body's appearance. At times, I felt this was such a limited way of perceiving yoga, instead of seeing it as an intricate art form. Going deeper into practicing yoga can you transcend the dimension of physicality by unlocking the doors of universal actualities.

## B. When in Little Lhasa

I settled in my temporary, new home with the sun starting to shine over the fantastic mountains. Ori told me that if I wanted to go to Dharamkot, I could follow the stairs further up to reach Upper Bhagsu instead of going back down them. Up there, a pedestrian path connected the two mountains on which the villages of Bhagsu and Dharamkot rested.

Dharamkot was much more spread out than Bhagsu and divided into three parts – lower, middle, and upper. The lower part was quicker to get to from Bhagsu. The middle part was a bit higher, and you had to follow a path from Bhagsu that went there. Upper Dharamkot was higher still, and although it did connect with Upper Bhagsu, it took a proper hike to get there. Not many people went up to Upper Dharamkot.

The famous sites of Gellu Temple and Triund were located further up from Upper Dharamkot. Trekkers had to climb the stairs through Upper Dharamkot, which acted as a stopover point for those hiking to either place. Triund was at about 7,700 ft (2338 m) above sea level. The hike was in the surroundings of a splendid mountain range.

By trailing through the village of Bhagsu and keying into Dharamkot, I was flying through a magical wonderland. There were obscure rocky paths all over the region conspiring chaotically to funnel my body through farmlands. Views of mountains encircled my eyes and carried me through concealed parts of the villages.

Vehicles had limited access to the upper parts of these villages, so I could only get around on foot. Trees drifted through the land. There were tapestries of green mixed with mud and stone *Himachali* houses and an increasing number of newly constructed concrete houses. It was all too immense for my eyes to take in.

The recent constructions were primarily for accommodating the travelers who stayed in these villages when visiting Dharamsala. Both Bhagsu and Dharamkot were the stage for international communities that ran tons of novel engagements and activities around the area.

I strolled along the rocky pathway that traveled slightly up from where I was staying. It joined into Middle Dharamkot, the most commercial of its parts, which could easily get away with being an imprint of an Israeli colony.

In large groups, Israelis who had just finished their military service could be seen everywhere in Middle Dharamkot. There were many restaurants and cafés in the region as well, where many Israelis hung out smoking *charas* all day.

To my surprise, a four-storied Chabad House (Jewish community center) stood alongside the main pathway in Middle Dharamkot. If I kept walking along that pathway, I would ultimately arrive at Dharamkot's main junction, where Dharamkot Road and the path to Triund converged at the recognized landmark of the Himalayan Tea Shop.

All the taxis and auto-rickshaws were parked in a line next to the Himalayan Tea Shop. It was where the meditators and students who did courses at the two meditation centers next door hung out – the Vipassana Meditation Center and the Tushita Buddhist Meditation Center.

Both centers were favorably active and ran myriads of meditation courses throughout the year, so people were always going in and out of them and promoting a busy environment around that tiny junction. It was packed with travelers, tourists, Buddhist devotees, and various people from differing parts of the world.

A friend of mine, Neeloy from Bangalore that I had also met in Ladakh at my Vipassana course, was staying in Dharamkot learning and practicing yoga. I had gotten in touch with him earlier that day before I started wandering around the area. He was staying in Lower Dharamkot in a guesthouse next to a place called the Himalayan Iyengar Yoga Center. He asked me to come by.

Neeloy was a tall man with dark skin, a long straight face, big round eyes, and silken lengthy black hair. He lived and worked in Dubai for several years before deciding to leave his job and take on a seeker's path. A very talkative man, he was also a struggling writer and was working toward deepening his yoga practice while traveling around disparate parts of India.

As a very humorous and charming person, Neeloy always found a way to get around issues using his tremendous outreaching ability and wit. He loved making fun of Israelis the most, as Israelis traveling in large groups around India could be a book.

He would do stand-up comic performances among travelers mimicking Israelis in India, a phenomenon almost. Israelis themselves could not stop laughing at the absurdity of large groups of young Israelis traveling to India after finishing their military service and just going wild.

It was probably a reaction to being in the military for many years and now getting the freedom to travel and do whatever they wanted. I would probably be doing the same thing if I'd had no choice and was involuntarily tossed into the army at the age of eighteen. What a tough culture to grow up in – especially when all you'd heard about since childhood was army and wars. Perhaps that constantly keeps your nervous system at the edge of survival mode. An opportunity to detach yourself from that could indeed call for a wild ride.

I walked down the main Dharamkot Road, passing the Himalayan Tea Shop, and then took a detour of several minutes into Lower Dharamkot. There were some fancier hotels around Lower Dharamkot, which I strode past to arrive at a guesthouse next to the Himalayan Lyengar Yoga Center.

I saw Neeloy as soon as I entered its grounds. He was standing right outside his room shirtless when he said to me, "Heyyy!" in an animated tone of voice with his round eyes getting even bigger. He hugged me as soon as I got closer to him.

Once I met Neeloy, I just knew my tour of the whole area was about to begin. He knew not only all the places but also the people who managed them. His several months of staying in Dharamkot had provided him with all the information there was to know – and more.

I was soon following Neeloy. We first went through the Iyengar Yoga Center, where yoga classes were going on. He asked me to enter one of the classes to check it out. "Are you sure I can go in?" I asked.

He replied, "Yes, yes! Just take a look," and so, I did.

I peeked inside the door where the yoga teacher, an Indian man, was not very pleased to see me as he was leading a class. I took it as a sign to be on my way out, saying to Neeloy, "I don't think that was a good idea."

With a smirk on his face, he replied, "Probably not."

We continued down the hill in the direction of Bhagsu through little creek-side tracks with no people around.

It was much quieter in Lower Dharamkot than Dharamkot's middle slice, which had a lot more going on. We passed by many guesthouses and farms on a narrow pathway that took us to people's homes and then to a place called Trimurti Garden. That place was run by devotees of Amma, an eminently renowned spiritual leader from the southern State of Kerala, who was famous for giving out hugs to people.

Trimurti Garden was curved around trees in a seductively insulated setting embodying silence. We swiftly cut through it and merged with a rocky pathway that led upward. We stopped at a place called Divine Nature, based on the roof of a *Himachali* family's house. Neeloy told me this was the place with the best food. That was great to know.

Shadowing Neeloy was a high, as he energetically guided me through the hilly ways of Dharamkot and gave me a proper tour of the place. My body was synched with his, and my mind was busy receiving new information as he spoke without interruption.

I told him he should be a tour guide, as he would excel at it. He laughed at that suggestion and continued the tour as we made our way up from Divine Nature, cutting through rice farms spread out in a ladder-like topography until we merged with a concrete pathway at a crossroads. If we turned right, we would end up in Bhagsu, and if we turned left, we would end up in Middle Dharamkot. We were in the heart of the mountain.

We turned left for Middle Dharamkot, where Neeloy showed me the places with the best food options and told me all about who specialized in what. I had already walked through that part earlier on the way to meeting him, but this time it was a whole new experience. We stopped at almost every place, and Neeloy spoke with everybody.

After crossing the village of Dharamkot, we traced down from the Himalayan Tea Shop toward Mcleodganj. I had not been there yet and was excited to see it. Two roads went to Mcleodganj from Dharamkot. Dharamkot Road was longer and on a level, and the Trail to Triund was much steeper and took way less time to get down. Facing the Himalayan

Tea Shop, the road on the left was the longer one, and the one on the right past the Tushita Meditation Center was the steeper one.

We took the longer route, roughly a two-mile zigzag walk on a concrete road. Vehicles were continually driving by us as we talked about our travels along the way. Tall pine trees accompanied us down until we started seeing houses on both sides. Eventually, we came out at the Main Square of Mcleodganj, which I had seen earlier in the morning from my taxi when no one was around.

It was almost mid-day, and Mcleodganj was rushing with people and vehicles alike. I kept on following Neeloy, who took a left from the Main Square to get onto Jogiwara Road, not Temple Road, which was parallel to it.

All the closed shops from the morning were now open, along with the restaurants, cafés, street sellers, assorted food stalls, travel agents, and other eye-grabbing amusements. Straightaway, it felt like India again, but with an atypical vibe as the Mcleodganj region was primarily owned and run by Tibetans. They had received the land from the Indian government on a lease when they first came as refugees.

Little Lhasa was now alive – monks in their red robes were walking past, and Tibetan people were sporting their traditional attire and selling all kinds of Tibetan artifacts on the streets. We could hear the chant of "Om mani padme hum" as we rambled along the road, looking at the sundry delights. Neeloy kept on pointing at places for me to check out. He even showed me his barbershop by the street.

We went all the way down that road until there were no shops and restaurants to be seen and then turned around to walk back up. As we were walking up on Jogiwara Road toward the Main Square, at some point, we took a left to cut into Temple Road. Pedestrians did not have to go all the way to Main Square to get onto Temple Road, as there were several pedestrian shortcuts between the two roads. There was insufficient space on either road for vehicles to turn, as the space was so compact; vehicles could only move in one direction.

We got to Temple Road, and rather than making our way toward the Dalai Lama's Temple, we continued walking toward Main Square, where all kinds of goods were being sold. Neeloy had shown me where the Dalai Lama's Temple was but said that I could go there later.

From the Main Square, we walked straight up to get onto the steep but slender road of Triund Trail, which also reached Dharamkot. I had not been on it yet.

"I want to show you a place, Common Ground. I'm meeting some friends there as well," Neeloy said to me.

"Common Ground?" I asked.

"It's a nice quiet café. Stands on its own. It's filled with writers, artists, and an interesting mix of people," he said.

"Perfect."

We walked for a few minutes up the road, after which a place with a board hanging outside saying "Common Ground" appeared on our right side. There was nothing else around the café – it literally stood on its own, with an unrestricted view of the mountains on the other side of the valley.

The café had an open seating area by the street from where you could simply watch the mountains. As you walked past the narrow, glass door, the ordering counter was on the left. Slightly above the main floor, a group sitting area was on the right with a large sharing table. The table's colorful cushions were for people to sit on the floor and share the table with others.

Past the group sitting-area were two detached tables and sets of stools. Up to six people could share each table, as six wooden stools surrounded each.

A couch adjacent to one table was placed next to the ordering counter, opposite the detached tables. Behind the couch and those tables were large bookshelves packed with an infinite number of reads.

An enormous glass wall was positioned by the group sitting area, admitting bountiful natural light and allowing everyone sitting inside the café a clear vision of the road outside and the mountains far in the distance.

I knew I had found my space to be in and write all day. I said to Neeloy, "This place is fabulous."

"Yes. It is. It's perfect for you," he said, and I smiled in agreement.

A friendly Tibetan family ran the café. As Neeloy told me earlier, I could see other writers and an interesting-looking mix of people sitting there working on personal ventures. In general, the place attracted a specific type of individual – those in Mcleodganj for more than just touring around.

A sense of community and understanding characterized the people who came to the Common Ground, which hosted a safe space for people from all backgrounds. I somehow always discovered such a space wherever I went, and a lot of eventualities materialized from them.

Stories would emerge.
Bonds would form.
Characters would create.
Ideas would share.
Walls would break.
Distances would fall.
Love would prevail.
Lies would uncover.
Eyes would fare.
Skin would disappear.
Mind would elevate.
Depth would mature.
Pain would become.

# VII. THE BROKEN SELF

*A* *FEW OF NEELOY'S FRIENDS* were seated inside Common Ground, a young couple from the US, an older Israeli woman, and a mid-aged Dutch guy. Neeloy introduced me to them. They were very welcoming and asked me to join them.

I sat in their company for a little while around the large table next to the outsized window where you could see the mountains settled across the valley.

I sat silently listening to the conversations eventuating on topics ranging from Buddhism to relationships.

Naturally, Buddhism was a very dominant topic of discussion around Mcleodganj in general. Many seekers came there because of their interest in Buddhism. It was also the home of His Holiness the Dalai Lama. Programs and meditation courses related to Buddhism were always going on in institutes and monasteries across the region.

I engaged in the conversation for a little bit before I began writing until the day ran its course. Then I told Neeloy, who was still deeply engrossed in conversation with his friends, that I was going to walk back to Bhagsu.

I told him I was meeting my friend Ori for dinner at the German Bakery in Bhagsu and asked if he wanted to join us.

"Why not!" he replied.

The group of travelers I was sitting with started to disperse with the sun's diminishing tone, and after we'd been at Common Ground for several hours, Neeloy and I left to make our way to Bhagsu.

We walked on Bhagsunag Road as the sky was turning grey, and the temperature was getting ready to drop. Neeloy and I were fleet-footed and soon reached our goal outside the legendary German Bakery of Bhagsu, where Ori had been patiently waiting for us.

Ori's yoga course ran all day, and was exceptionally exhaustive in its outline. By evening she was starving. We went into the German Bakery, which adjoined plenty of other eateries, and was more of a restaurant. It was packed with a blend of travelers seated at plump tables.

I introduced Neeloy to Ori, and then we three had dinner. Neeloy knew a bunch of other travelers seated around us, so we ended up interacting with more people as the night uncoiled.

After dinner, I thanked Neeloy for showing me all around the area. He then left for Dharamkot while Ori and I climbed the stairs toward Upper Bhagsu.

I told her that Neeloy had taken me all around the area that day. "Yes, we walked so much that I completed a circle passing through the whole of Dharamkot, then Mcleodganj, and now ... I am finally back in Bhagsu."

She asked how it was.

"I loved it," I replied, "Especially Mcleodganj. I love the Tibetan spirit over there. It feels so real. Bhagsu and Dharamkot are also nice, but I think Mcleodganj is my favorite."

Since it was October, Mcleodganj was no longer that busy and had a very chilled atmosphere about it. There were hardly any tourists, and the travelers who were there had been staying in Mcleodganj for a long-time studying Buddhism or working on specific projects, so it was a very non-overwhelming environment.

"I might move to Mcleodganj in a few days," I said to her as we arrived in our guesthouse and were seated outside our rooms, gazing at the eternal valley.

"Why? You don't like it here?"

"I do like it here. But I think I need to be on my own for a while, and near a suitable venue where I can dedicate myself to writing," I replied.

"You will find that in Mcleod?" she asked.

"Yes. Neeloy took me to a café called Common Ground today, and I think it's perfect for me to write in, so I'm going to find a guesthouse near there."

She replied with assurance in her voice, "I understand. You need to do what you feel like."

Ori was a wonderful girl and had been processing a lot of stuff recently. The yoga course she was in was bringing her deep embedded wounds to the surface, and I felt she wanted me to stay near her, as she could talk to me and easily express her vulnerable side. However, I knew I had to focus more on what was happening within me because of my circumstances. I was processing a lot of change and being around the mountains was making me feel more aware of everything – the power within them was so potent that it amplified all human emotions.

The mountains were starting to make me feel more vulnerable than before and further my state of devastation. My body was physically reacting at regular intervals. My heart pounded severely and at length. Simultaneously, my gut felt like emptying itself into the open.

These physical outbursts lingered for several minutes and could hit me at any time during the day and left my whole body in a state of shock – which then triggered a release with tears dripping out through my eyes.

---

The next day I left for Mcleodganj early in the morning to visit His Holiness the Dalai Lama's Temple situated at the end of Temple Road.

It was a large monastery. You could walk in and be in the presence of Tibetan monks anywhere. It was busy with many visitors, Tibetans, Indians, foreigners – everyone. It stood elegantly on several floors with the main temple on the top floor. It also had an enormous outdoor seating area with trees and a panoramic view of the Kangra Valley beneath it.

The Dalai Lama's residence could be seen past the large open area with police personnel stationed outside the main gate to guard him as he has some enemies.

The large open area was where His Holiness conducted a lot of his teachings. On those days, it was almost impossible to breathe inside the temple; it was crammed with Tibetans and others from across the globe.

It was a typical Buddhist temple with a golden statue of Buddha inside, in the presence of which the monks would sit and pray for incalculable hours. Outside the main temple, small prayer wheels were set in a continuous line along the temple walls, which visitors would keep on rolling with a touch of their hands as they circled the temple on their way out.

I visited the temple several times over my stay in Mcleodganj, usually more in the evenings when the monks would sit in unison just outside the main temple for their daily chants. I liked sitting there on my own, either meditating or simply being and hearing the chants in the background.

His Holiness's temple in Mcleodganj probably came nothing close to Potala Palace in Lhasa, commonly referred to as the Winter Palace, where the Dalai Lama lived before he escaped to India. I had only seen pictures and videos of it. I could not imagine being there back in the day or how religion and spirituality would have been when that was all there was to Tibet.

After my first temple visit, I walked to Common Ground and wrote on my laptop for several hours before hunting for a room nearby. Behind Common Ground was a vacant area of land with trees rooted into it. If you kept strolling downhill, you got to the main Dharamkot Road.

The two roads that went up to Dharamkot from the Main Square formed a stretched triangle. If you wanted, you could cut through the forested area in the middle to get from one road to the other.

If you walked further up from Common Ground and cut through the middle part of this imaginary triangle toward the main Dharamkot Road, you came across an old fire escape style staircase. It was like the ones I was used to in New York. The staircase led to several guesthouses, built side by side above a few structurally linked buildings. There were entries on each floor from the staircase.

The complex was only a few minutes' walk away from Common Ground. Even though they were in Mcleodganj because they were placed slightly above the Main Market on the way to Dharamkot, they missed the blast constantly blaring from Mcleodganj's market area.

I got to the top of the staircase and started reading the names of the different guesthouses, whose entrance doors were on various floors. My eyes were singularly captivated by the Tibetan symbols engraved on a green colored wall outside one of the entrance doors on my left as I slowly went down. It said "Kalsang" beneath the Tibetan symbols.

A young Tibetan woman was at the reception, who could speak Hindi as well. I asked her, "Are there any rooms available here?"

She replied, "Yes," with a shy smile on her face, and then took me to the floor above, where several rooms were constructed next to one another with a lengthy balcony that took in the whole view of Mcleodganj and the valley beneath it.

I was not expecting that kind of view, and before seeing the room, I had already decided that I would stay there. She gave me a simple room for rs 500 a night, which I was happy to take. I discovered later that mostly monks lived in this guesthouse, as it used to be a Buddhist temple. An old Tibetan man sheltered in a red robe was always praying on the building's bottom floor next to flames burning in copious, golden lamps decorated with numerous Buddhist symbols.

There were two entrances to the building. There was the one I first came in after walking down the old stairs, and there was another entrance from the main Dharamkot Road. If you rambled that way for several minutes, you were in direct contact with the Main Square of Mcleodganj.

I told the young Tibetan woman as I was leaving that I would check in the next morning.

I then walked to Main Square and got on Jogiwara Road to trail down until I passed a building called "Tibet World" on my right. A place called Café Budan was just ahead of that on the left.

I visited Tibet World quite often, as they always had cultural activities going on. They also had delicious food in their café. It was a meeting point for other writers, Buddhist scholars, and artists.

Café Budan was much smaller than Common Ground. It had an open seating arrangement directly fronting hectic Jogiwara Road, so it was a perfect place for engaging in some people watching. During my days in Mcleodganj, I would sit there on my own, not really doing much but simply observing people's impeccable and synchronized movement.

While in Mcleodganj, my world was to revolve around these few spots. I moved from Bhagsu to Mcleodganj the next morning after saying goodbye to Ori and wishing her the best for the remainder of her yoga course.

I immersed myself back into writing while slowly disconnecting from the world outside. I followed the simple routine of waking up, meditating, practicing yoga, writing in Common Ground, walking around the town, conversing with travelers at times, and then being on my own at night. As I stared at the moon draped in the solemnity of the night, I would wonder what I was doing in life.

I had started feeling a lot of doubt in myself in recent days. All the moving around in India and earlier in Peru had taken a toll on my mind and body. Seeing my grandmother's pain and constantly being asked to justify my actions to others on my recent visit to Gwalior had weakened my spirit.

The weight of these externalities was starting to seize my mind. The question of survival had started kicking in as well. Some doubts were all that were required for the darkness within me to capture my senses.

All my work from the last several months to detoxify my mind, body, and spirit and realize our being's truth was now being tested to the utmost.

My deepest fears and insecurities had no form or words attached to them. They were just excruciating sensations that were surfacing and paralyzing my body. Not only was I constantly feeling like throwing up – my mind was simultaneously vanishing into a crushing, dark space where hellish feelings and visions overcame my every sense.

The roots of darkness were being uncovered, and it was all I could do to struggle to keep up with the ferocity of what was happening.

I was not sure how much longer this would go on, as months had already passed, and it only seemed to be getting worse. The only thing keeping me alive was the belief that I had to go through all of this to surpass my preceding self.

It was not something I could talk to anybody about; neither did I have any guidance. It was a battle of the self with the self, in which the self was getting destroyed.

## A. Unexpected Encounter

I stayed in Mcleodganj for a few weeks. In the interim, Neeloy left Dharamkot to continue his travels around India. Ori was still in her yoga course, and I had recently met some people that I mostly came across while sitting in Common Ground writing on my laptop.

My writing was the only thing that provided me with strength, as I was not writing to impress anyone or change the world, for that matter.

I was writing what was flowing through me. Expressing the extremity of all the change I had been through. Feeling everything there was to feel as a human. Life was slowly whirling me into a being who wanted nothing to continue in himself and was willing to let go of everything he could.

I did not go and explore anything beyond the town of Mcleodganj. I just stayed in my bubble over those days of unwiring, except that one day I went on a day's hike with a woman I met at Common Ground.

One day, I was sitting cross-legged at the corner of the large table next to the bookshelves away from the outsized window. That was my usual spot where I sat for countless hours drinking French pressed coffee and letting the stream of words take over my mind.

A woman with golden, lustrous hair, light green eyes with a tint of hazel on their insides, was seated across from me. With her back supported by the glass window, she was comfortably settled horizontally on the wooden surface beneath her body with her legs crossed over one another. She was wearing a loose shirt and blue jeans and reading a book. The sun's rays reflected through the glass behind her and struck the inside pages of her book.

She would momentarily peek curiously in my direction. I had noticed her doing that several times before the moment I decided to say to her, "I have read that book. It's a good one." She jumped in my direction and sat right in front of me as soon as I delivered those words. It was almost as if she had been waiting for me to say something.

An older woman seated beside me, but at a distance, could not stop herself from giggling at the other woman's spontaneous gesture. She was now sitting right in front of me with her burnished green eyes gazing candidly into my big brown eyes, and asked me in an excited tone of voice, "You have?"

"Yes," I replied, though I remained unmoved by her spontaneous gesture. I was so consumed by my inner world in those days that not much externally got a reaction out of me.

She asked me what I was doing on my laptop. "I am writing a book about my travels in Peru."

She said, "Wow!" and we exchanged our names. She could not pronounce my name, but I could easily say hers. "My name's Kensey," she told me, "and I'm from Australia."

We talked for a while, and I felt a sense of kindness in her heart as we continued. So, when she asked me if I would like to join her on a one day hike the next day, I agreed without any reluctance.

I had been restricting myself from unnecessary socialization. After so many months of moving around, I'd gotten a bit tired of continually meeting more people and was happy being on my own and focusing on what I needed to do – writing and processing everything I had been going through, especially during the prior month.

It had been a feeling of repulsion, almost, where my mind did not want to meet somebody new. My mind was keyed into a box of its own making; it wanted to be closed in and taken away in a noiseless dream-like state without having to be bothered by any human creation.

I could feel a deep sense of camaraderie between Kensey and me – as if we had been friends for a long time. So, when she left Common Ground and I returned to my world, I felt good about going on the hike with her the next day. *It will be a good break for me from all the writing and processing*, I thought to myself.

---

We met at the Himalayan Tea Shop at the top of Dharamkot the next morning. From there, I mostly followed her as we walked past Dharamkot and Bhagsu and then randomly made our way up the mountains.

We were not thinking about where we were going, just going upward along the unsystematic paths, while talking about worldly things and India in general.

*She has a busy but highly intelligent mind,* I thought, as she continued to lead the way and in our endless conversations would proclaim things such as, "These mountains can feel so overwhelming at times," or "How chaotic India is ... opposite to Australia in every way. Everything there is so organized. Here everything runs in a completely unorganized fashion, but somehow it still works."

A lot of what she said was how I looked at things as well. So, it was stimulating to notice this similarity in our thought processes and perceptions of the world. When I asked her, full of curiosity, what she had studied in university, she told me anthropology and psychology.

"That makes a lot of sense, considering how you look at things relating to people and disparate cultures."

It was almost precious to me when I met anthropologists, or psychologists – or anybody – whose curiosity was aroused by how people's minds functioned based on the environment they grew up in. Or how dissimilar cultures were formed. Or how the world operated the way it did. Or what factors contributed to making the world and bringing us to where we are today.

These are questions about the world and our selves that we never wonder about ordinarily. We are so busy being consumed by the pointless distractions we have delicately devised, which keep our minds occupied by things that won't matter in the long run.

In this century, we continue to live ignorantly, which brings about a disastrous future long term. We lose the essence of having the gift of this gorgeous life. What is it for? For living as if we were dying? For dying without knowing that we had been living?

The green surrounding the tracks, along with the warmth of the sun shining over our heads, made a perfect day for spending out.

Kensey was great company. I felt like I would meet her again at some point in my life. We were trailing down the mountains after having spent some time by a small temple built alongside a tiny village sheltered in the mountains.

A *Himachali* woman from the village was thrilled to see us and tried to invite us for lunch in her house, but we had to gracefully decline as neither of us were hungry. We were ready to make our way down as we had been hiking for several hours by then and knew it was time to get back.

It did not take long to get down. I then took the lead and showed Kensey the lower part of Dharamkot, where we halted at Trimurti Garden for a *chai* amid the oasis of trees before we went up to Middle Dharamkot. We had dinner together and finally went our separate ways as Kensey's guesthouse was in Dharamkot itself.

"Thank you for today. I really needed a break from all the writing," I said.

"Of course. I had a great time, as well," she replied.

"Me too! Hopefully, we will get to see each other again," I said to her as we hugged, and she said, "Yes, absolutely."

Tracking through the darkened streets in the earnestness of the night while hoping the vicious monkeys would not attack me, I felt broken in myself.

It was the lowest of times.
My spirit was hurt.
My heart was heavy.
My mind was lost.
Pain is all I could feel.
Suffering is all I knew.
Darkness is all I saw.
Broken by the shackles of life.
I was ready to give up.
A hint of light was keeping me alive.
Except.
I was losing hope.
As I was losing time.

# VIII. TIME TO CALL IT QUITS?

*T*HE DAY HIKING WITH Kensey was the only day of those weeks in Mcleodganj when I was out in the open lost in the sublimity of nature with a wonderful companion by my side. The next day, she left for Rishikesh.

I was in Tibet World the following afternoon sitting inside their small café, Crepe Pancake, on its first floor. It was less of a café and more of a library with monks and scholars always occupying the space along with an expanse of books oscillating between the varying topics preserved inside its minuscule space.

There were more books than the place could hold, and with the café interiors enveloped in darkish wooden layers, it was almost like a living bookshelf. When seated inside, I felt like I was one of the books in their fabulous collection.

I had always believed that every single person had a story to tell – a story lurking under the self's layers waiting to be scripted into a book. Now that I was writing a book – which I had never thought I would do – I started conceptualizing the possibility that a story rested within every single person I met.

The art in telling the story was becoming of sheer importance to me, not the story itself. I had come to understand it was not so much about what I was saying, as how I was saying it.

This declaration of how to narrate my story was to become my source of inspiration in the world.

Listeners' ears and readers' eyes were to be an outpost for the spirit, which could lose itself when those ears and eyes were altogether in synch with the burning of the rivers.

Kensey came to see me before leaving for Rishikesh before she booked her bus ticket.

"I'm going to see if there's a bus leaving for Rishikesh tonight, and if there is, I might just hop on it," she said to me. She was seated in front of me on the floor cushions inside the café. We were in a rectangular nook carved into the wall to form a box, where two people could sit with their backs resting on the wall.

"That sounds good. I was in Rishikesh before coming here."

She asked me how it was. "It was good, but I prefer it here. It is more chilled here. Rishikesh was too busy and sometimes unnerving."

"Well ... I gotta check it out," she said and continued. "I have this strange feeling in me today that I need to go somewhere else."

"I get that. Let me know if you do leave for Rishikesh," I said, as she stood up to leave while sending me the most heartfelt smile.

She messaged me later while I was still in Tibet World that she had gotten on the overnight bus for Rishikesh and was very glad to have met me. I sent her a message wishing her the best for her travels.

I somehow knew I was going to see Kensey again. Ours was one of those connections that was not just a one-off thing. Having traveled extensively and met so many people in the previous months, I had developed a good sense of when I met somebody special. It was an intuitive grasp that could not be described in words. It can only be experienced when you let yourself go down the path of breaking your self-perceived limits and being open to the possibilities the world has to offer in its tender form.

## A. Terrifying Night

Feelings of despair and doubt had conquered my mind of late. Even though I wanted to continue writing and finish off what I had begun, worries about the future, exhaustion from my travels, and constant work with deep meditative practices had brought me to an unhinged point bristling with embodiments of darkness and fear.

My body could not cope anymore and was on the verge of collapse. My mind struggled to handle the flow of information; every day evolved into a combat zone.

After a few weeks of being in Mcleodganj, I decided to return to Delhi and stay with my parents. I could not think beyond that as the depths of my mind were being unraveled. I felt compelled to wonder what was holding me together through that time.

It was mid-October of 2017 when I left Mcleodganj on foot with my backpacks strapped to my shoulders. I walked past the Dalai Lama's monastery and down Jogiwara Road to Dharamsala, where I got on an overnight bus to Delhi.

That was one of the most terrifying nights of my life.

All elusive forms of fears and darkness that had been brewing within me since I left New York exploded onto the surface while I was trapped inside the bus, threading through the mountains. It felt like death had embodied my being, and my mind could not make sense of anything. I lost all hope and thought to myself, *I am done ... I can't do this anymore.*

I was not sure what I was "done with," but nothing made sense in that unbearable collapse. I had no control over my mind, and my self-assurance was fading, as I could not see past that terrifying moment.

It seemed that I was forever utterly contained by that horrific moment. And I could do nothing. I was stuck inside a bus with a strong impulse to jump out. All I wanted was not to be trapped by that endless moment of hell, wholly consumed by my infinite darkness.

Somehow, I survived the night, which seemed to slog on forever. I could not remember how many such nights there had been in the last many months, but every time I overcame such a dark, imposing time, something within me changed.

## B. Lonely by the Days

This was the first time in my life that I was going back to my parents' home without having any thoughts of when I would be leaving again or where I would be going next. No signs of those thoughts were in my mind at all.

I arrived in Delhi very much broken in myself. I was unsure if my parents could tell when they first saw me, but I sure couldn't tell them about the state I was in. No words would suffice, and it would not be pleasant for them to hear. So, again, I kept it all to myself.

It took me a few more months to finish the book I was writing at the time. For those months, I barely left my parents' ground-floor apartment of four rooms as well as a living room, dining room, and kitchen.

A single passageway from the entrance linked the entire apartment. The dining and living rooms were across from each other, with an open kitchen attached to the dining room.

There were three rooms away at the far end of the passageway, their doors next to one another in a square-like formation. The fourth room stood on its own next to the apartment's entrance. That was where guests stayed, and my parents being very sociable, it always had guests in it.

I liked that room the most, as it was on its own and had a window I could see through into the garden outside accessible to everyone who lived in the whole complex. These private housing options within a complex were known as "societies" in India. They had become very trendy over the previous decade, especially in the major cities. Many people lived in residential complexes like that.

That room became my home for the next few months. I hardly came out of it and even ate most of my daily meals in it on my own.

My parents and my sister, who was also staying in the apartment at the time, were glad to have me back but knew something had drastically changed – not because I said anything, but because they could sense how I was.

I cut myself off from the external world in every way possible and only interacted with a few people during that time through my phone. Kensey, who was traveling around Himachal then, was one of them. I saw her a few times when she passed through Delhi before going to Rajasthan and other parts of India. I even met her mother, who had come from Australia for a month to travel with her.

When visitors came to my parents' house, I contributed only minimal conversation. I listened to whatever they had to say but did not give anything away about what was going on in my mind.

Many thought it was a time of loneliness.

More so, it was a time of reflection and reconciliation in myself.

Months raced by, and I finished writing my book by the end of January in 2018. Then straight away, I gave in to parental demands to start working in my father's business. The day after I finished writing my book, I moved to Gwalior, where I was to stay with my grandparents while simultaneously doing that.

His business manufactured water storage tanks and pipes. The tanks were installed above individual houses with pipes inside the walls linking them to the bathroom taps.

The manufacturing facility was situated in an industrial area called Banmore, a 30-minute drive from Gwalior.

"I started the company from a small room in Gwalior. So, you need to start working from there as well," my father said to me the day before I was leaving for Gwalior.

In my parents' eyes, I could see that they were thrilled I was going to start working with my father. I had never really thought I would work with him because from an early age I always did my own thing and moved to the US when I was seventeen.

I had studied and simultaneously worked all through my years of living in the US, and right after finishing university, I moved to New York City to pursue the American dream. I started climbing the success ladder hurriedly while working for a solar startup company before unexpectedly jumping off the ladder to go traveling – not knowing at the time what was coming.

And now that it was close to a year since then, it was a big swing for me to give in to my parents' genuine desire, which arose from a respectable place in them.

I sincerely thought that I should give this fresh chapter a fair shot and try to learn from it as much as I could, even though deep in myself, I knew that it was not the path for me. Still, I didn't want to step into that untried life without being willing to embrace the virtues of surrender.

---

I got on a train from New Delhi for Gwalior to begin a fresh chapter of my Indian journey. I would be working again in the business world and had to snap out of the seeker's mindset to bring my focus back to the realities of the relative world.

My grandparents were thrilled when they found out that I would be living with them. The Gwalior railway station has a palatial exterior. Gwalior is a historic city famous for its old fort, Man Singh Palace, now a remarkable museum, and several other historical sites, providing some pleasantries to visitors' eyes.

It was almost as if there had been a glitch in the system. A year before, I had been living a fabulous life in New York. Now I had returned to my family's roots and where I was born. It marked the completion of the whole cycle of leaving behind an old life and starting a new one.

With the clear intention of wanting to spend time with my grandparents, I alternated my days – I went to the factory one day and my grandfather's office the next to work under him.

My grandfather, Gopal Das Ladha, was one of the most revered chartered accountants of the city. He had built his accountancy firm all on his own, contrary to his father's wishes. The latter wanted him to handle the family clothing shop, the only source of livelihood for countless members of our entire extended family.

He had a dominant personality, my *dadu*. He always wore the customary Indian attire of a *Kurta Pyjama*, all in white, which contrasted well with his dark skin and bulky spectacles. The crown of his head was bald now, but some wild, white hair still dribbled outward from his temples.

In the last few years, my *dadu*, an empathetic man, in collaboration with a few of his friends, had started a non-profit organization in Gwalior called *Samarpan*, "complete surrender" in English. Its primary intention was to feed the underprivileged and offer them affordable health services at minimal rates possible. They distributed food packets for 5 rs each and the health services were on a break-even financial basis to cover the organization's running costs.

My grandmother, *dadi*, was truly delighted when she found out that I would be living with her. Even though she was struggling with Parkinson's, having me around motivated her to prepare meals for me, which she had loved doing when I was a kid. It was the celebrated love of the grandmother that I could see bubbling in her, as she felt energetic enough in the mornings to get out of bed and cook for me.

Both my *dadu* and *dadi* were phenomenal human beings, and now I was getting to spend some precious time with them after years of being away.

My grandparents lived in a two-floored house, which was built under their supervision in their earlier days. The floor above was mostly unoccupied nowadays and came in use only when relatives visited. My parents' previous room was up there, so they stayed on that floor whenever they visited Gwalior.

A sturdy, metallic gate connected the house directly to the main road, which had become cripplingly busy and noisy over the years as commercial activities grew in the area.

As you walked inside the metallic gate, a small garden was to the left of the pathway with a parking space for my grandfather's car. Asoka trees shielded the boundary walls on the perimeter, stretched over the front gate, and then turned inward away from the main road to fashion a unified plot.

An entrance door took you inside a closed verandah past the pathway near the garden. On the verandah, a hefty wooden door with a slab of glass in it was the last barrier you had to get through before entering the house.

There was a hallway with a dining room and an attached living room on the left beyond the wooden door. Straight past the dining table, a plain white wall greeted you, and at the left corner of this wall was the entrance to the kitchen. If you walked around the dining table to the right was the door to my grandparents' room.

The wall next to the kitchen entrance was thick. It had wooden steps thrust into it, which led to a tiny room on a mezzanine floor at the top-right corner of the hallway overlooking the dining table.

This misfit of a room on the mezzanine floor used to be a cramped storage space back in the day with its entrance door on the house's rear. When the house was renovated a few years ago, they'd broken the walls inside the hallway to join the storage room directly to the hallway and thus converted it into a room that could be used by guests when needed.

With this box of a room now attached to the bottom floor, there was no need to go to the upstairs floor; its stairs were on the right side next to the main entrance door.

I stayed in that tiny mezzanine room. It had a sliding glass door for an entrance, a low ceiling, a mattress on the floor, an old desk, and steel cabinets in front of the mattress. These cabinets were crammed with my grandfather's books, which were mostly related to accounting and taxes.

It was interesting for me to notice the kind of shift that was taking place in the external world and how my mind, which had until now been out in the world seeking answers, was observing this domesticated life I was now part of.

That instantaneous transition initiated a strange feeling in me. After finishing my book, I was gearing up to work in the business world in just one day's time. I was not trying to fight what was happening but merely giving in to whatever spontaneously cropped up.

───── ❄ ─────

The factory was a 30-minute drive away from my grandparents' house. I used to ride along with the factory manager, Sidhwani, who came to pick me up early in the morning. He was a loyal and hardworking employee who had been working with my father for a long time.

He was a tall and dark fellow who had a sharp mind and a direct and cut-throat managerial style. He used to be a trainee under my grandfather in the early days before my father hired him at his factory. So, I had known him from way before when I was a young kid and saw him around.

India is a country of relationships and emotions. This is also part of the business culture, so employees are almost like family members and stay with just one company for their whole lives. It is quite different from the western world, where, in my experience, everything is very professional and straight to the point. But in India, things work a little differently.

In 21st Century India, relationships among business partners, and the countless parties involved in the trade have priority. Relationships and understanding are equally responsible for the proper functioning of a business in the country.

In India, people always prefer working with someone they can trust and build a long-term relationship with. Loyalty is highly valued in the Indian way of running a business.

Having worked in the US earlier, my working experience in India was limited. Even though I came from a business background and had seen my father build his company from childhood, for some reason, I had never really taken an interest in getting to properly know what my father did. I had visited his factory many times, but just as a casual observer. I had never been aligned with any details.

Sidhwani managed the manufacturing unit for pipes and its fittings, and another manager managed the unit across the road for manufacturing tanks. I spent time in both places, learning about the manufacturing, supply chain, and operational processes.

It was a business with immense competition in the market as the manufacture of pipes and water storage tanks is not that complicated.

The key parameters that provided one company with leverage over others in this industry were the sustained quality of the product, the service provided to the business partners – the "dealers" – competitive pricing of the products along with proper branding, and at the same time, management of a healthy relationship with the high performing dealers.

It did not take long before I understood how the business worked. When I was in the factory, I spent my time going around every department, learning how they functioned and the tasks they handled. I also took the time to learn how the manufacturing process worked to have a good understanding of what we were selling.

On the alternate days, I was with my grandfather in his small accountancy firm, located near one of the most celebrated temples of the city – Acheleshwar. It was a sacred temple for Hindus and on Katora Tal Road, Gwalior's most prominent road with famous colleges, hospitals, and old temples built around it.

At the start of this road was Scindia Palace. The Scindia royal family had lived there for centuries ruling over the City of Gwalior. Most of the palace had been transformed into a museum, but the Scindia family still occupied a part of it.

After a few weeks back into the business world, I felt reasonably grooved in my skills. I guess having studied business in university and having been involved in other businesses in the US still held onto me subconsciously, and my mind only needed some refreshment.

Although it all came naturally to me, something else deep within me was being suppressed in the meantime. What was it? I was not inquiring yet.

At nights, I would sit in the company of *dadu* and *dadi*, who shared stories with me from their past, while I listened to them sincerely as they opened their hearts.

"I used to take pills that could keep me up at night, so I could study by night and handle the shop in the daytime," said *dadu* one of those nights, when I asked him how he'd managed to pass the Chartered Accountancy (CA) exam when his father wasn't for it.

And my *dadi* told me, "I was the only woman enrolled in the college in Gwalior, where I studied political science. And because I was already married, I had to go to college with the front of my face covered with the *sari's pallu*[39]."

I was always amazed by their stories about the kind of India they grew up in. *It was literally another world*, I would think while listening to their stories of India during the 1950s and 60s.

By the time I was lying down on my mattress looking at the white ceiling above my eyes, having gained a plentitude of information over the day, my mind felt stimulated. However, a part of me, which I think I was consciously suppressing, was not entirely satisfied.

I would note that feeling until my eyes closed without letting it develop into anything – I wanted to give this business thing a fair shot before arriving at any given conclusion.

---

39 A *pallu* is what women in India call the extended cloth of the *sari* that they wear. It usually falls down the back of their shoulders toward the ground.

# THE LOST SOUL

Losing my eyes.
Flinching my toes.
Twisting my nose.
Deathening my hold.
Bursting my floors.
Blocking my doors.
Deepening my soul.

# IX. SUITS AGAIN

*S*OMETHING ABOUT WEARING A suit makes humans feel powerful or influential. It's a style of clothing that has been comprehensively adopted by the world today. Leaders worldwide, business folk, lawyers – and all those with highly esteemed job profiles – share one thing in common. In suits, they appear professional and cosmopolitan.

It is intriguing how clothing and fashion play their unique roles in the human world, while all other animals roam around with their bare skin in direct contact with the breeze. We, humans, are restlessly consumed by the madness of the million ways of dressing we have construed for ourselves.

Depending on someone's attire, perceptions are sparked in our minds. If somebody is wearing a suit, we automatically consider them important. If we come across somebody in torn, dirty, old clothes, a feeling of disapproval might flit through our minds.

We are so thoroughly schooled in the look of what we wear and how it represents our image in the human world, we have added these additional layers onto our already heavily layered self.

We wear different sets of clothes depending on our deceptive society's demands to play our roles.

---

Having spent a few weeks in Gwalior working in the factory and my grandfather's office, I felt primed to begin working with my father in his Noida office. My grandparents were very sad when I left Gwalior. They had tears in their eyes as they modestly posed outside the metallic gate of their house when it was time for me to go to the railway station.

*Dadi* whispered to me, "You didn't stay long enough. *Thoda aur ruk jaa.*"

I smiled at her comment, and after touching my grandparents' feet to receive their blessings, I sat inside the car to be on my way to the railway station, where I got on the Gatiman Express, the fast train for Delhi that had recently started. It covered the total distance in just a few hours, only pausing mid-way at Agra.

Squeezing into working mode, I started going to the office with my father the morning after I arrived in Delhi, thereby fulfilling his long-held dream.

"Every father wants his son to join him in his business," he had said to me one day many years ago, and now that I had joined him in his business, it was almost a cliché.

I was now doing what most sons in India had been doing for generations. It was a tradition that was not questioned by most families in India. People felt it was a safe assumption – our son will take over the business or the farm after us. And if they were not from a business or agricultural family, the assumption was – our son will become an engineer or a doctor and fulfill our aspirations and provide a better future for our family. Playing into these sacred assumptions, I had now become a part of this tradition.

After working in its Finance, Operations, Manufacturing, and Purchasing departments, I had learned how the numbers flew and what was entailed in the proper functioning of all the systems to ensure the company's accountability and profitability. Once I had gained this thorough understanding of the business back-end, I was on my way to fulfilling the ideal Indian son's destiny.

Wearing suits again when the situation demanded. Sitting with lawyers and financiers in stressful and ferociously long meetings in conference rooms. Going through and analyzing the company's financial sheets. Shadowing my father and his business partner – also his cousin, my uncle. Seeing how they worked and dealt daily with everything involved in the steady running of a business in India, where, with its changing scenarios and complexities, things never ran smoothly.

I forgot what I had been through in the months after leaving New York. I seemed to have no time to think of anything other than all the business stuff going on. There was no space for anything else.

A cloud had encased my body, and I was purposely choosing not to see past it.

Once I strode into the Sales and Marketing departments, I had jumped fully into the business wagon. Sales and marketing were what I was familiar with because that was what I had done in New York, and that is where my skill set's strength.

I had purposely kept those two for last because I knew I had to first understand how Finance, Operations, Manufacturing, and Purchasing worked in this business. I told myself that once my grasp of the business back-end was fortified, it would not take long to get myself going on the sales side of things. And that's exactly what happened.

"The best way to learn sales is to start selling. Once you are in the field, the field teaches you."

That was my philosophy when it came to sales. I had embodied it in all my sales jobs in the past and was always among the best performers. In New York, especially in the solar company, I was working for, I had broken all their sales records as a door-to-door salesman.

Previously, I had only done B2C, i.e., Business to Consumer selling. In this business, it was all B2B selling. The dealers were the ones we dealt with, and although the end product was for a householder, we didn't sell the products directly to consumers, but always went through our channel partners, known as "dealers."

These were the guys who ran hardware shops across the country, and as sales professionals, our job was to find extra dealers and keep the old ones happy.

Once I jumped inside the sales wagon, I began touring around the country with the sales heads from differing regions to develop my understanding of the dissimilar markets. I met with old channel partners and hustled to acquire additional ones while sharpening my sales skills at the same time and observing how people worked in other parts of the country.

Based on the state I visited, the means of conducting business varied. A new learning curve in terms of dealing with each market's specific challenges always presented itself.

I was no longer a seeker in India but a salesman.

So, I was not aimlessly moving around the country looking for answers anymore but had sales targets in my mind while accompanying the senior sales managers who had been working as sales representatives in India for decades.

It did not take long before I was well versed in my selling abilities. Once I figured out what the dealers liked to hear and how it was not so much about selling as maintaining/creating a healthy relationship, I experienced a fluid transition into India's sales world.

Power dynamics play a unique role in every stream of India's society, from politics to business, community to family.

Some play of power dynamics governs all the country's structures. Socially, it can be based on somebody's caste. In business or politics, it can be based more on what position the person holds in the hierarchy – which puts them above others on the food chain in terms of designation, power, influence, or pay.

Most organizational systems that I came across in the country were pyramidal with a top to bottom hierarchical arrangement – not a very flat one. Nepotism also played into the power dynamics, which I had now become a part of.

For instance, now that I was working in my father's company, and because I was his son, I was automatically treated uniquely by his employees and got easier access to departmental heads or senior managers. And even though I tried not to play into the power dynamics by working along with all the employees on an equal footing, the power dynamic was still rooted very deeply in their minds.

Not giving much weight to the whole power dynamics equation, I tried my best to work with all the senior sales managers on a human-to-human basis, which allowed for healthy relationships with the sales personnel. Even though they knew I was the son of their boss, with time, they started to acknowledge that I didn't want to be treated like the boss's son, but as a colleague who was working with them while simultaneously learning about the intricacies of the business.

During my first few months in the sales world, I toured through the states of Madhya Pradesh, Chhattisgarh, Orissa, Rajasthan, Gujarat, and Maharashtra with their respective sales heads and visited their remote parts. We traveled by car, train, and plane to cover them and meet old channel partners and potential new ones.

When I was done with the daytime business-related stuff, I would try to visit the region's famous sites at night – or meet some relatives or acquaintances who lived in the cities I was passing through. They would then take me out to show around their city.

If not with locals from the city, I would be with my sales colleagues, and together we would scout the region while improving our relationship.

A lot of exploring happened, along with all the selling. I visited the Mahatma Gandhi Ashram in Ahmedabad; Gujarat to Gateway of India in Mumbai, Maharashtra; the astounding temples of Jagannath in Puri, Orissa, and Mahabaleshwar Jyotirlinga in Ujjain, Madhya Pradesh, where my spirit could reminisce. I drove past the dense forests of Chhattisgarh and Orissa in the startling darkness of the twilight.

I was scintillated by experiencing India's contrasting flavors in their full intensity while devoted to playing the role of salesman.

Months went by, and my days were fully occupied by either attending meetings in the office or being out in the field with salespeople while simultaneously taking calls from other sales recruits from other regions. It took me through the ups and downs of being tangled in a business in India.

My parents were happy to see me getting involved thoroughly in the trade. The many questions from relatives and other family members about "What is he doing in life?" and all that stuff had stopped coming my parents' way. Everything had started moving in the direction it was always supposed to.

It was not until half a year later, when I was on a sales tour of North India and was driving up from Delhi, pausing through States of Haryana, Punjab, and then Himachal Pradesh before going all the way to Jammu and Kashmir, that a hiccup arose on the ride.

When I was passing through Himachal, I decided to do a ten-day course at the Tushita Meditation Center in Dharamkot. A break in between my sales tours appeared. So, after a day of meetings with several channel partners in the region of Dharamsala, I went straight up to Mcleodgangj and then to the village of Dharamkot to attend a ten-day meditation retreat.

It was a Buddhist retreat. I went to use those days for going deeper within myself in my practice while in complete silence for those ten days. It was a much more relaxed environment than in the Vipassana retreats I had done the previous year.

It was in those ten days that all the busyness of my mind halted, and I was left with no choice but to face the questions I had been avoiding until then.

The entrance gate to Tushita Meditation Center was next to the Himalayan Tea Shop at the top of Dharamkot Road. It was an appealing center with tall pine trees around it. The buildings inside the center were mostly painted in red and had colorful Buddhist patterns carved into them. The main meditation hall had a golden statue of Buddha and many cushions on the wooden floor in front of it. Students sat on them to meditate or listen to teachings from a Buddhist monk.

Downstairs, a garden lay outside the entrance of the main hall. Many residential options around the meditation hall offered shared rooms and dormitories for students.

As it was not a very rigorous course like the ones I had done before, it attracted a more extensive and relatively younger crowd, who were only starting to discover more about meditation or were interested in Buddhism.

All students had to do "karma jobs" as part of their stay, which is how most of these places operate across India. They provide cheap lodging and food in exchange for your services while you get most of your days to study and meditate without any external distractions infiltrating your mind.

Only once a day did I have to complete my responsibilities for the so-called "karma job," to clean the toilets. Somehow, I always got stuck with "cleaning the toilets" whenever I went to such places. Still, I did not care much as I was getting the rest of the day to devote to my meditative practice.

I just wanted to be in that space, which offered a serene environment where I could do my own thing. I was not interested in what the others around me were doing. It was a perfect setting for me to disconnect from the world outside and look inward.

## A. Touch of Silence

It was that time of the year when we were closing in on monsoon months with the rain gods starting to indicate their presence. Those days of meditating in silence, hiding amidst the trees on the mountain top, brought up all the questions I had not asked myself since I joined my father's business.

"Is this really what I need to be doing?" and "Am I being true to what I was born to do?"

Examining such questions, I kept on going deeper in myself, where I could see the moments of illusion clearly in front of my sealed eyes.

I had been standing on one side of the river consumed in my darkness and waiting for a push. But nobody else was going to come to push me forward - I had to do it myself.

And as I walked past that river, all that remained on the former side were the observer's eyes, observing the projection of my mind's creation, now standing on the river's other side.

I stood beyond the darkness to simply observe it and no longer be affected by it.

During those days of transcendence, erasing the last bits of fear and darkness and finally letting go of the gravest fear – the fear of death – I concluded that this business thing was not the way forward. And I had to tell my parents I couldn't do it any longer.

I could not continue pretending to be somebody I was not.

I had broken free in myself and needed to keep growing in this freedom that I had by now experienced many a time. With its effect on my being only getting stronger over time, I had to start sharing it with others in any way I could.

By the end of those ten days, I had decided to tell my parents I would not continue working with them and that it was time for me to dedicate myself to walking a nameless path.

⸺ ⧈⧈⧈ ⸺

The day after the retreat in Tushita, I continued with the sales tour moving up from Himachal Pradesh to the State of Jammu and Kashmir. I knew I had to finish the sales tour as I had committed myself to attend several meetings, but once I returned to Delhi, I was sure in myself that I had to start cutting away the strings – no matter how tough it seemed.

I arrived in the City of Jammu the next day, where most of my meetings were scheduled. After the meetings, I was supposed to take a bus to Srinagar with the head of the region's sales personnel.

That was in 2018, in July, when many Hindu pilgrims made their way up from Jammu to the Amarnath Temple. In the Pahalgam region not far from Srinagar, a cave, referred to as the Amarnath, contained a famous Shiva shrine.

The Amarnath pilgrimage was controversial because it was in Kashmir territory, a victim of terrorism for many years.

On the day I was supposed to leave for Srinagar, terrorists attacked one of the buses transporting a pilgrim group. The Indian military shut down the highway from Jammu to Srinagar, and I had to miss out on Srinagar.

Instead, I flew from Jammu to Leh to finish off the last bits of my meetings and end the sales tour of North India. It was interesting to return to Leh in Ladakh as a professional a year after having been there as a wandering seeker. That parallel reality was almost unreal.

I was revisiting Ladakh as a business professional who had recently completed ten days in a Buddhist retreat in Dharamkot, having concluded that I would stop working in the business world and start focusing on:

*How do I make the most of this life by continuously doing something that allows me to fully express a sense of freedom in what I do while simultaneously wanting to inspire others through my actions - not just words - to live their best lives?*

If we study the whole human trajectory from the last several centuries to the present, undeniably, our actions concerning the natural world around us have been very destructive. They are not conducive to the well-being of anybody on this planet. They are destroying ourselves and our only planet.

---

I was scared about telling my parents my decision, that I was unable to fulfill their expectations of me as their only son. But I knew I had to do it because if I did not do it now, I would explode from holding everything inside.

During the evening of the very day I returned from my sales tour, I went into their room and said, "I need to tell both of you something."

My mother was lying down on her bed, and my father was seated in a wooden chair looking outside the large window several feet away in front of their bed.

"What happened?" they inquired.

I replied, "Nothing has happened. But I need to tell you both that I cannot work in the business anymore." The room toppled into an awkward silence.

I continued speaking with a stammer in my speech and a pounding heart, "After being through everything that has happened with me since

I left New York, I cannot lead this falsified life. For a moment, I thought I could, and that's why I gave all of this a fair shot, but after spending these last days in a retreat, it has become clear to me that this is not the path for me – I cannot continue pretending to be somebody I am not."

My parents had tears in their eyes.

"I knew this was coming... I had started sensing it these last few months," said my father in a cracking voice while holding his sobbing eyes. "You weren't wholly in it lately, and I could see it."

"I will always be there for you guys as your son and be of support in your lives, but I cannot take on these deceptive responsibilities society has contrived for me to fill. This is not who I am, and this is not what I am supposed to be doing," I replied.

"How will you make money? You need money in life," said my father, still crying.

"I don't have an answer to that question ... but I know money isn't what speaks to me. It provides for my necessities – fulfills them – but it can never be my end goal, and I cannot pretend that it is. I must continue listening to what is in me. I cannot avoid it any longer," I replied as I wept tears too.

My mother was quiet the whole time. The dialogue between my father and me faded off with our sobbing.

Our bodies stayed frozen past time – silence had won the battle of the knights.

# X. WHAT NEXT?

*THE WATER FROM CLOUDS* started stormily pouring down over Delhi's carbon-induced air as we approached the end of July in 2018. Hardly any conversation between my parents and me followed the night we sank in our sorrows.

The monsoon can be an appropriate time for complete introspection. It is a period when profuse rains prevail over the land, demonstrating the force of the mighty power nature holds.

In the weeks after that night of solemnity in my parents' room, I began to distance myself from my father's business unobtrusively. I gradually ventured back into the unknown, beginning by leaving my parent's apartment for a short while to again make my way up to the Himalayas – this time to another destination.

It was a small village called Bir Billing, another Tibetan settlement in Himachal Pradesh. It was about 25 minutes away from the hill station of Palampur and a few hours' drive from Dharamsala airport. Many Buddhist monasteries had been established in Bir since 1966.

I went to live in the Deer Park Institute, founded in the early 2000s to reinvigorate the deceased spirit of the ancient Nalanda University by converting a former Buddhist monastic institute into a center for the study of classical Indian wisdom traditions.

A month-long rainy season retreat titled the *Dathun* was in progress there. It was another Buddhist retreat inspired by Buddha's time. In the monsoon season, Buddha and his disciples gathered in one place and meditated together because it was too demanding to travel during the rainfall.

The *Dathun* was an intensive meditation retreat, and without thinking much about it, I went straight into it. Two weeks of the retreat had already ended by the time I arrived in Bir, which had become relatively famous for paragliding in the last few years.

A narrow road was all there was to the village with sizable Buddhist monasteries situated far and near. Bir was not as commercial or as vibrant as Mcleodganj, but much more grounded in its appeal. Besides, as it was the monsoon season, all paragliding was temporarily shut down, so the whole village was virtually empty when I got there.

I could not keep track of how many retreats I had done in the last year or so. Everyone I knew thought I'd gone crazy, and they had a fair reason to believe that – because I had gone crazy, in some ways.

I had gone crazy in a way that meant nothing seemed to matter anymore. I could no longer think of being part of life's usual charade because none of it made sense to me. In those months, I felt very detached from everything, including my own humanness.

The illusion of a reality so deeply ingrained in us had taken its final toll on me. I could no longer pretend it was the way forward, as I knew through my core that it was not appropriate, and none of it was going to matter in untold years.

Nobody could alter that realization for me; it was not up to anybody to do that. It was something I had observed time and again in an absolute sense.

I stayed in Deer Park for the remaining two weeks of the retreat. It was a large complex with a Buddha temple, a meditation hall, and gardens floating around in between the buildings accommodating basic rooms and dorms for students.

It was a very noncommercial and authentic institute hosting students from across the globe who came to seriously devote themselves to studying ancient eastern texts or practicing meditation to gain more clarity in themselves.

The *Dathun* focussed primarily on Vipassana meditation sessions for countless hours a day, with additional morning and evening Buddhist chants, walking meditations, silent meals, silent periods, meetings with meditation instructors, and *dharma* talks.

There were only a small number of students sitting in the retreat, and because the institute spread over a sizeable area, it delivered plenty of space and time.

The charismatic mountains and raging clouds accompanied my weeks of immersion in the retreat. The clouds boomed thunderously while bursting open to release uncountable tears of blood, declaring war against humans and asserting that the sky was ready to collapse on the land we had been busy destroying.

It called for a tenacious uptake to survive those howling nights facing the fury of nature and the days beholding the endless rage in myself. It denoted a definitive stamp in my heart and a clear directive that there was no going back from where I had now arrived.

It was time only to move forward.

## A. The Enlightened Yogi

After finishing that thunderous retreat, I went around Bir visiting Tibetan monasteries from various lineages of Buddhism. I was not trying to go anywhere but tagged along with other meditators or teachers I met in the retreat. Whenever an invitation came to go somewhere, I said, "Yes," without knowing where I was going.

One morning, I was seated in a local Tibetan eatery having breakfast when the teachers who had organized the *Dathun* entered and sat beside me. They were from all over the world but had been living in Canada for as long as they could remember. They had come to India specifically to manage this retreat.

As we were having breakfast, the eldest teacher, a Japanese-American woman named June, said to me, "We're going to visit a monastery after this ... would you like to come with us?" She was a small and aged woman, but the depth in her eyes and the finesse apparent on her face contradicted her physical appearance. She was one of the wisest and humble women I met in my travels.

I replied, "Why not!" and soon enough, we were on our way toward Palampur to visit Tashi Jong Khampagar Monastery, about a thirty-minute car ride away.

It was an enormous monastery, mounted along the appealing mountains of Dhauladar. A courteous Tibetan woman named Rinzin accompanied us to assist the teachers whenever she could. Rinzin was a well-connected woman. It was her eatery I was in earlier having my breakfast when the teachers arrived.

It did not take long to arrive at the monastery, never-ending in its size. A friendly young Tibetan monk named Jimmy covered in red robes was waiting for us and took us on a walking tour around it.

I was not sure what was so special about this place as it was far away from Bir, and the teachers had explicitly gone there to meet somebody. I hadn't asked anything and was happy to go with the flow.

Soon enough, we were standing outside a room's door. Jimmy asked us to wait outside as he gently entered. He came out a few minutes later and said to us, "We can all go in now."

An old Tibetan man with a cream-colored vest suspended over his chest was sitting on a single framed bed. He smiled at us with his magical eyes, and I knew, right at that moment, he was fully enlightened. There was no doubt in my mind. I had been roaming around India for over a year by then. I had met hundreds of people, and not once I had encountered a being like him, where I had to think twice about whether this person was enlightened or not.

It was a definitive thing, and somehow, I just knew that was the case.

He belonged to a specific lineage of Tibetan monks designated as *Togdens*, which translates as "the realized ones."

I cannot explain what happened to me when I was sitting beside him. I could not come out with a single word while people around me were asking him questions. He didn't speak English or Hindi, so Jimmy was our translator.

We sat on the floor next to Jimmy in the very compact room. The *Togden* was comfortably seated with his long hair wrapped in an ascending circle spiraling up over his head.

"He has never cut his hair," said Jimmy, who was narrating to us how he escaped from Tibet when the Chinese military started assassinating yogis like him.

"It was a very tough journey crossing those mountains," Jimmy translated. "Many people died on the way."

A fellow student sitting next to me asked him, "How can somebody become enlightened?"

He didn't say much, just a few words as he nodded his head and whispered them to Jimmy, who then told us, "He says it's tough ... very, very tough."

Jimmy continued the narration. "He's done several twelve-year retreats, where he stays in just one room and doesn't ever go out."

We were all in total shock after hearing that. I could not believe what I'd just heard. Somebody asked in confusion, "Twelve years???"

Jimmy replied while smiling, as if he could not believe it either, "Yes ... multiple times."

That moment in the presence of this Tibetan yogi became a highlight since my return to India. It inspired me in a way I could not express. I thought to myself, "Wow! How incredible!"

After having met this divine being, Jimmy took us to another astonishing chamber. We climbed up some monastery stairs to a small meditation hall at the top. Inside this room, something was conserved that I never expected to see – the mummified body of a deceased enlightened monk. His body was wrapped in decorative clothing and secured inside a glass box.

People visited this space to meditate in the company of the departed monk. Many also believed that he was still inside the body. It was a breathtaking prospect and something I did not anticipate seeing in a Buddhist monastery.

That day could not become any better than what it already was. After seeing such human marvels, Jimmy took us around the core temple, situated further down the mountain.

Jimmy held my hand as we walked down the stairs as if we had been friends for a long time. It was a sweet and unconditional act of love.

It was funny, I thought. If I had been in the US and some random man held my hand while walking, I would have been like, "What the hell?!" or would have associated it with a sexual thing. That is how it would have been perceived in the US, and I used to share that mindset. But in India, it is common to see men walking around the streets, holding hands. It is not seen as something "gay" or "sexual," but simply as an expression of the human-to-human bond, with none of our conditioned ideas attached to a guileless act of friendship between men.

After exploring the monastery's remaining parts and thanking Jimmy for showing us around, we left for Bir. *It could not have been a better day,* I reflected and thanked June for taking me along.

That was my last night in Bir, Himachal Pradesh. I left the next morning for Delhi braced and ready to face anything that came my way. At the same time, I fully intended to devote my time to creating something of real significance, which would make my every breath, my every second living on this planet genuinely worth it.

## B. City of Thugs

As the following months went by, I gradually distanced myself from the business and returned my focus to writing. *I must get my first book published,* I thought to myself, and started figuring out how I could do that. The sales personnel continued calling me to update me about everything and asking me to join them on sales tours. It was initially tough for me to decline. Considering how we had developed relationships with one another, I wanted to support them, but I knew I had to put my complete focus on other things.

Starting with how to get my first book published.

I had never thought I would be doing the things I was doing, and writing was never part of any life plan, but with time, I understood that life is not something we can plan. We try to plan everything and want our lives to go in an explicit direction based on what we think fits our desires, but life doesn't work that way.

It works in its own inimitable and mystical way, which we have no control over. It is better to surrender ourselves to its organic functioning instead of trying to plan and control everything.

The best we can do is to keep on giving our best to what we know best without worrying about the results and consequences. The more we start living in the act rather than what it will result in, the more we start creating and rejoicing in our day-to-day.

That was the simple philosophy I adopted for myself.

I contacted many book publishers in India and sent them samples of my first book but didn't hear back from anyone. I guessed, *why would somebody respond to a nobody* – especially in a country like India where everything worked through contacts. If you knew people, you could get your foot inside many doors, but not knowing anybody meant endlessly knocking on walls.

Now that I was moving away from my father's business, I had no choice but to dive deep into making my first book a full reality. I put continuous and diligent effort into starting something of my own, which emanated from a place of truthfulness in me.

Months went by with me trying to reach out to people to get the book thing going, but it all concluded in dead ends – nothing seemed to work.

I started touring around Delhi to socialize and build a network, hoping that would help me get my foot inside some door.

It was almost like being a door-to-door salesman again. This time rather than selling solar panels to New Yorkers, I was selling myself to the people of Delhi, possibly the most formidable people on the planet to sell anything to. I was meeting new folk every day and exploring Delhi in the meantime.

Walking around specific regions of the city, I started seeing a side of Delhi I had never seen before.

The arbitrary historical sites, splendid gardens, architecturally sound religious monuments, wild timeworn markets, and the elite modern ones. Simply winding through Delhi, I met all kinds of people. Some owned a palace to accommodate their endless luxurious needs. Others slept in the open underneath the city's bridges with the turmoil of traffic driving by.

It was diverse in every sense of that word. I met people from all parts of the world – many expats[40] as well.

With so much history resonating in the city's walls, there was nothing the City of Delhi did not have to offer. But something about Delhi that made survival very difficult.

---

40  Expats are foreigners who live and work in India (or any country), other than their own.

*It's tougher than New York,* I thought to myself many a time. Everybody was always trying to step on my toes to get ahead, and that trend was too prominent for me not to notice.

Darkness and light blended in the city with toxicity rooted in the blood of many – and concurrently, simple acts of kindness could be observed in passing.

A city of contrasts, Delhi could be easily called the "City of Thugs" or the "City of Saints," depending on what unexpected incident you spotted drifting around in that intense place.

## C. Dead End

Things were not going anywhere; all my efforts went in vain. I was left with no choice but to self-publish. I told myself, *I'm going to connect with people face-to-face through human-to-human interaction. I'm going to use social media for its benefits and reach out to people with a message filled with purity from my heart – not try to manipulate or convince anybody. I'm going to speak with only truth in my words.*

*I am done living a life built around lies.*

*I can't continue living like that any longer. It's killing me every day. So, it's only the truth arising from the ashes of my burning spirit that I'm going to speak.*

*I've no intention of trying to get people to do something. It's simply about sharing with them the real-life stories of everything that has come about in my life – and in the lives of others – that got us to walk on a path of courage and bravery so we could live with complete freedom in our hearts.*

Rejection and opposition had become my two best friends a long time ago. They were the two who had faithfully stayed with me since I graduated from university and began my career as a door-to-door salesman in New York.

*Life without them would have been too boring,* I always reminded myself. Every time facing rejection or opposition made me want to improve my craft and give more than previously.

Whether it was sales or writing – or anything else – every obstacle I faced along the way helped me strengthen my spirit, and once I decided to fully jump down the rabbit hole with no strings attached to my back,

I didn't care if the world collapsed at my feet. Nothing was going to stop me from going at it.

The silence from the night when I confided my desire to not work with my father continued for months. Both my parents were taking their time to process what I had said. I could see their internal struggles on seeing me act the way I was. I knew I had to be very patient with them. Only with time could they accept – if not understand – what direction their son was heading. Our conversations had minimized, and the silence played out for as long as it could.

I had nothing left to say to them. And they did not know what to say to me either. I had stopped giving in to the demands of anyone else and utterly focused on what I needed to do.

A lot of judgment and advice came my way from people visiting my parents' apartment. But I did not take on any of it because it was not mine to take. I had become indifferent to what people thought of me – none of it mattered to me, and none of it got to me.

I stayed silent through all of it and meanwhile found a publisher who could help me print and sell my books. I did all the work to create a website and got all the required framework ready for launching the book online.

With a "sell on-demand" model, I hardly had to invest any money. I started creating all the marketing content for social media and handling everything to get the book out in the market.

Alongside this, something much more powerful than myself had started coursing through me. Even though I could feel the rising of that expansive sensation in me, I didn't know it then, but in the months to come, my life was about to change forever – more than I could have imagined.

# XI. HIDING IN AN OASIS

O NE EVENING I WAS strolling through Lodhi Gardens, a serene oasis concealed within Delhi's viscera.

Named after the Lodhi Dynasty, which ruled Delhi and parts of Northern India in the 15th. Century, Lodhi Gardens was home to numerous tombs of several members of its dynasty. With gardens sweeping alongside the enormous Islamic domes, Lodhi Gardens was not so much a garden – as its name suggested – as a historical park spread across a broad area.

A pedestrian walkway encircled its rim with several entrance gates in it. Towering trees were rooted along the way, and a rich array of flowers blended in. Many unmarked paths spread throughout the gardens.

The entrance gate on Subramaniam Bharti Marg guided you inside the gardens, where you walked over a bridge built of hefty stones across a pond. This was home to a large group of ducks, whose quacks could be heard as your feet marched across the bridge.

It was October of 2018, and I had worked out most of the details for publishing my first book, titled *Dream Beyond Shadows*.

I received a message from a friend, Irfan, while I was sitting inside Sikandar Lodi Tomb, situated on its own in a secluded part of the gardens close to the pond, not visited by many people.

I liked going there to sit alone – and frequently did – inside the tomb's eclipsing walls to contemplate the thought of death, as it helped me gain perspective on how the material body's death was an inevitable truth of life.

Coming to terms with our own death can inspire us to live our lives the way we truly want, doing the things we love doing, and making the most of what we have to offer.

In the message, Irfan had asked me to come to the café he managed in Khan Market. I had been introduced to Irfan by my sister a few months previously when we visited his newly founded space called Immigrant Café.

A tall, dusky fella with a thick beard, Irfan had been in the restaurant business for quite some time and was an expert in the food and drinks industry. He had overseen many brands over time and recently established this stately restaurant in the Khan Market.

An artist himself, Irfan, was a passionate and interesting fellow who had done all kinds of things while living in different parts of the country. A knowledgeable and literate man, he was impressed when we first met to find out that I had written a book and was trying to get it published.

Leaving behind my contemplation of death, I made my way out of Lodhi Gardens to stroll in the direction of the Khan Market, only a few minutes' walk away on Subramanian Bharti Marg.

The Khan Market was the plushest market in Delhi. It was built in a U-shape across three parallel lanes with restaurants, cafés, exclusive brand outlets, specialized bakeries, and other such amenities for human pleasure. It also expanded through three vertical floors in a complex configuration.

Situated not far away from the embassy borough of Delhi, it was a go-to spot for the ex-pat community living and working in the embassies, along with other high-profile Indians on the top of the country's food chain.

In some ways, I always felt out of place going in and out of Khan Market because I knew my feet didn't belong there, but I still loved going in just to be reminded of the kind of material wealth resting on the shoulders of the people, who visited.

I loved sitting on the edge of the walkway built alongside the market's innermost lane. From there, my eyes looked toward the parking lot, and my body was next to the road where the sports cars drove in to drop off people whose clothes could be auctioned at an art museum.

It was astonishing to see these parallel realities in India. You could come across people with such wealth that they didn't know what to do with it, and a few miles away, you could find a slum, with people living hand-to-mouth trying to secure their physical survival.

In both scenarios, I saw one thing in common. The people in both places could not be free in themselves and were bound by our world's illusions. Both were surviving one way or the other – one by their need to secure the necessities of food, water, and shelter, and the other because they couldn't get enough of what they already had and kept on craving more.

Both were miserable. The only difference was that the misery of one was easily visible, but it was not for the other because it was more internal.

The certainty remained – no one can escape the misery of being bound by our lives' physicality and not being able to see life beyond our human-initiated distractions. All are kept aloof from realizing the reality of our existence.

I entered Khan Market through the front entrance into the outermost lane. Passing several bookstores on my way, I tottered along its bricked path through the middle pathway linking the three adjacent lanes. In the immediate presence of boutique designer stores on both sides of the ground floor and restaurants lining the floors above, I took a right onto the central laneway.

I kept walking until I was standing outside a half-glass, half-metal door, with the name Immigrant Café transcribed at its top.

A narrow wooden staircase past the metal door led to the first floor of the two-floored café, with its spread-out seating arrangement and an elongated window at the end. The window embraced a view of the front lane of Khan Market. There were photo frames of illustrious travel icons from around the world hung across the white textured walls playing on the theme of Immigrant Café, that all of us in some ways are immigrants in the land we currently reside in.

The core of any human civilization was founded on immigration. Our ancestors always migrated from one land to another in the hope of a better future. Immigration has been one of the single biggest factors in defining human history for thousands of years.

Wealth creation in the material world also fundamentally derives from the migration of people. Our recent history over the last several centuries holds enough evidence to support this. For instance, the United States of America, a nation considered to be the wealthiest of all economically, is built on human migration.

It's sad to see that we have not realized that immigration is natural for humans and that we are not supposed to be bound by borders or nationhood, although that is what we have made of our world today.

We have struck imaginary lines everywhere to segregate and distinguish people based on various identities and ideas. We have thus made it harder to realize that all humans are the same on an absolute level.

We are products of the earth's soil. We were born from it, and we will die on it.

If we were all to realize this in an absolute sense, none of the propaganda that politicians promote to divide people based on immigration issues and put them into boxes twisted to dehumanize them would exist. Yet, it is not the politicians' fault. It is ours because we easily give in to this divide-and-rule strategy that people in power have been using for thousands of years to control the masses and promote an us-versus-them mindset.

We are still bound by this mindset and fail to see beyond the human-devised identity boxes governing us daily.

All these boxes – be it religious identity, or nationality, or cultural heritage, or any of the countless human conceptions we use to define our existence – won't mean anything at the end of the day when we are dead.

We are not born with an identity, and we die without one.

All the human-made madness goes on between the two certainties of birth and death. If we were to get rid of this madness, we could escalate the evolution of humanity.

What an ideal world that would be, where questions such as, "Where are you from?" or "Where were you born?" or "What's your religion?" or "What's your caste?" or "What's your race?" or "Where are your parents from?" or "Which country's passport do you hold?" etc., etc., would not matter.

Imagining the layers of human madness disintegrating all over the world seems preposterous enough. But if it really did manifest on a global scale, someday in the future, how incredible our world would become!

I may be a fool to think this way, but I would rather be a fool and believe in such a magnificent possibility instead of continuing to play along with the human madness we have turned our world into today.

## A. Hint of Light

I turned around at the top of the narrow wooden stairs to climb up another floor.

Fleetingly past a wine cellar on my right with the kitchen arranged just behind it, I scrambled up the slender stairs to the café's top floor, where Irfan could be found. He was typically seated on one of the three bar stools fixed in front of the bar positioned in the corner.

This floor was narrower in outline, with plenty of open space in between its round tables that ascended to my lower chest, alongside chairs with long metallic legs.

It was an exquisite and elegant space. It had white textured walls, dark timber furniture, grey patches in specific spots to contrast with the white walls. There were dangling old-fashioned carbon gold-line light bulbs – the insides of which could be seen – and an antique Kashmiri tiled pattern covering the floor, further enriching the refined vibe.

A narrow, foldable glass door attached by the bar steered patrons to an exposed terrace hosting a view of Khan Market's front lane.

Irfan had designed the space himself, and as I entered, I could see him standing outside on the terrace, burning a cigarette through his lungs. He was a chain smoker and went through a whole pack in a day sometimes.

As he saw me enter and make my way out on the terrace, he asked his customary question in his thick, manly voice, "*Kya piyega?*" What will you drink? to which I replied, "*Chai?*"

He then laughed in his usual, wildly appealing way and said to me, "*Kabhi kuch aur bhi pee liya kar.*" I smiled at his remark, and we then conversed over a *chai* sitting at one of the tables inside at the front of the bar after he finished smoking his smoldering cigarette.

In the middle of our usual conversation, he said to me, "I want to launch your book."

"Here?" I replied and then continued. "That would be great. I thought we would be able to collaborate to devise an event. Along with launching my book, we could also showcase works by other artists."

He thought about that for a second and voiced his opinion. "For anything travel- and art-related, I'm in. Let's do it."

I replied, "Great. We can start preparing and do it in a month?"

"Ok. I have some artists in mind. This should be fun," he said.

"Yes! Absolutely. Thanks, Irfan!"

We spoke for a little while, figuring out the hows and whats for the event. As the dimness of night began to linger in my eyes, I said to him, "I have to get going ... I'm leaving for Gwalior with the family tomorrow for Diwali celebrations."

"What's in Gwalior?" he asked.

"My grandparents live there. We're going to spend Diwali with them."

"*Acha*, ok then ... happy Diwali. Call me when you're back."

"*Pakka*. See you!" I replied.

I left Khan Market to get a shared Uber back to Noida. We were leaving for Gwalior early in the morning. Happy about my interaction with Irfan, I was also excited to see my grandparents and celebrate Diwali, one of the most prominent Indian festivals.

Regarded as the Festival of Lights, Diwali is celebrated across India by people from varying faiths. The festival symbolizes the victory of light over darkness, knowledge over ignorance, and good over evil. It would be my first Diwali with my family in many years, and I did not know then that this Diwali would spark the birth of a life-changing pursuit.

## B. Cryptic Message

We drove to Gwalior the next day. The silence between my parents and me had faded by then, and we had begun conversing again. They were slowly digesting the fact that I would not be working with them, but I remained patient as I understood it was not easy for them.

That night we celebrated Diwali in my grandparents' house. Many relatives also came for the *pooja* (prayer rituals), followed by an *aarti* in the small *mandir*[41] next to my grandparents' room.

My *dadi* spent most of her days inside that *mandir*, praying and chanting while seated in front of the idols of Hindu deities.

It was a colorful evening, which ended with all of us sitting in the living room and conversing through the night about random topics.

2018 was a year when I spent a lot of time with my immediate family – and it granted me deep and powerful insights into family life in India. There were many pros and cons to Indian family dynamics compared with the western individualistic way of living. However, one thing was sure – family dynamics in modern-day India still play a pivotal role in shaping Indian society.

The morning after Diwali I was meditating in a room on the first floor of the house. This floor consisted of two rooms, the main hallway, a verandah, and another room at the end of the main hallway, primarily used as a storage room in earlier days.

When I was growing up in that house, we used to refer to that room as *kala kamra*, meaning the black room – mainly because it had a black-colored floor and was very creepy with all the material stored in it. My sister and I used to scare our younger cousins about that room whenever they visited us. We used to tell them it was haunted and that ghosts lived there. Nobody liked going into that room.

In recent years, my grandfather had cleaned up the room and converted it into a bedroom, where I stayed for Diwali. How ironic was that? I was staying in a room referred to as the black room during the ongoing Festival of Lights.

While I was sitting inside the preserved silence of the black room, a message appeared inside my head: "You have to go walk through South India."

I did not know where that message came from, as I had never thought about something like that before. Somehow, the message grew stronger as I continued meditating. I sensed a sort of power in

---

41 A *mandir* is a room dedicated to the worship of god.

it that I had never experienced before, which said to me that this was something I had to do.

It was almost a directive of sorts that I had received from a mysterious source that left me with no choice but to follow through with it. It was so random but so clear at the same time.

The message was direct and substantial, and without any doubt in my mind, I knew I had to go on that walk.

*Why this walk? What this walk? How this walk?* were irrelevant questions in that spell. All that mattered was that I had to do it.

I went downstairs later to share this with my grandparents over breakfast. They started freaking out. *Dadu* said to me, "What do you mean you're going to go walk through South India?" After a moment, he continued. "Like a *padyatra*[42]?"

"Yes, kind of like that," I replied.

His eyes became larger, and in a trembling voice, he said to me, "You are going to go on your own? You cannot do it without a team or proper planning. Anything could happen."

"Nothing's going to happen to me," I replied.

*Mummy* was sitting beside me at the dining table silently listening, while my *dadi* said to her in a freakish speech, "*Iska dimag kharab ho gaya hai? Kaha se aise ideas aate hai?*"

My mother replied to her swiftly, "*Kuch bolo mat... apne aap time ke saath idea drop ho jayega... hum bolenge toh aur karna chaheyga yeh.*"

I didn't tell them that it was not my idea, but a directive that I'd received and had no choice but to follow through with.

My grandparents kept on insisting that I drop the idea by saying things like, "It's absolutely irrational," and "It's very dangerous."

I silently listened to them and said at the end, "I'm going to do this no matter what."

We left Gwalior that evening, and *mummy* told *papa* about the walk during the car ride. He had not been there when I made the revelation that morning.

He reacted the least of all and stayed mute for several minutes after hearing my mother out before he asked me, "How are you going to do it?"

---

42 A *padyatra* is a pilgrimage to sacred shrines traveled on foot.

"I don't know... I haven't figured anything out yet."

⸺✖⸺

November came in, and I got busy with Irfan preparing for the event we had planned.

On one of those days, while we were on Immigrant Café's terrace, I told him I would leave Delhi after the event and walk through South India. He replied in shock while exhaling smoke out of his mouth, "Walk??"

"Yes, I'll probably start from Kanyakumari and make my way up."

He replied, "*Tu pura pagla gaya hai*," and both of us started laughing.

My first book, *Dream Beyond Shadows*, was launched in December of 2018 in Immigrant Café. Alongside my book, we showcased the works of other artists. The entire top floor was filled with people with no air to breathe. The event, named the "Nomad Hour," attracted a range of people – artists, travelers, and people from varying fields of work I had met during my last few months of socializing in Delhi.

I spoke my heart out that evening in front of a wonderful crowd and knew from that moment onward that there was no going back from there. I could only move forward.

The book started spreading like fire after several campaigns on social media, with no foresight about what was coming a month later.

In early January of 2019, I left my parents' house with a tiny backpack, a few sets of clothes, and other key essentials to board a one-way flight for the City of Thiruvananthapuram in the southern State of Kerala.

In an emotional statement, my father said to me the day before I was supposed to be leaving, "In the olden days when people left for such *padyatras*, they were sent off after a celebration because many of them didn't return."

I replied, "Don't worry. I will be fine."

My mother said, "Please don't go," while crying ferociously. "Why do you have to do such a thing? Why can't you be like others?"

"I cannot explain it to you, but I have to do this. And do not worry – I will be ok," I replied while caressing her back.

Both my parents had tears in their eyes as I left their apartment. This time they knew, I was not going to return as the same person.

"We will pray to god for you," they said to me as I left their weeping sight, knowing in my heart that a storm was coming my way.

PART THREE

# THE NAMELESS WALK

# I. WHERE INDIA ENDS

*I* ARRIVED AT THIRUVANANTHAPURAM AIRPORT late at night to begin an unknown triumph over the oceans.

I was determined in my weeping that I had to let go of everything that could hold me back from moving my feet.

Nothing was needed but my own strenuous belief that there was something to seek. I was to seek – not to find or look for anything. Solely to immerse myself in what was encompassed by the flavors of the sea.

Straight away, I found a taxi outside the Thiruvananthapuram Airport that could take me to Kanyakumari, a small town situated at the southernmost point of India, where the land came to a halt with the divine merging of three oceans – the Indian Ocean, the Arabian Sea and the Bay of Bengal.

The merging of these seas is auspiciously referred to as *triveni sanganam*[43].

An inspiring, dreamy coastal town, Kanyakumari is part of India's culturally rich State of Tamil Nadu, which neighbors the State of Kerala – known as God's Own Country – where I had just landed in its Capital City of Thiruvananthapuram.

I had just landed in and was going to depart from Kerala by crossing its border and entering Tamil Nadu.

---

43 *Triveni sanganam* means a place where three sacred water bodies meet.

Tamil Nadu was a state where I found a temple on every lane, a man wearing a *lungi*[44] and selling coconuts on every street corner, and women walking around elegantly, displaying their bright mottled *saris*.

It is a state roaring with diversity in religion. You can easily find yourself in the company of marvelously erected Hindu temples, churches, and mosques dotted through the tapestry of the groovy land.

That was where I saw the sunrise from the southernmost tip of India the first time.

I sat in the taxi with a Tamilian man driving me to my destination. He asked me in his strong Tamilian accent and broken Hindi outside the airport, *"Aapko kaha jaana hai?"*

*"Vivekanandapuram,"* I replied.

*"Ok. Ok ... challo. Main le jata hai aapko,"* he answered.

Driving through the darkness of the night, we seemed to merely inhale a few times before we reached Kanyakumari on National Highway 66.

I was not precisely sure when I would begin walking. *Maybe in a day or so*, I thought to myself.

I had been living day-to-day, not thinking about anything to come, and that's how I would walk as well – not worry about the destination but be fully present with my breath's every moment corresponding to the rallying ahead of my feet.

It was close to midnight when we entered the gates of Kanyakumari. The driver dropped me in front of an open-door reception set at a building's entrance with the sign "Information Center" ascribed to it.

A sleep-deprived Tamilian man stood behind the reception counter – his red eyes and sunken face, easy giveaways of his tiredness. Simultaneously, many young visiting Tamilian students were rambling around the city streets, talking, and producing a lot of merry noise.

Kanyakumari became famous across India primarily because of Swami Vivekananda. He was a Hindu monk who is profoundly celebrated across the country's length and breadth by many Hindu devotees for the teachings he bestowed during his brief material existence in the 19[th.] Century.

---

44 A *lungi* is a delicate ankle-length garment men wrap around their waists.

As was conveyed to me, Swami Vivekananda became enlightened while meditating in a lotus posture seated on a soaring, enormous rock several hundred yards away from the tip of Kanyakumari out in the ocean. The rock was later named after him and is now known as Vivekananda Rock.

It is said that with crashing waves separating the mainland from that rock, Swami Vivekananda meditated incessantly for three days after having made a pilgrimage across India as a *bhikshu* over a few years. The story of Swami Vivekananda's quest was recited to me the next day by a man who was referred to by everybody in Vivekanandapuram as *Mama ji*[45]

Vivekanandapuram was founded in the fond memory of Swami Vivekananda. It is a combination of township and *ashram*, where many Hindu monks and nuns reside. Vivekanandapuram was also a vibrant spot hosting the tourists who visited Kanyakumari for its many attractions, such as the Bhagavathy Amman Temple, one of the primary drawcards for pilgrims. A large statue of the prominent Tamilian poet and philosopher, Thiruvalluvar, was also constructed on top of the tiny island beside the Vivekananda Rock Memorial.

The town of Kanyakumari was home to a few other memorial sites – one dedicated to Mahatama Gandhi and another to the countless victims who died during 2004's deadly tsunami.

---

Most of Vivekanandapuram was booked out when I arrived. Only that one room, located far from everything, was available. On my arrival, the Tamilian receptionist told me that he could move me into another room in their main lodge the next morning at 7.

"That's ok," I replied. "I just need a place to sleep for the night."

So, I went to sleep that night only to wake up early the next morning to check out and then check in again for another room. The new one was inside a building called Vivekananda Lodge, beside the Information

---

45 In India, *mama* is the word for an *uncle* on your mothers' side, i.e., your mother's brother. And on your fathers' side, an uncle is referred to as *chacha*. Commonly in India, even strangers are called *uncle*.

Center, where the reception was. Across from the lodge was the visitors' dining room called Hotel Chitra.

I had only just moved rooms when I heard a tentative knock on the door.

I was sure that it would be *Mama ji*, who had been informed by a family friend of mine, *Shailja dadi ji*[46], that I was going to Vivekanandapuram. A social worker and a well-connected woman, *Shailja dadi ji* had been a frequent visitor to Vivekandapuram for many years. She was somebody I had known for a long time, as I had met her in my early teens. She was like an older sister to my mother, not by blood but by heart.

When she found out that I would be in Kanyakumari, she had informed *Mama ji*. She asked if he could show me around Vivekanandapuram and advise me about anything to do with Kanyakumari.

"*Mama ji* is an encyclopedia of Vivekandapuram," she said to me on a phone call I had with her just before flying from Delhi.

An elderly, skinny man with dense wrinkles on his face, bald head, hulking frameless glasses, a simple *kurta pajama*, and a bag made of delicate cloth hanging down his right shoulder stood outside the door of my room when I opened it.

His eyes were bluish, and his face was sunken inward because of his wrinkles. He came across as a straightforward and learned man, which I would find out later was true.

"*Mama ji?*" I asked inquisitively.

He replied with a firm, "*Haan.*" Yes

"Please come in."

He slowly walked inside my room and grabbed hold of a plastic chair beside the bed next to the window, looking toward the Information Center. I sat down on my bed, facing him while he sat cross-legged on the chair.

He asked me in his low, quavering voice, "*Aap Shailja ko kaise jante ho?*"

---

46 A *dadi ji* is an esteemed grandmother. The word *ji* is a mark of respect –*dadi* means grandmother.

I replied, "I know her through my mother."

"*Acha.*"

"How do you know *Shailja dadi ji?*" I asked.

He then went on to tell me the story about how he had met *Shailja dadi ji* back in 1989 and how he had been living in Vivekanandapuram since 1974. He had devoted 45 years of his life to the service of others.

"That's very admirable," I said and asked where in India he was born.

He replied, "I'm from Ahmedabad."

To which, I said, "Ahh ... *Gujarati!*[47] That's why you have a connection with *Shailja dadi ji* who's been living in Ahmedabad for the last many decades, even though she still considers herself to be *Marathi*[48]."

He replied with an assuring voice, "*Haan ... haan ....*" Yes... Yes ....

Our conversation went on for a little while. He told me that I should visit the Vivekananda Memorial built on top of Vivekananda Rock. He also told me that the Kanyakumari Devi (goddess) Temple located next to the Vivekananda Memorial on the same rock was worth visiting as well.

"I will possibly see you in the evening for *chai,*" *Mama ji* said to me as he was leaving the room. I replied, "That would be wonderful, *Mama ji.* Thank you for coming."

On *Mama ji's* suggestion, I left in the direction of the Vivekananda Memorial. The port where I could get a ferry for Vivekananda Rock to see the memorial was a few miles from Vivekanandapuram. I decided to walk there through Kanyakumari, which was built around the main road that escorted people straight to the end of India.

---

It was my first day in Kanyakumari. What could have been a better way to start the day than visiting the memorial of a monk who had walked around India as a *bhikshu!* And seeing as I was soon to begin walking

---

47 A *Gujarati* is somebody who comes from the western state of Gujarat.

48 A *Marathi* is a person from the State of Maharashtra. *Shailja dadi ji* was born in Maharashtra and grew up there before moving to Gujarat.

on a directive from an unknown entity through the southern part of the country, it only seemed fair to receive Vivekananda's blessings.

After drifting along the prevailing waves on a ferry ride packed with visitors mostly from Tamil Nadu itself, my feet landed on Vivekananda Rock. I then wandered about, adrift in the sublimity of the flowing wind.

Vivekananda's statue was inside an imposing, outsized edifice built on top of the rock. It was a marvelous piece of architecture. After glimpsing a statue of an eloquently standing Swami Vivekananda inside the memorial, I sat in a meditation hall beneath the memorial and meditated alongside others. Heaps of people continuously circulated by the statue in a striped formation, their palms folded together to pray with their hearts as they moved.

A square building with darkened stone pillars to complement Vivekananda's Memorial stood in front. In it was the statue of Kanyakumari Goddess.

A cheerful and relaxed atmosphere flowed over the rock's broad surface. Children were running around, and families were sitting in circles in the shade of the sacred buildings.

The tall statue of the Tamilian poet, Thiruvalluvar could be seen on a tiny island next to the rock I was on. The tip of the mainland was just beyond, along with its ageless temples emitting their steady light.

I stayed on the rock for a while before taking the ferry back to the mainland and returning to Vivekanandapuram, where I had an evening *chai* with *Mama ji* inside Hotel Chitra.

It was a mess hall with three long pairs of seats with tables in between. People were sitting by your side and further at a distance looking in your direction and chatting endlessly, while the servers hurriedly delivered the inexpensive food orders.

While *Mama ji* and I were having a *masala chai*, he said, "I have some work to finish today, but tomorrow I can show you around Vivekanandapuram and tell you the story behind the construction of the Vivekananda Memorial."

"That sounds good to me," I replied.

"You could go watch the sunset tonight, and I will see you tomorrow then," he suggested.

"Perfect," I replied and left his company to again make my way down from Vivekanandapuram toward the sunset point at the land's edge, where other tourist attractions such as the Mahatma Gandhi Memorial and the Tsunami Memorial Park were.

The town of Kanyakumari was much busier in the evening; more people surfaced along with the sun's drowning.

The streets were filled with bare-chested pilgrims, covered in black cloth from the waist down and walking barefoot. Hardly any western tourists or people from Northern India could be seen. I stood out vividly among the crowd because of my appearance and got a lot of attention from people walking by.

A massive difference exists between Southern and Northern India, not just in culture and ways of life, but also in people's physical attributes.

In the southern part of the country, people have relatively darker skin, and both men and women commonly wear their traditional attire. In the northern part of the country, that isn't always the case. The people there have lighter-colored skin, and even though most women wear *saris* and *salwar kameez*, most men have adopted western clothing such as long pants and button-down shirts.

Only the younger crowd walking around me was dressed western-style – the rest were wearing traditional outfits.

I had relatively lighter skin in comparison to the local people around me. Because I was dressed in casual western attire and nursed long hair on my head and tattoos on my arms, many locals mistook me for a foreigner on my very first day of walking around in the southernmost part of the country.

They would ask me spiritedly, "Which country are you from?"

I replied with an affirmative voice, "I am Indian!" to which they reacted with a lot of astonishment in their eyes.

This was a dominant question throughout my whole walk, where my external appearance deceived observer's eyes and left them flabbergasted many a time.

The next day was my last day in Kanyakumari before I commenced my nameless walk – an act so simple that it was to require nothing but the moving of my feet. I was to eventually discover that all the power for self-transformation rests in the simplicity of an act.

———◦⟨⟨⟨◦———

I met with *Mama ji* around noon the next day. He'd asked me to follow the central pathway inside Vivekanandapuram that led into the campus where all the monks and nuns lived. There were no outsiders in that part of Vivekanandapuram.

I had just returned to Vivekanandapuram after visiting several temples in the morning. They were crammed with devotees and pilgrims. I'd stood in long lines bare-chested before getting a glimpse of the gods. Most temples in South India had a rule that men took off their shirts before entering, so the sign, "Please take off your shirt before entering," could be seen outside most of them.

That was not something I had come across in North India, so that inclination was noteworthy. The priests and security at the temples were also strict about implementing their rules and regulations. I almost felt tense at times when setting foot inside a temple.

I had visited many famous temples in India by then and it was always an intense experience. They regularly had influxes of thousands of people.

In pure devotion, people would let go of their guard while standing in the long lines for innumerable hours to get a momentary glimpse of a god's statue, which meant everything in the world to them.

They would helplessly cry, shedding blood through their tears while simultaneously bowing down to a power much greater than themselves.

It was always a powerful and unimaginably abiding experience, where my body felt deeply both exhilarated and susceptible at the same time. My mind was not able to make sense of anything. Its rationalizing ability vanished somewhere along with the crusade embedded in those long lines, carrying you without your having to decide to move your feet.

It was holiday time when I was staying in Vivekananadpuram, so other than the monks and nuns, few people were on the main campus.

Activities relating to children's education, agriculture, animal rescue, wellness, and other such endeavors ensued.

*Mama ji* took me on a tour through its administrative block, which is where he worked. I saw the school for children, the cowshed, the residential quarters for the monks, and finally, the dining hall built exclusively for the monks and nuns, where we indulged our senses in a mild *thali* consisting of *dal,* rice, *roti,* and *sabji.*

It was a life of service and simplicity that people living in Vivekandapuram practiced, and it was pleasing for me to appreciate that coin of the world.

*Mama ji* and I parted ways after that delightful lunch. "I will tell you the story of Swami Vivekananda in the evening over a cup of *chai,*" he said to me as I was about to walk away.

"I am looking forward to hearing that," I replied.

Rather than returning to the Information Center, I continued walking in the opposite direction to go explore what was at the other end of Vivekanandpuram.

I walked to the boundary walls from where a small gate opened onto an empty slender lane. I took a right on that lane and walked toward the end of Kanyakumari.

Gigantic trees surrounded me with an ample silence resonating in the air. The end of the lane opened out into an expanded space of red soil with trees popping up around it. There was a clear view of the ocean and the Vivekananda Memorial and Thiruvalluvar Statue from that spot, hosting nobody else except some birds channeling their usual chirping songs.

I sat under the shade of a large tree to gaze upon the Vivekananda Memorial and Thiruvalluvar Statue. That was when it finally hit me: *I am starting to walk on my own through South India tomorrow.*

Until that instant, I had not really thought about what I was doing. I was simply following a cryptic message I had received the morning after Diwali.

I still had no clue where the message came from or its origin. Without considering what the future held or what could happen to me, I had packed my bags and left everything behind. Now, I was seated under a tree rooted at India's end, thinking to myself:

*I have no idea how I will do this walk or what will happen to me. Still, I promise that I won't stop moving my feet until I have exhausted my every breath and have let go of everything I think I am, and am truly experiencing life without any of our human layers attached to it.*

# II. THE WALK BEGINS

"*VIVEKANANDA ARRIVED IN KANYAKUMARI* after wandering through India for a few years," *Mama ji* said as we were seated inside the Information Center with a cup of *chai* in our hands.

"He arrived here all lost in himself and didn't know what he wanted to do. So, he asked the Mother Goddess (referred to as *mata* in India), 'Mata, tell me what I should do now.'"

I was intently listening to *Mama ji*. He was reciting the story with a glimmer in his eyes and animation in his voice.

"He saw a huge rock far in the distance from the tip of the land and suddenly had a powerful urge to get onto it. A fisherman was on his boat by the shore, so Vivekananda asked the fisherman to take him to the rock. The fisherman told him, 'The waves are very powerful, and I can only take you there if you give me some money,' Vivekananda said to the fisherman, 'I am a *swami* and have no money. You will have to take me there without money.' The fisherman refused, so Vivekananda dived into the ocean and swam toward the rock. Unafraid and untouched by the sturdy waves, he swam all the way while the villagers were screaming for him to come back."

I was unsure if the story was accurate, but I was enamored by it.

I asked *Mama ji*, "And then what happened?"

"Vivekananda meditated on that rock without moving an inch for three days through the dates of 25, 26, and 27 December, after which he became fully enlightened."

When *Mama ji* mentioned those dates, I recollected a memory from my visit to the memorial the day before. The same dates were engraved on a stone outside the memorial.

I asked *Mama ji*, "In the photos, you see of Vivekananda everywhere, he's sturdily standing on a rock in the same stance as his statue inside the memorial. Is that trying to capture the essence of the moment after he became enlightened?"

*Mama ji* confirmed, "Yes, exactly."

I stayed quiet for a stretch and then inquired, "Who started Vivekanandapuram?"

"A man named Eknath ji," *Mama ji* replied.

He then recounted Eknath ji's story, whose primary intention in life was to spread the teachings of Swami Vivekananda throughout the country.

He started by first getting Vivekananda's Memorial built on the rock. For that, in 1963, in a mere three days, Eknath ji managed to get the signatures of 323 MPs (Members of Parliament) on the petition for its construction.

"That was unheard of at that time," *Mama ji* said to me.

"How did he manage to do it?" I asked.

"Eknath ji was very good with people, and his catchphrase for getting so many MPs from diverse regional parties to sign the petition was, 'I am not a politician. I am just a social worker,'" *Mama ji* replied.

"That line must have made all the difference," I said.

"In those days of post-Indian independence from the British, most politicians used to be social workers themselves before joining politics," *Mama ji* continued. "Of course, things have changed now, when most of them are in politics for personal selfish reasons."

"That's very true," I said. "Most of them get into politics either for power, money, or fame. Rarely anyone wants to serve anymore. They want to rule and are willing to do anything and everything to be in power."

The sky was losing its color while *Mama ji's* stories relating to Vivekanandapuram sustained their flourish. I remembered with amusement *Shailja dadi ji's* statement when I was leaving Delhi that *Mama ji* was an encyclopedia of the place. After spending most of my day in his company, I realized she was correct.

I had no choice but to interrupt him during his storytelling. "I want to get some rest tonight before starting my walk tomorrow," I said to him.

"*Haan ... haan,*" he replied.

We then stood up from our chairs. I thanked *Mama ji* for showing me around Vivekanandapuram and narrating all the stories related to Swami Vivekananda and other dignitaries such as Eknath ji, who had contributed their lives for the betterment of people and society.

———— ∞∞ ————

I spent a vigilant evening of solace and reflection inside my room before embarking on the journey of a lifetime early the next morning.

Nothing was fixed about the walk.

*What distance will I walk? How many hours per day will I walk? Where will I stay at night? What will I eat?* I left the answers to these questions for the world beyond me.

I was not carrying a tent or enough food and water. So, finding a roof to cover my head at night and garnering food and water during the long hours of walking under the sun's scorching rays and South India's cruel humidity were all left to the mercy of strangers.

I never walked at night and covered as little as 14 km to as much as 36 km a day. For a little over three months, I journeyed through the south-western belt of India. I covered over 1000 km alone lost in the sublimity of the land while passing through the States of Tamil Nadu, Kerala, Karnataka, and Goa.

Not once did I get on a vehicle to shave off the slightest distance through the countless villages, towns, and cities I marked on my way.

It was not a walk for charity, or to achieve an athletic feat, or to prove some point. It was a purposeless act following the footsteps of a mystical voice enticing me to walk my life to dissolve it in the fortress of a boundless dream.

I was unable to sleep for the night before I began walking from Vivekanandapuram in Kanyakumari.

With my eyes closed, I was breathing in an awakened state, asking the divine power beyond me to protect and support me during the walk's progress – which I didn't know why I was doing.

I was shadowing a noiseless roar bursting in the depths of my core, wanting to bleed out of my veins into the sea's abysm.

With no planning or research into the walk, I would soon be out in the world living by the day and not knowing what the next day held in store for me. Distanced from the past and unconcerned about the future, I would walk in the entirety of the universe with all my heart at its disposal.

## A. Day 1 – A Pilgrim?

I got out of bed around 4 am to meditate and practice yoga before making my way outside the walls of Vivekanandapuram by 6. This was the usual time frame I followed on my walking days.

Rising before the sun with darkness clouding the sky, I would wake up for the prime hours of activating my inward-looking practices for strengthening my mind, body, and spirit – the three pillars of self-transformation.

It was merely a warm-up for the three pillars so they could surmount the unknown challenges that would confront me on the unseen road ahead.

By the time I started walking, I could see a perfect blend of the night's darkness and the day's light. With the sun commissioned to ascend, the redness of the light would gently spread over the shying darkness to bring clear vision to my eyes. Birds sang along every step of the way as I moved ahead, leaving behind my old self and continuously embracing the novel nameless self.

I left Vivekanandapuram to start my walk on the 16th of January 2019. I walked along National Highway 66 against the traffic. That allowed me to be aware of vehicles coming in my direction, as there was no space beside the highway for pedestrians. It was a narrow highway, so I had to be relentlessly mindful of the fast-moving traffic that could drive over me.

After a few miles into the first day, I had solemnly left the town of Kanyakumari and was passing green terrain on both sides, with countless temples fading by. I was maintaining a decent pace effortlessly, neither too fast nor too slow.

Since it was only my first day of walking, I was letting my body get accustomed to the land's conditions and letting my mind ease into the reality of this groovy but straightforward act.

The scenery accompanying my footsteps was picturesque, with lakes and emerald hills feasting along the way. I slipped into walking so naturally that it almost felt as if I had been doing it all along.

It didn't seem like a beginning, but more like a continuation that had been paused a while ago – and someone had re-pressed the play button.

I wore a round hat to protect myself from the sun's ruggedness and carried a stick in my hand for guarding myself against any unwanted terrors. Ferociously aggressive dogs would turn out to be a significant threat during the entire walk.

I had my first meal on the walk at a small eatery outside the temple of Sai Baba, a beloved saint born in the 19th. Century who lived through the early years of the next century.

The eatery had just opened for the day, and I was the first one to walk inside, dripping with sweat and looking like a comical character from a movie.

I was wearing casual sports attire over a severely soaked body. I had a backpack hanging over my shoulders with a blue tube emerging from it just close to my face that I drank water from; a cream-colored round fisherman's hat over my long tied-up hair to protect me from the sun; a stick in one hand, and a smile beneath my thick beard.

It was an intimidating and unexpected encounter for gentle South Indians to come across at 8 in the morning.

The eatery was run by a Tamil family, happy to host me and serve their freshly prepared meal of *idli* and *sambar* – prime delicacies of South Indian cuisine. Their eyes were suffused with curiosity and excitement. It was a look I got used to seeing on my walk.

As they served me *idli* and *sambar* – which I would ingest too many times by the end of the walk – another Tamilian man entered the eatery.

With eyes shocked on seeing me, he started inquiring about what I was doing there. This was a question that was to float in my direction perpetually in the upcoming months. My response was usually, "I am walking through South India."

This always triggered a pause followed by a change of pitch in the person's voice, enlarged eyes, and hastily voiced questions. "Walk??" or "Just walk??" or "No car?" or "Nothing??" or "For how long??" or "Alone???" or "In this weather??" or "Why??"

I would mostly smile at such reactions without really getting into the whole gist of it, which would arouse the listener's curiosity more and have them further inquiring about me. I used to navigate past the rapid-fire rounds of questions and steer into talking about their outlook on life – to learn about and understand their life's intricacies within their minute bubbles.

## B. Trace from the Past

I was always an inquisitive child, curious about the world's happenings. With my parents unable to answer my whys, I tried to find answers to my unending questions from books or teachers at school, but nothing ever fulfilled my innate desire to get to the root of everything.

As I grew up in the robot-engendering schooling system of India, that curious childlike spirit started dying. It did not fit in with the mundane things taught in schools. And if I were to become successful in life, I had to learn to act logically and responsibly – to cope and fit in with all the other children, who were also being converted into mechanized humans.

Only in the last few years of traveling around India as a nobody did I realize that everything I had been taught and had braided into my being was one big old lie.

It did not matter to me anymore if most of the country – and the entire world – believed in this lie. From rekindling that curious childlike spirit in myself, I reckoned that striving to convert children into adult-like robots was an appalling error that we humans have been participating in during our lives.

It is an unbearable crime. Instead of nurturing the child's spirit of curiosity, creativity, and freeness, we kill it all.

We let them become miserable adults who spend their whole lives at the mercy of shooting themselves in the head while sluggishly approaching their graves with fear intact for every second of their existence.

Something about people and unique cultures had always fascinated me. It always helped me gain more perspective and allowed me to look at our human world with a much broader understanding and eventually reach a realization in these last few years.

*Everything we humans have invented relating to our lives is so temporary. Everything we think is right or wrong, good or bad, is simply a creation of our mind. It doesn't exist beyond the mind. We live our lives attached to so many laws, rules, and regulations we've devised for ourselves – about how we need to act and behave in a particular society or community or tribe – but we've failed to grasp that, at the end of the day, they don't matter. None of it does.*

*Everything we think our lives are worthwhile for won't mean a damn thing when our bodies start giving up on us and start deteriorating and preparing themselves to return to the soil they originally came from.*

Where did this realization come from?

It came from simply walking my life while traveling around India as a mere seeker, not giving in to the norm – walking while fighting with my heart to break out of the vicious human-composed way of living relating to life and death. This entraps us; we do not see the world beyond the illusion we've been conditioned to believe for our entire lives.

⸺ ◈◈◈ ⸺

I concluded my first day of walking at Thanumalayan Temple in the small temple town of Suchindram.

Thanumalayan Temple was a prehistoric marvel of Hindu architecture. Its workmanship was as profound as I had ever seen on the stone walls of any major Hindu temple. I strolled past its majestic ancient gates with layers of sweat dripping down my whole body from having walked close to five hours on my first day.

Everything was stemming from the roots of spontaneity, so I had no idea this temple was approaching. With dungeon-like darkened passageways resonating with the sound of mantras and people walking by, I went all the way inside the enormous temple to receive the blessings from the core *linga*[49].

This temple had a unique *linga*, a representation of all three principal gods of Hinduism: Brahma, Vishnu, and Shiva. It was the first time I had encountered this, and it was just when my mind was beginning to grasp the reality of what I was doing.

This was not just a casual walk I was on. It was a pilgrimage: a deep unsolicited journey into the unknown.

I was not following a path that led to some renowned pilgrimage site. I was letting the world take me through it as a mere pilgrim who had surrendered himself to the causality of all things.

There were appealing sculptures engraved around the temple's walls. After strolling through its chambers, I made my way outside, passing by the charming temple pond on one side beside the temple's main building and some food joints on the other.

A lodge – the sort of place I stayed in for most of my nights during the walk – was on the main highway, just a few minutes' stroll away from Thanumalayan Temple.

---

49  A *linga* is a symbol that represents the ultimate reality in Hinduism. It's usually made of stone and is egg-shaped. It can be easily seen around India, even under trees, with Hindu devotees worshipping it.

Lodges in South India were dwellings that offered cheap accommodation for passersby. I could easily find a room for 300rs ($4) per night in one. The rooms never had anything more than the basic requirements - dirty sheets and colorless walls. I did not care about the room's condition, so long as I got a roof to cover my head and a flat surface to sleep on.

Lodges were customarily sleeping places for laborers or truck drivers. It was only in South India that I came across the term "lodge" so frequently. In North India, the cheapest accommodation is called a hotel or guesthouse. The differences in terminology in the region were noteworthy.

A cage-like box is what I would get used to sleeping inside throughout my walk. It was a constant reminder that it was the prison of my mind that I had to free myself from - not the physical caged boxes my body would take respite in.

We live in our palace-like cages today, thinking we have achieved what there is to be achieved in life without realizing that the only real cage is inside our minds and that we do nothing to free ourselves from its bars.

It is a prison that bars us from experiencing freedom beyond our understanding of it.

Each of us is a slave to our mind's prison.

I walked inside the narrow doorway next to a *chai* shop by the highway to enter the lodge. An old Tamilian woman wearing a stunning *sari* was cleaning the floors by the reception desk. She was small and had curly white hair. She greeted me with a big smile when she saw me. She spoke no Hindi or English but knew I was there for a room.

She was trying to explain to me in Tamil that the owner was unavailable and asked me to hand over some identification before giving me a room, which was nothing less than a prison box on its own with colorless walls and a hard single bed.

Even though I spoke no Tamil, I never had any problem understanding what the locals in Tamil Nadu were trying to say.

I loved how so many states of India had their individual language and unique set of dialects across their land. It always captivated my mind and made me feel like I was traveling through a new country. Even though similarities relating to the whole country prevailed, every state had its inherent peculiarities.

These included things like language, topography, cultural variations, and divergent traditions. Each state had its own matchless identity. By embracing these different identities and cultures, I was relinquishing myself in the complexity of whatever came my way.

Though I enjoyed observing and learning about the differences that humans attach to themselves relatively, I had stopped caring about human externalities in the absolute sense. I did not see their color, religion, or any label they hung about themselves.

I did not attach myself to any label; neither did I put other people in specific boxes. They were all the same to me.

When I was walking through Hindu constituencies, I became Hindu; when in Muslim, I became Muslim; when in Christian, I became Christian. Temples, mosques, or churches were the same to me. I did not see any difference. They were all creations of the human mind, and I saw them like that, as I was learning to stand free and independent of everything and everyone.

Only the name my parents had given me stayed with me when I interacted with people, yet in my mind, even that name had no relevance any longer.

I stood detached from all human conceptions regarding the self. I was becoming label-less and devoting myself to the true divinity of being fully connected with the sublime.

~

# III. LOST DIARY AND UNWANTED STRANGER IN MY ROOM

*I* WAS DRINKING A SAVORY *masala chai* sitting on an old ligneous bench inside a teeny *chai* shop run by a friendly Tamilian woman beneath the lodge I was staying in. The shop was alongside the highway, so I could see vehicles transiting by. Frequent visitors came in to drink a *chai* or get a *gutka*[50].

On seeing me inside the *chai* shop, some locals got excited and asked for a selfie, to which I happily agreed.

It was only the beginning of everything, and I had brought a diary with me as my companion. Sipping my cup of *chai*, I was scribbling thoughtless words in my diary. Other than my phone, this diary was the only tangible possession I cared about. Before starting the walk, I had debated whether I should carry it with me – or wholly drench myself in the act of walking while receiving everything the world had to offer. Was I to write or think about anything else, or simply be present with every shimmering moment?

Somehow that is what ended up happening anyway. A few weeks into the walk, I lost my diary, along with all my writing inscribed within it. That served as a validation for me. I was not meant to be writing during the walk, as it was not for that.

---

50 A *gutka* is chewable economical tobacco crammed with chemicals.

*The walk was an act of pure surrender and devotion. It was to disintegrate my physicality into becoming a channel with no layers attached to it and to grant me the radiance of blissful energy through my mutating cells.*

Other than the essentials, the only material possession that stayed with me for the entire walk was my phone.

I used my phone to stay connected with the world by sharing sincere updates on social media about the walk and my first book, *Dream Beyond Shadows*. It was starting to receive attention from readers across the country who deeply related to the story inscribed in its pages.

As the sun was starting to melt away, I went back toward the Thanumalayan Temple in the evening. The locals were dancing on the streets, celebrating the birthday of a certain Hindu god. *Sadhus*[51] were dipping in the temple pond and chanting mantras as the sun flickered its shadows on the water.

Food joints were preparing their jumbo metal stoves suffused with immeasurable amounts of cooking oil on top of oversized burning flames or frying large meals for the people dancing around.

Music and the recitation of mantras in unison were echoing from inside the temple walls. A festival ensued through the night in a country that is notorious for its infinite procession of festivals.

I did not dive too deep into the celebrations but got a taste of them from joyously watching the energetic demonstrations of the people congregating and rejoicing. Later, I went back to the lodge to end my first day's walk by lying down inside my prison box.

I was animated in myself and willing to bring out my spirit to let it burn and howl past the irons of time and the delusions of my forbidden mind.

## A. Day 2 – Strange Encounter

I was walking past the coconut trees by the ocean and along the heated concrete road in my torn old shoes. Feeling the charge of the earth funneling through my feet, I was walking in synchronicity with the sea's changing tides.

---

51  A *sadhu* is a religious ascetic or holy person.

It was the life of a pilgrim that I was leading - gracefully accepting food, water, and sometimes, even money from strangers, and resting under wise old trees embedded within the perimeters of temples, churches, or mosques.

With every step of the way, I was letting go of my ego and a sense of belonging. I kept on unwinding within myself from the sheer grace of what others had to offer.

I was becoming an instrument of reflection as I walked past the uncountable numbers of eyes that stared through my heart and chiseled it by exposing it to everything there was to receive.

I would observe every thought surfacing in my mind about the people I came across. Every day, I reminded myself that each thought cropping up in my mind about another person was just a projection of my mind, triggered by a layer within myself I needed to let go.

The projections could have come from the roots of anything - anger, sadness, judgment, aversion, pain, love, hatred, and so on. The key was not to disown them but to get to their origins - a childhood memory, specific conditioning, or an experience from the past.

Whatever the derivation for the projection's eruption, that was what I had to let go.

I started treating every thought that arose in my mind about the people I encountered as a reflection of myself, which made me realize that every thought we have about others - negative or positive - emanates from a source within ourselves.

By beholding the observers' immovable eyes while thinking of them as mirroring my soul, I began detaching myself from every single thought that emerged.

With time, the relevance of these thoughts relating to other people dissipated as I consciously chose not to give them any importance. That sponsored the creation of space for nothingness in my mind.

It was a momentary space of pure joy where none of our human creations existed. This space of nothingness kept on growing over the ensuing months of walking countless miles. It allowed me to dwell at further depths in myself and experience the all-embracing rawness of my being.

It would be a prolonged state of utmost existence, which I had previously experienced only for brief moments. The walk spurred me to breathe through it with every new second.

I spent so much time on my feet the soles of my torn shoes eventually disappeared. There was no separation between the outside of my physical body and the world beyond. Both merged in the sense of oneness with all of life surrounding me. The human-made objects and the natural world around me became a part of me, and I became a part of them. Subsequently, I understood there was no separation between anything.

We came from the soil and will eventually disintegrate into it. In between those two realities, the opportunity exists for us to transcend what we think is possible.

I walked along National Highway 66 on Day 2 before I momentarily halted in a quaint Shiva Temple around noon. It was outside the administrative City of Nagercoil. I had navigated through Nagercoil early in the morning and was stopped by several college students who were thrilled to learn that I was walking through their state.

They referred to me as *"baba ji"*, which I thought was hilarious, and shared a laugh about it with them.

It happened all along the road as I walked. People constantly stopped me to inquire about what I was doing. I would tell them, "I am just walking," and they would want to converse with me. I used to ask them to walk and talk with me.

Interacting with young students with so much spirit and vigor in their hearts was remarkable. That was my favorite part of the walk – young people joining in when they saw me pass by their homes.

My afternoon was taken up by resting my body under an enormous banyan tree rooted next to the unoccupied, antiquated Shiva temple. It was nice to be lying down under the shade of the tree. It provided some much-needed relief for my body that had been walking for many hours in the heat.

I had not finished walking for that day and continued rambling at 4 pm for a few more hours until I arrived in the small town of Thucakalay by 6. I had covered over 20 km that day and got my legs warmed up for the coming days when I would be managing longer distances.

This town had various churches, mosques, and temples scattered around, but it was primarily Christian dominated with sizable, stunning, white churches in the area.

I was looking for a place to stay for the night when I came across a small eatery on my way. I asked the ancient man sitting outside, "Do you have a room?" He replied with an unclear nod of his head while pointing toward its inside.

I walked inside the eatery not sure if they offered accommodation. A young, skinny, dark-skinned man approached me as soon as I entered and asked me in his broken English, "You need a room?"

"Yes. Do you know where I can get one?"

He answered with eagerness in his voice, "Yes! Follow me."

A stack of stairs led to the eatery's dingy basement. I sensed the young man was overly friendly in an unusual way as I followed him inside a small office in the dim basement. An old computer sat on a table with a few chairs next to it.

He asked me to take a seat and queried, "You have your country's passport?"

I replied, "No passport. I am Indian. You can see my driver's license."

He responded with astonishment in his eyes, "You're Indian?"

"Yes!"

Something did not feel right – the guy was getting very intense as he continued speaking. I was unsure what it was, but was trying not to presume anything or project any of my thoughts onto him. I gave him my ID.

As he was writing my details on a tattered register, he whispered, "I can also give you a massage later at night, and we can watch a film together."

That's when it hit me. *Ahh! He's gay! That explains the excitement.* I laughed at his proposal and said, "No, thank you."

He looked disappointed. After writing down my details, he asked me to follow him to the room. As we approached it through the creepy basement, he again asked me if I wanted a massage at night. This time I said, "No," with some seriousness in my eyes, making it extremely clear that I didn't want anything from him but a room. It turned out to be another caged box quartered in an uncanny basement with no lights and cracked walls with the paint peeling off.

Even though he did not stop fussing over me, I didn't think he would be any trouble. All I needed was a room to crash in for the night before setting out again on my walk early the next day. I took that tiny box in the strange basement.

I quickly washed my clothes after taking the room, which I did every day after concluding my walk. They were so drenched that when I squished them with my hands, the sweat from walking all-day in such steamy conditions almost filled half a mug.

Severe dehydration would surface in the upcoming months.

Tired from that day's walking, I went to bed early that night. My body was begging for rest, but my mind was thoroughly stimulated from being continually introduced to new surroundings and repeatedly conversing with strangers along the way.

It was late at night when my survival instincts kicked in to raise my shaking body from the waist up. I promptly turned my neck to look at the door, barely a yard away on my right.

I had locked the door earlier that night, and as my senses burst into life to grasp what was happening, I saw the door handle gradually moving – someone was attempting to get inside the room!

I was stunned for a moment, and my survival instincts immediately kicked to protect myself. *Who is it?* I thought to myself. *Is it the same guy from the reception?* I wondered. *Or could it be somebody else?* A few seconds later, somehow, I was sure it was him – the guy from the reception.

Anger started rising from my core, which I tried to observe. *This is going too far. How dare he!*

These thoughts surfaced along with anger mounting through my belly. *Should I teach him a lesson?* I asked myself, with my body getting all fiery. *What if he has a weapon on him?* I wondered and hurriedly grabbed my stick.

*If I open the door and hit him, that could wake up other people: the restaurant owner, neighbors,* I thought to myself. *He could get into serious trouble for trying to do this. I'm in a very traditional town, and I don't know how they would react on finding out he is gay and tried to enter my room forcefully late at night,* I contemplated, while he kept on trying to enter the room.

*This is too aggressive, though. He has crossed the line!*

I was not sure what to do, but after a few minutes of observing the rising sensation of anger in myself, I decided not to do anything and went back to lying down on the bed while holding onto my stick, just in case if he could break in.

I was unable to sleep anymore because my survival instincts had been triggered. They could not let me sleep knowing that somebody had tried to enter my room forcefully and could try again – although I gave him the benefit of doubt by thinking, *He will not do it again.*

My mind brought up the worst-case scenario. If he does try to do something that could be physically dangerous, I will just take him down. He was a short and skinny guy, so I was unconcerned about him being a threat to me. At the same time, given the kind of frame of mind I was now in, it would have been very difficult for me to physically attack somebody, as I didn't want to resort to any violence. I was really hoping it didn't come down to such a scenario.

The rising anger in me was unable to understand what this man had just tried to do, but I made a conscious effort to let go of it and generate forgiveness for him.

Some time passed, and the anger melted, and just when that happened, he again tried to enter my room. This time I was already sitting up on my bed observing the door handle moving. I really could not believe my eyes while he kept on trying to break in.

With my anger having melted away, I no longer felt affected by his actions, which allowed me to try to understand why he was so relentless.

I realized he was not in control of himself at all. He was commanded by his sexual impulse and had no awareness of how to control it. As a result, he did not recognize that what he was doing was so aggressive. Not that being piloted by his biology allowed him to carry out such an act – not at all – but at that moment, I understood where it came from. And there was more. He must not have recognized that his actions were outrageous and inappropriate.

Something odd happened to me just then. I began to imagine myself as a woman in this precise circumstance. *What if it was my mother or sister here – not me?*

How traumatizing and scary would this be for a woman with a strange man trying to enter her room to assert his dominance over her, thinking he could do whatever he wanted. I began to feel the sensations that many women worldwide must go through in their everyday lives, always being forced to live in survival mode – being made to feel physically vulnerable and defenseless because of threats in their surroundings.

This encounter with a man trying to enter my room forcibly led to a night where I sketchily felt what it meant to be a woman in today's extremely derailed world. Things men cannot imagine; women must face every day just because they are women.

Simply take India's example, where we segregate the sexes at a very young age and raise children so unnaturally in most parts of the country. There is no formal sex education in the school curriculum from one end of the country to another. Children are not familiarized with this subject at school or at home. People don't openly talk about sex even nowadays, as it is still considered a taboo in a country with over a billion people.

In the coming decades, we are primed to surpass China and become the world's most populated country, but still, we fail to talk openly about the most natural process there is in the world. It is the seed of creation for everything. We would not exist if not for sex.

Not schooling our populace about sex, especially when we have a significant population control problem on top of inequality in the male to female ratio – males outnumber females. There is a sad history of female feticide, violence, abuse, and rape of both women and men. There is a plentitude of tribulation about sexuality – no, or only improper, awareness of it as well as violence.

Sexual energy is one of the most potent energies for driving a species. It is the seed of creation for all and learning to harness it has been considered pivotal for spiritual growth by profound sages over thousands of years. It profoundly affects our psychology, as well as overseeing our biology.

But somehow, we have managed to turn sex into a taboo subject in India and attach so many layers of false conditioning to it. We label sex as an "evil act" or a "vile act," even though it's the sole reason we were born in the first place.

Suitable sexual education can lead the way to a more awakened society. It will also bring about a much more harmonious society. Young men would not try to enter a stranger's room late at night because they cannot control their sexual impulses and aren't aware of how aggressive their actions are or that it may traumatize the person at the receiving end.

My survival instincts didn't let me sleep that night. The stranger tried to breach my room forcefully several times throughout the night. Without reacting to his actions, I observed them and tried to go beyond them while understanding why he would do such a thing.

It was not the only time a stranger would try to enter my room. It happened a few more times on the whole walk.

Every day of walking on my own with nobody to support my back was only going to make me stronger in myself with my spirit blazing more and more through my whole body.

Somehow, I just knew nothing would happen to me; I felt protected.

However naïve this belief may have been, I was convinced that whatever unknown source had asked me to do this walk, it was also looking over me and would not let anything happen to me. Even though a stranger vehemently tried to enter my room on only my second night of walking, my determination was not affected. It was only going to get sturdier every day until the arrival of the moment when I would know, "Why this nameless walk?"

# IV. WHEN IN GODS OWN COUNTRY

*I LEFT THE TOWN OF* Thuckalay early the next morning to continue walking. The same guy from the reception, the one who had most definitely tried entering my room during the night, woke up on hearing me walking out the eatery's main door.

It was as if he had been waiting. He hurriedly came out to see me before I left. I gave him a furious look, conveying all that I had to express through my eyes to make him recognize that what he did the night before was unacceptable.

He tried to hug me as I was leaving, but I sternly brought my hand up and stopped him before he could get any closer. *What an aggressive fella*, I thought to myself, as I left the absurdity of that night behind while advancing alongside National Highway 66 closer to the State of Kerala, a state commonly known as God's Own Country.

I finished walking that day in the City of Marthandam, a major trading hub. It was also my last city in Tamil Nadu, as I was to cross the state border the next day and slide into Kerala.

Famous for its striking CSI Church[52], a dated stone building next to the main highway, Marthandam had a clear sense of busyness about it because of all the trade materializing in the region.

I had been surviving my last few days of the walk predominantly by eating *idli, sambar,* and *dosa,* the staple food of South India. It was all I could get my hands on in the small eateries on the way, but in Marthandam, I got to treat myself with a multi-course traditional South

---

52 The CSI is the Church of South India.

Indian *thali* bursting with a variety of flavorful options. Just looking at the untouched *thali* was a delight for my eyes.

It was a reward presented to me by the welcoming people of Marthandam for having crossed over 50 km on foot. In the next few days, I would touch the 100 km mark while propelling myself through Kerala.

I didn't keep an exact count of how far I walked each day, but as I moved past the road signs with the names of the approaching towns and cities and the distances on them, I always had a rough sense in the back of my head of the approximate number I trod.

And as I kept walking consistently with time at my disposal, I started developing a natural ability to figure out the distance I was covering without the need to look at the road signs or the GPS on my phone.

I was not setting targets while walking but treating every day as a new day.

No planning was necessary, as I was listening to my spirit, my true, and only guide. It sometimes went too far, though, directing me to keep walking even when I had no physical strength left or had run out of water. But regardless of any emerging challenges, I continued walking while pushing myself beyond my perceived limits.

I could not defy the declaration of my spirit raging through my core and guiding me every step of the way.

Sometimes it conveyed to me I should take it easy and relax my body to let it heal, and at other times, it insinuated that I keep going no matter what.

By listening to my spirit, I was learning to distance myself from repeatedly being shattered by my mind's enchainment. Instead, I was being stirred by the vitality exalting through my core.

Every day of that walk was like a year, as my being received infinite teachings from the universe. Simultaneously, I was getting to see and experience the changing world around me. It was all too real at times as my senses' capacity had been enhanced so enormously.

### A. Walking into heaven

It was on the fourth day when I crossed from Tamil Nadu into Kerala. It was a paradisial land with boundless coconut trees; an immense enclosing green; a synthesis of flourishing culture and arts; the richness of Ayurveda; serene beaches; pulsating oceans; impeccable backwaters, and a myriad of other splendors. All this made the state live up to its signature of God's Own Country. That title truly reflected the kind of sanctified beauty captured by the land of Kerala.

The primary language spoken by the people of Kerala was Malayalam, so they were commonly referred to as *Malayalis* by people from other parts of the country. I didn't know it then, but I was going to walk through Kerala's entire Malabar Coast, part of the southwestern belt of India, covering nearly 600 km in the state of Kerala itself.

Walking through the State of Kerala would be a phenomenal experience. More importantly, it would be one of the most defining times of my life. The simple act of walking transformed into a movement of sorts when word of it spread in Kerala like wildfire.

In the weeks to come, I was invited to speak at events while passing through the major cities of Kochi, Kozhikode, and Kannur. Journalists from national and local newspapers would come and interview me about the walk and my first book, *Dream Beyond Shadows*.

"Why are you walking so much? How are you surviving this heat? Why alone?" the journalists would inquire.

I replied with answers such as, "Life is for walking through," or "Life is meant for us to experience first-hand and give everything we have," or "What I am doing may seem unnatural to the world of today, but this is who we are in our deepest selves," or "I am simply trying to live an authentic life by being sincere and honest in myself."

I would be given the title of "The Philosopher on Foot" by *The Hindu Newspaper*.

News of the walk eventually went viral right through the State of Kerala with people recognizing me on the streets, stopping me on the road to talk and walk with me. They showered me with enthusiasm and kindness.

"Trailing the Nameless Walk" is what *The New Indian Express* termed it.

Local *Malayalam* newspapers published several articles about the story of the walk. I could not read Malayalam, but wherever I went, people would stop me and say heartily, "It is you!" or "We read about you in the newspaper."

I had no idea that all of this was going to unfold when I first stepped into Kerala.

---

Leaving National Highway 66 and taking inner routes passing through little villages on the way, I arrived in Poovar on my fourth day. Poovar was a tourist destination – as was most of Kerala, a state that thrived on tourism, especially in its southern parts.

Its pristine natural beauty and eccentric aspects of wellness and holistic living drew visitors to Kerala from around the world.

Poovar was between two water views with backwaters on one side and the Arabian Sea on the other. It had delighted the eyes of seers with an exquisite natural blend.

It was my first sunset in Kerala by the backwaters. I watched it sitting in the serenity of the backwaters while hiding under some trees.

I stayed the night at a local family's house after having covered over 20 km that day. They gladly provided me with a room for the night. On their recommendation, I continued my walk early next morning on the Poovar-Vizhinjam Road toward Kovalam Beach, the first major tourist destination I arrived at in Kerala.

I encountered many old churches on Poovar-Vizhinjam Road and trailed past tiny fishing villages next to the ocean in the morning. Most of the fishermen were returning to the land after having been out at sea all night. People stared at me as if I was an alien, while their minds pondered about what I was doing walking past their villages.

That was the first day wild dogs attacked me on the walk. It made me recognize that I had to be wary of them whenever I was walking through the land's interior parts, away from main highways.

The people of Kerala were friendly from the get-go, even before they found out about me from newspapers. Hospitality was rooted in the land, and even in areas where no outsiders went, there was no hostility.

It was always curiosity more than anything else, even though I could initially come across as intimidating to the locals. But as soon as I smiled

at them and was open in my approach, their sense of intimidation died. A space for honest interaction was generated.

I arrived in the major tourist spot of Kovalam Beach on Day 5. Many elderly British tourists were hanging out in the area among other western and Indian tourists.

A lighthouse was atop a small cliff at one end of the beach. I had to walk down the street away from Kovalam's main town to get to the beach area, where many restaurants, shops, and all kinds of tourist attractions captured panoramic views of the ocean.

Even though Kovalam Beach was quite touristy with many foreigners in the area – which always increased the prices of food and accommodation – it was still a gorgeous spot to have come across. I was told later by a local restaurant owner that Kerala's tourist season that year had been deficient, which was bad for the businesses that were entirely dependent on it.

But in some ways, that worked in my favor as there were fewer crowds, more silence, and I could easily find cheap accommodation even in the tourist areas, as there were plenty of occupancy options.

When I asked around about why there were fewer tourists that year, people didn't know. They usually suggested, "It could be because of the bad press Kerala received from the floods last year in 2018, even though the floods happened mostly in particular areas of the state's northern part," or "It could be because of the news about the outbreak of Nipah virus."

Both of these had received a lot of attention from the media. When the floods happened, most Indian media channels made it seem like all of Kerala had gone underwater, and the apocalypse had begun.

It is one thing, to tell the truth as it is, and a whole other thing to stretch it so far that it becomes sensational and grips people's attention in front of television screens – and boosts media channel ratings.

Headlines and breaking news are what sell in the world today. While I was walking through South India, I felt as if I was living in two worlds – the one shown on our TV/phone screens and the one playing out on the ground.

At that time, the country's general elections were a few months away, starting in April 2019. People would vote for who would become the Prime Minister of India.

All the political parties were actively running campaigns with the principal intention of dividing and polarizing people – in the name of the religion, ideology, identity, and the labels we humans so dearly love. It was done to maximize the parties' votes because democracy is based on popular demand.

To attain power in a democracy, all you need to do is get most people to vote for you. It does not matter how you do it because winning is all that matters in politics. If you can strategically market yourself to specific constituencies in a country by including tag lines in your speeches to convince the masses to listen to you and believe in what you are selling, you can win the election.

Inserting fake news into numerous social media posts and creating propaganda to manipulate the voters has become extraordinarily easy to do in the digital age.

A country such as India has such an enormous population, an incredible wealth gap, vast numbers of people living below the poverty line, a stark divide between rural and urban settings, and a sizable number of uneducated people. (How someone in India is assessed as being educated is another book!) Regardless of their socio-economic condition and section of society, most Indians now have access to a phone and the internet, as they are so affordable.

Using the armaments of fake news and targeted marketing is perfect for today's marketers. They can manipulate and influence people how they want by creating the desired perception in their minds.

Most statistics we fight about are made up. The facts we argue about are not facts. The primetime political news we talk about is nothing but a false conjecture of words.

It is hard now to distinguish in the relative world between what is real and what is not.

Throughout my whole time of walking, and previously when I was traveling around India, I saw more people glued to their phones all the time than not. From what I observed, they were mostly on social media platforms receiving information.

"What was that information? Was it true or false? Right or wrong?" are not the questions we need to ask here.

We need to ask, "How is our mind getting affected by endlessly receiving information like this?"

Most of what our mind receives nowadays from our interaction with technology is rubbish. What we need more than ever in the digital age is to be wiser.

Only wisdom can provide our minds with some peace. Wisdom equips us with the ability and awareness to accept what we want to let inside our minds.

More information is not what we need in the 21st. Century. We need to cultivate more wisdom – and especially among young people.

We are currently being ruled by technology, and technology on its own is not the problem. How we interact with it makes the difference.

If we use technology for its benefits, it can make our life more comfortable and convenient. But if we keep on using it for its disadvantages, it can mentally degrade us, leading to an increasing number of mental health glitches. Global trends suggest this is already happening.

People aren't happy. They aren't satisfied with what they have – young or old, rich or poor. It doesn't matter where people are smeared on the food chain. Anger, frustration, and dissatisfaction are rising.

Extremism and polarization is growing, and we can clearly see this by acknowledging how politics is shaping across the globe. People stand at different ends of the pendulum's swing with polar-opposite views.

For the pendulum to return to the middle and balance things out, we need to unite in these dark times. We need to see behind the curtain and past the stage sets where the powerful hide – those who promote chaos and uncertainty among people. It is easier to organize and manipulate large groups of people who have been made to feel lost and trumped by turmoil.

Even if turmoil may not be the reality on the ground, that is what we are shown on our phones and TV screens. Amplified confusion, fear, and anger are attached to a barrage of strategically contrived propaganda.

This human-concocted propaganda infiltrates our minds and makes us believe in a false reality, which either confirms our false notions about the world or invokes our deep-seated fears. In either case, it causes an eruption of anger and insecurity about who we are, what we believe in, and what we stand for.

It makes our identities feel threatened. It methodically activates our defense mechanism and compels us to act from our stoked, primal survival instincts, rather than from an evolved and truly conscious place within ourselves – where we can learn to look at things with a thorough and deep understanding of the whole game.

That whole game stems from the core philosophy of divide and rule, which we have been succumbing to for the entire course of our history – and still fall prey to.

We don't realize that on an absolute level, there is no Us vs. Them. There is only oneness without any labels or identities attached to these battered bodies of ours.

The day all humans on the planet comprehend that there is no separation between who we are and the world around us, no conflicts will exist. The root cause of any conflict derives from the Us vs. Them notion.

Only when we can reject this notion and embrace the truth of oneness in everything and everyone will there be no space for separatists promoting their extreme ideologies and infiltrating our minds to corrupt our souls, so we do not see the truth of what binds all of us.

<hr/>

I had been walking steadily for five days when I arrived in Kovalam Beach, so I decided to take a day to rest my body before moving on to the next destination.

I was starting to notice some changes in my body. My muscles were getting looser, especially in my legs and parts of my body were sore with swelling around my ankles and knees.

As I was wearing worn-out shoes with no soles, my feet were distressed from walking such long distances on boiling concrete roads. The agony was transmitted up from my feet to my hips. The skin on my feet was beginning to rupture, and their surface was getting calloused. They were becoming less sensitive to touch.

I could feel the pain increasing in my legs, while, simultaneously, there was pain from a neck injury I had from before the walk. Since I was carrying a ten-kilo backpack on my shoulders, my neck was only going to get worse.

It was almost too extreme for my body; it had been put into this unfamiliar situation without preparation. But, somehow, I did not care what would happen to my body.

All my spirit wanted was to keep moving forward.

I found an affordable room for a few nights in a guesthouse in one of the internal lanes at a right angle to the main road along the beach, Light House Head Road. All the fancier resorts, hotels, and restaurants were on that main road – obviously because they offered an uninterrupted view of the ocean. Things got cheaper as you went inward away from the beach along narrow lanes.

These constricted lanes linked with one another in a chaotic mess took you past people's houses, most of which had been converted into guesthouses or yoga and Ayurveda healing centers. They were separated by hotels, resorts, cafés, and restaurants. There were small shops, too, selling touristy stuff such as the legendary elephant pants, funky accessories, loosely fitted Indian-style clothing, and jewelry – the items many foreigners bought as mementos of their trip to India.

It was an arrangement I would be familiar with when passing through tourist beaches in the coming months.

———— ∞∞∞ ————

Entering this tourist center after walking past remote villages and local towns in the previous days made me feel like I had entered an unfamiliar world altogether, a world within a larger world ... a bubble within a bubble ... derived worlds split with visible paradox.

I had gotten very used to noticing this constant paradox in all parts of India. The way people lived varied theatrically from one region to another according to their socio-economic status and accepted identity. Sometimes the physical distance between these altering realities could be a mere few miles, but it almost seemed like I was hauling past scattered planets.

On one planet, I saw how the kings and queens lived in their palaces with their endless luxuries and numerous helpers running around. On another planet, I saw how heaps of people lived in their communally integrated villages.

My wandering through India as a nobody, experiencing, and living these varying paradoxes spread over the land kept providing me with clarity and perspective into the illusion that governs our world.

It is an illusion so deeply ingrained in our systems that we do not see the nameless reality of our true nature.

It is an illusion that keeps us tied to all our human-devised constructs. It does not let us experience freedom from everything we think is real. And it does not let us experience the freedom of what is real – which is nothing.

The reality of the human world, whatever we may think of it concerning our conditioning, ideals, or values, is merely a construct of our mind. Only when we start breaking past our mind's devious constructs can we experience the absolute truth of our lives.

# V. SUNKEN FEET

*S* *TANDING IN THE OCEAN* with waves caressing my naked chest, I was staring at the red sun while requesting the sea to heal my swollen legs and requesting the sun to rejuvenate my body's cells.

I always submerged like this whenever I was going past a beach on my walk. It always rendered me the opportunity to merge myself with the ocean and become one with the elements of creation.

While the sun became masked below the ocean, flashes of sunlight compelled my mind to remember the simplicity with which the sun carried the burden of our planet's nourishment.

If we receive too much sun, no life can survive – and if we receive too little of it, no life can revive.

It must do the same job every day while maintaining a course of perfect balance.

---

I went to sleep that night, knowing in my heart that the most significant changes had begun moving through me. It was becoming more apparent that everything that had happened in the last few years since I left New York was for me to be on this walk.

It was almost bizarre. The pieces of the puzzle had started coalescing without me trying to bring them together, but simply because that is what life had in store for me.

All I had to do was keep moving forward.

The next morning, I was chanting the *Gayathri* mantra[53] along with the sun gleaming as it stirred, while the seas were summoning my body.

With my feet sunk in the sand to balance my posture while standing tall and not letting the strong waves carry me away, I was fully immersed in listening to all life thundering around me.

I strolled around Kovalam Beach after my morning prayers, and as it was still very early, few people could be seen. The Statue of Mahatma Gandhi, aka *Bapu*[54], his wooden stick in one hand and in a walking position, was near the lighthouse end of the beach.

Seeing his walking figure was a great way to start my day. It reminded me of how, as part of India's struggle for freedom from the British Empire, his powerful marches – such as the Salt March, also known as the *Dandi* March – had unified people nonviolently by using the strength of civil disobedience.

Not that I was walking in a movement, but there was this underlying parallel – freedom.

Freedom from the prison of our mind
Enslavement by our sorrows
Evils of our spirit
Triumphs of our anger.
And most importantly …
The delusions of our self.

⸺⸺⸺

I found a quiet rooftop café facing the ocean after my morning stroll around Kovalam. There I could sit and write in my soon-to-be-lost diary while reflecting on the changes I had been going through in just a few days after having begun the walk.

It was not the usual passing of a day because my mind had thoroughly distanced itself from the concept of time and was getting lost in the crevices of my departed self.

---

53  The *Gayathri* mantra comes from revered scriptures, the Vedas, and is dedicated to the deity of the Five Elements.
54  *Bapu* means father in Hindi. This is how Mahatma Gandhi was referred to by Indians – "Father of the Nation."

The dungeons of my heart were exploding onto the surface, bringing the oldest of vanished memories alive, demanding my mind to process everything.

I was consciously aiming to observe everything surfacing and not pay any attention to the noise that kept on drifting through my mind. I was practicing the art of letting it all go.

A group of older, white-skinned women dressed in casual Indian attire were sitting at the table next to me.

I asked the one seated closest, "What brings you all to India?"

She replied, "Most of us live here."

I got curious and asked, "Really? Where?"

She replied, "We are Amma[55] devotees and move around with her wherever she goes."

"Amma? The woman who gives out hugs?"

She smiled and said, "Yes, that Amma. And she is not just a woman. By the way, my name is Christina," and then she asked me, "What are you doing here?"

---

55 *Amma* means mother in India.

"I am walking through South India. I started five days ago from Kanyakumari."

Her light green eyes became animated, and she said with her melodic voice as she turned her head to look straight at me while displaying her tightly-curled brown hair. "You must come to visit Amritapuri on your way."

I inquired, "Amritapuri? Where is it?"

She replied, "It's *Amma's Ashram* and is about 100 km up from here on the Malabar Coast near the town of Karunagappalli." After a moment, she asked, "You know Amma?"

"Ahh, yes. I know Amma. She's very famous in India. If it is by the coast, then it is probably on my way, as I am following the coastal line."

She gave me her details and asked me to get in touch if I was passing by *Amma's Ashram*.

She inquired more about why I was doing the walk, and after hearing me out, she said, "It is very inspiring, what you are doing."

The other Amma devotees sitting beside her also asked me to visit the *ashram* and told me Amma would be returning there soon, and I could receive a hug from her.

*That sounds interesting – a spiritual leader known for giving out hugs. Couldn't hurt to get a big loveable hug from her,* I thought to myself.

Millions of people followed Amma. Even though I was not into the *guru* and devotee thing very much, I did like exploring this side of India and observing how these *ashrams* functioned and why people followed *gurus*.

In most situations, whenever I came across a devotee who followed the teachings of a known guru, they always told me that so and so was not human – but beyond human.

Rather than judging their viewpoint, I admired their devotion to their *guru*. Nevertheless, I had discovered for myself while wandering through India over the last few years that seeking through the world and not following a particular *guru* or a specific lineage or revered ancient scripture provided the conditions for genuine realizations.

*Guru*, a word from Hinduism, describes your teacher or guide, someone who can show you the path for self-realization – a path you have to walk yourself, even if you have somebody to guide you.

In the last few years, I had met plenty of teachers and guides on my path, who did provide a lot of guidance and advice. Ultimately, though, I had the most profound experiences and connected with the highest form of myself when I was by myself in nature, connecting with a power beyond me.

I did not follow a *guru*, a god, or any scriptures, for that matter. Simply tuning into the freedom within myself while surrendering to a higher self with no attachment to any image, symbol, stories, or scriptures delivered the strength in me to break away from the shackles of this world truthfully.

---

Christina and the other *Amma* devotees left soon afterward, and I continued with my wanders around Kovalam later.

Being in Kovalam Beach was a good break from all the intensity I was beginning to experience on the walk.

Halts like this in tourist spots furnished my throat with an opportunity to share my experiences about the walk with people who were on a somewhat similar path to me, seeking more from life than the usual.

India has attracted seekers from across the world for thousands of years. Even in the contemporary world, where spirituality and religion have become commercial commodities, India continues to magnetize them. Seekers want to break out of their hardbound shells and willingly dive with pure audacity into the unknown to explore what comes.

Being a seeker isn't just about traveling and seeing what the external world has to offer. It is much deeper than that. It's more about walking away from everything you thought you knew before – the person you assumed you were – and being willing in your heart to prevail beyond everything while being open to whatever comes from the unknown.

Sadly, today's world is unsuited to such an undertaking. It does not accept people who don't function by society's rules or the establishment's orders.

We are supposed to live by human-contrived guidelines and work at a job, get married, raise a family, buy a house, and adhere to the rest of the façade that goes into making the capitalist world. Even if we have no desire to be part of that, we must because our physical survival depends on it – money is the prime source for securing physical survival.

It is not that people don't want to get out of this broken and greed-driven system. They are in a predicament. The system discourages them from breaking out of it by continually aggravating their survival instincts, so they act out of fear and unremitting anxiety about securing their future.

The system is masterminded to enslave people in cages with debts, mortgages, liabilities – any form of the ax that can be wielded to stop them from realizing the pure actuality of life without human interference.

I faced all this because choosing to follow the seeker's path required me to go through it all. I had to let go of my ego and be ok with the fact that it didn't matter who provided for my physical survival, so long as I got to keep walking on the path of ultimate freedom.

Accepting donations in the form of money, accommodation, food, and water from strangers whenever I could on my walk made me recognize that help would always be given to me as long as I stayed authentic and resilient in my determination to continue walking.

There was a clear picture in my head that, for whatever reason, I was now trailing on this unknown journey and able to sustain myself through it because of the kind support from my family, friends, and strangers. They were all instruments in the grand scheme of things providing the means I needed to keep my physical body alive and secure its basic needs. As a result, I could fully devote my energy to creating and then sharing the sincere impressions of what ensues from leading the life of a seeker.

It was not just about me anymore. I understood that my body, which I used to be obsessed with, was soon going to perish. Hundreds of years from now, nobody would remember it.

Humans have such a short memory.

We want to achieve a lot in our lifetimes so that other humans will recognize us. We continuously look for external validation, but forget that all the recognition we regularly crave will mean nothing once our bodies crumble.

This need for recognition only impacts us superficially because our minds have been made to believe all the elusive stories sold to us since our birth.

We live our lives fully occupied by these imaginary stories while simultaneously creating new ones, not recognizing that none of what we do today is going to matter thousands of years from now. In that case, why don't we do something with our every day, so we feel truly alive?

When questions such as, "Aren't you worried about your future?" and "How can you live without getting married and having children?" and "Why do you not want to own a house?" and "Why are you not living the way other people are living?" were thrown in my direction, it always made me laugh. This was not because they weren't fair. It was because they were all related to the future, while I was trying not to be in the future but in the present moment.

This constant mindset about achieving in the future can take us away from appreciating life without any human filters attached to it or acknowledging that much of what we think we're achieving today isn't going to matter hundreds of years from now.

We only truly stand our ground in the present moment when we realize that the future isn't real. When we attach so much importance to the future, we lose sight of why it's imperative to start being more present in the NOW.

The more we are present with the arising moments, the more we can live fearlessly in our selves away from the world's delusions and not succumb to the false ideas about everything we have invented over the years.

Life isn't about living in the future; it is about living in the now.

Sure, we can live by the system – get a secure job, tons of money, and plenty of real estate; have children, and do what everybody else is doing. There is nothing wrong with that, but we will always have to make allowances for the feeling that something is missing in the deepest part of our being.

A sense of being in a vacuum will prevail, which we might try to hide under the covers or choose to ignore in our lives. However, it will somehow manifest through us, and keep us distant from experiencing the blessed satisfaction of realizing the actuality of what is passing through us.

Whatever we may think of life based on our limited understanding of it, the ultimate fact of being born as a human is to work out why we were born in the first place.

As clichéd as this may sound, without getting to the root cause of our existence, we will never be able to experience life in its full sovereignty.

———∞∞∞———

Being on my own for entire days and nights while melting into the ground catered to my groundedness.

As a result, when I found myself in the proximity of social environments, such as Kovalam Beach, which hosted travelers from differing parts of the world who formed a very open and interactive atmosphere, I was immediately confronted by an upsurge in interactions with people from other countries. They were leading fascinating lives traveling around India and had varieties of tales to tell.

They had profound insights about India, accumulated while moving around the country with a pair of observant lenses from having been raised in another part of the world.

Even the foreigners I came across became extremely curious when they found out from conversing with me that I was walking through South India.

Travelers from the western world were intrigued to meet a young Indian man who had lived in the western world but had consciously chosen to leave that life behind to follow an unconventional path in his motherland. Most Indians were busily chasing the growth story pitched to them by the western world.

Blindly following this growth story adopted from the western world, we lost sight of the real freedom that originated and flourished in India. That had occurred under the guidance of great sages and saints from thousands of years ago, who narrowed down a path for us so we could live with freedom intact in our hearts.

We have now forgotten all of that and have recklessly assumed the western world's ideas about development. We don't question any of it while simultaneously distancing ourselves from true spirituality and adopting blind faith in religious propaganda. That doesn't make us conscious in ourselves but succeeds in keeping us distant from life's true essence.

Travelers from what we call "developed nations" come to India to learn more about themselves and dwell more deeply in the idea of wellness, so they can learn to lead healthier and happier lives. The developed nations whose primary focus is to provide their citizens with a high standard of living and security for their social and economic needs, cannot provide their citizens with a well-balanced approach to living. That happens because we humans have a one-dimensional way of looking at things when thinking about development and progress.

From looking at the trend of growing mental illness in the western world, it is evident that merely focusing on amassing material wealth is not the answer to humanity's problems. We need to put equal weight on our wellbeing with a keen focus on all aspects of our creation – physical, mental, emotional, and spiritual.

The idea of infinitely growing our material wealth but not raising our collective consciousness is a recipe for self-disaster.

The natural world is now a genuine reflection of that. We are doing nothing but destroying it.

In economic terms, the world, as of today, has accumulated more material wealth than in our entire previous human history. But it is controlled by the top percentage on the food chain. That way, they can keep dominating the world as they please and always have a working class to carry out the basic jobs. That way, the people on top can continue adding ever more to their bizarre amounts of stockpiled wealth.

I am not saying if this is right or wrong. Looking at this from an observer's point of view, it seems to me that when artificial intelligence and robots take on the jobs of all the working class, vast numbers of people will be left without jobs.

A country such as India already has an unemployment crisis among most of the young population, because large numbers are not appropriately trained or skilled to carry out what is required in a rapidly changing job market. And the dynamics of growing mental problems and dissatisfaction levels among people could prime a perilous scenario to burst.

There was no part of the country that I had been to in the last few years where the young people were not constantly telling me how lost and depressed they felt because they could not live up to the expectations of their parents and society in general.

When I say young, I'm even talking about kids as young as thirteen! They told me how confused they felt from not knowing what they were supposed to do in life and insecure from the pressure from their families to do well in the exams, so they could get admitted to a reputable college and then get a job.

At some point, I had to ask myself: "How did we manage to produce a society such as this, where children as young as thirteen are depressed and afraid to be alive?"

Isn't this something that needs to be thoroughly investigated?

If we fail to address this deepening issue, I think we have failed as a species by being so adamant that ignorance and greed define our world.

Life isn't meant for us to be sad and depressed about. It is for us to be excited and inspired by. It is not for us to be like the so-called mature adults, but to be more like free-spirited, carefree children, who aren't consumed by the hows? whats? and whys? of life but are totally involved in the madness of experiencing life.

More like free-spirited, carefree children who are distant from the blackened adult world, where adults can't see they have lost touch with their absolute nature.

# VI. FIRST MAJOR TOUCH

*U*NTIL THE TIME *I* arrived in Kochi, a major port city in Kerala, denoted as the Queen of the Arabian Sea, I walked through plenty of tourist spots meeting all kinds of travelers from across the world.

A trail of famous destinations starting from Kovalam Beach all the way to Kochi was followed by most travelers while exploring Kerala. I continued to run into familiar faces whenever I crossed the tourist spots until I arrived in Kochi. Many were shadowing a similar trail to me – except they were traveling by car or train, and I was at the mercy of my legs.

Even among traveling circles, word about my walk had started getting around. There were many instances when I would be interacting with some backpackers, and they would go like, "I heard about you from another traveler! You're the one walking through South India?" This always made me see how the synchronicity of it all was too uncanny at times to comprehend.

———

I had several interactions that day in Kovalam Beach, including one with two older Italian women, also *Amma* devotees, who asked me to visit *Amma's Ashram* on the way.

It almost seemed like all *Amma's* devotees were in Kovalam Beach, as I kept running into them. These two had been visiting India for over two decades. They told me how much India had changed since they first came in the 1980s.

"It is really, really changed now," one of them said, a woman named Bhavia in her broad Italian accent, while her friend Betti, who didn't speak much English nodded her head in agreement. They told me more of their friends would join them in Varkala Beach, the most arresting beach I would come across in Kerala. It was about 50 km up from Kovalam Beach.

Bhavia asked me if I would be walking past Varkala, to which I replied, "Varkala is up from here? Yes?"

"Yes. It is close, and we're going there tomorrow by taxi. So, maybe we will see you there?"

"Who knows, but it is quite possible."

Early the next morning, I walked again through the empty streets of charming fishing villages before winding my way along with National Highway 66.

With train tracks on one side and vehicles speeding by on the other, I was on my way to the Capital City of Kerala, Thiruvanthapuram, commonly identified by its former name of Trivandrum.

I had walked more than 100 km by the time I arrived in Thiruvanthapuram, which was highly commercial in its setting. My eyes were greeted with the sight of elongated concrete towers along the way, many inside the campuses of IT companies.

As I wanted to keep on walking, I did not stay in Thiruvananthapuram. I found a room for the night along the highway a few miles past the exits heading toward the city's central part and continued the walk the following morning, thundering away on the road.

### A. Almost a Marathon

Now that I was feeling acquainted with the land's topography and breathing more deeply, I started experiencing a surplus of rage rising through my core into my heart. It was a spirit of rage I had never experienced before.

A mix of anger, fearlessness, madness, and freedom combined in a bursting ball of fury and poured over every part of me.

It was flowing through my veins and constantly exploding through my chest and making my whole body turn into a bursting flame. It was overpowering and regulating my every breath to move my feet under the brutality of the torrid sun.

That was the day I covered the longest distance in the walk – around 36 km for close to ten hours of fleeting through villages. I also stopped on the way to interact with students at local schools; curious householders, who, on seeing me walk by, asked me where I was going; strangers who offered me rides, and even a policeman who questioned me about my whereabouts.

It was a day packed with unbounded socialization while I simultaneously acknowledged the rage surging in my body with every step forward.

I took breaks in the shade of colossal churches, as most of the villages I was walking by in that part of Kerala were predominantly Christian. This was the day I started noticing images of Fidel Castro[56] painted on village walls. Politically, Kerala was strongly influenced by communist ideas. Communist parties had had a major influence on the state since India's independence from the British in 1947.

It was thought-provoking to see the paintings of Fidel Castro there – he was revered as a revolutionary among many in Kerala.

With most of India having adopted capitalist values in the last several decades, it was intriguing to notice a communist aspect in this state. Kerala probably had one of the highest standards of living, education, and healthcare in the country, along with lower rates of poverty and crime and other such features that go into bettering ordinary people's lives.

It initiated a question in my mind. I wondered if adopting specific communist policies would help achieve somewhat better functioning in an over-populated country such as India.

But instead of letting political thoughts consume my mind, I didn't dwell any further on that or any other political-type question. In those moments, I knew that politics was a distraction for my mind, as an

---

56  Fidel Castro was a former president of Cuba and an iconic communist leader.

eternal rage was overtaking my being and activating the most distant parts of my mind, body, and spirit. They were parts concealed in my deepest cellular pockets, that hadn't been touched since birth.

With my eyes wide open and my body having transmuted into a ball of fire, I moved through the outside world, experiencing the awakening of cells throughout my body. This triggered the emergence of realizations from a lifetime while instantaneously conveying me to a state of consciousness that endured beyond me.

The world in all its flavors became abundantly alive before my lucid eyes while my mind expanded through the sky.

By the time I was nearing Varkala, my body was somehow moving even though my legs had become numb, and I could no longer feel them.

The observer inside my mind was not a part of my mind any longer. It had deployed outside my mind to observe this alien body moving through time in the misty silence of the land – which, as I approached Varkala, became secluded and jungle-like.

My feet touched a street called Temple Road around 4 pm. Fancy resorts started popping up on both sides as I kept walking along it and flowed into Varkala's southern part. I was led straight down toward the Varkala Balu Mandapam Temple at the edge of Varkala Beach.

My feet were implanted in Varkala Beach's malleable sand while the sun's presence was scintillating on the sea. There were no sensations left in my body as I walked onto the sand. My eyes took in the sea on one side and the illustrious Varkala Cliff at a distance on my right.

It was a moment of complete detachment from my body and being at one with the sublime beauty nested in front of me.

Most of the restaurants, cafés, and guesthouses were settled on top of the lengthy Varkala Cliff. Further north, it was more for backpackers and therefore much more affordable than the southern end, where all the fancy resorts were.

I climbed up the stairs from the beach with no energy left in my body and disembarked into an open car park on the clifftop, offering a complete view of the lingering beach and the far-reaching sea.

The sun was fading as I sluggishly walked across the open parking space to a narrow pathway built on the clifftop where all the restaurants, cafés, and shops were next to one another in an endless line. It was a similar kind of a touristy arrangement to Kovalam Beach with laneways running between the restaurants and cafés away from the main pathway.

As I was dragging my feet along the main pathway, I saw the two older Italian women I'd met in Kovalam – Bhavia and Betti – walking in my direction with their other friends.

All were looking at me with excitement in their eyes and said to me as we got closer, "You made it!!"

One of the women I hadn't met before said, "We've heard all about you from these two. Your spirit arrived here even before your body. Wow! We can't believe it! You have walked through this heat – it is amazing!"

"I don't know how I'm walking either," I responded.

They warmly invited me to follow them and helped me get a room in a guesthouse, situated in one of the lanes running away from the sea and run by a friendly Keralan woman.

After getting me the room, they asked me to meet them for dinner later.

By the time I took off my backpack and went inside the bathroom to sprinkle water on my body, my legs were almost paralyzed. As I slowly washed the dirt and dried sweat off my body, I could not feel my legs at all, but I was not worried.

Instead, in that physically excruciating but internally liberating moment, I knew I was a long way away from the turning point when I would stop walking.

I met with the older Italian women later that night for dinner at a restaurant on top of Varkala Cliff. It encompassed a full view of the drifting sea, with the moon reflecting its solid presence over rippling waves.

The other two women who had joined Bhavia and Betti in Varkala were Cecilia and Caterina. All four of them had been *Amma* devotees for over the two decades since they'd first visited Kerala.

"There used to be nothing here in Varkala when we first came here. Just a few huts and nothing else. No lights and none of these buildings. Only stars and the sea," said Cecilia, the most fluent in English. Betti and Caterina spoke little; Bhavia spoke some.

But by this time, I didn't feel the need for language to communicate with people. My eyes were enough. The silence rolling through energetic bodies conveyed more than the words coming from our mouths.

Their description of Varkala from back in the day reminded me of my time in Zanskar, where there had been the least human involvement in the land, so it was still preserved in its raw state of creation. But that would not continue for long because greed had infiltrated human minds even there in Zanskar.

Wherever I had been in the last few years, this question always bubbled in my mind about the human world's rising madness:

*If our intentions were governed more by need, not greed, would we be able to preserve the balance between our natural world and our lives in general?*

---

I didn't stay out for long that night as my body felt exceedingly stressed from what it had been through. Even though what I was enduring looked physical from the outside, it was more than that. A storm was raiding the bleakest concealed layers of my mental, emotional, and spiritual self to bring everything up to the surface, leaving me with no choice but to deal with it all.

Separating from the enlivening company, I dribbled back toward my room to wrap up my thoughts about that riveting day. I was unsure how long I would stay in Varkala, but I could not think any longer.

Varkala was undoubtedly one of those places where you could end up staying for a long time. Other than holding its compass on sacred land with views as impressive as possible, people from across the world lived there. It was an international community of artists, yogis, musicians, healers, travelers, and a variety of curious people hanging out in the area and involved in numerous engaging activities.

It was a night of solemnity for me. All the rage that had been coursing through me for that day of walking had dissipated. I was merely lying down on a hard bed with my body static like a firm rock and mind intently simmering through it all.

The next morning, I was up on my swollen feet before the sunrise to go down onto the beach in the secrecy of dawn. I wanted to merge with the ocean and ask the divine to heal my legs and provide me with the strength to keep walking.

I sang prayers and meditated in the sacred hours of the morning, along with the sun's rising while my being was embedded into the land unconditionally.

I continued this morning routine for the remainder of my three days in Varkala and spent time on my yoga practice. My physicality continued dissolving, and my mind continued expanding.

During those days, I met several travelers and interacted with readers. I had informal story-telling gatherings with people from varied backgrounds at trendy cafés run by owners who were thrilled to host me. It was an exciting way to spend my days around Varkala, during which I got the chance to connect with loads of original people who gladly welcomed me into their spaces with open hearts.

Just about when I was beginning to get comfortable in Varkala, I decided to continue walking. On the recommendation of a bunch of Israeli travelers I met there, I left the paradise of Varkala behind on

Day 12 to move toward Munroe Island with legs that were getting worse by the day.

I stopped for a night on the way in the City of Kollam, a trading hub situated on the Malabar Coast – and chockfull of trash. Its beach was covered with more plastic waste than sand. It was so disheartening to witness after coming from Varkala, where the beach was clean.

Seeing such magnificent locations trashed by humans always made me feel sad. I could not understand why people trashed their land, which was so outstanding in its natural setting.

It always made me realize how humans are why this world has turned into a garbage manufacturing machine. Our madness has taken us so far that we can't see how destructive we've become. We fail to operate from our true creative nature and instead keep on giving more energy and power to our destructive selves.

The simple example of weaponry and the military is enough to understand this madness. We describe people who develop weapons of mass destruction as "geniuses." A huge percentage of our economies' growth and our investments go into developing and selling these weapons, whose purpose is to destroy.

Our inability to see beyond our ambition for more power, wealth, and influence has caused so many wars globally, and even in this century, we have failed to understand a simple prescription – wars don't solve anything.

It almost sounds idealistic. However, when the consciousness of humans around the planet collectively expands, we will be able to admit that we don't need to manufacture more weapons or keep developing our armies. We will be able to stop calling ourselves "powerful nations." Only the expansion of our collective consciousness will allow us to move beyond this highly destructive way of living.

We cannot allow ourselves to keep living by these false ideas about what defines national power and strength. These are not just bows and arrows; they are nuclear. They can easily destroy the whole planet and all life on it with the pressing of a button.

It doesn't matter what any war is for or how it's sold to us as a glorious battle of "evil" vs. "virtue." Nothing good comes of it.

There is nothing but destruction for all the parties involved.

―⊶⊷⊷―

This was the first time in my walk that I had a destination in mind before I left Varkala. To get to Munroe Island, I had to get off the Malabar coast and go a bit inland into the State of Kerala.

I walked about 25 km away from Varkala to arrive in Kollam.

On my way, I saw some stunning old mosques near Varkala, a more Islamic territory. It was astounding to see the influence of Hinduism, Islam, and Christianity play out in Kerala. The villages and towns were easily distinguishable by these religions – everything external altered other than the land's topography and people's physical attributes. Names, religions, clothing, buildings, and other such externalities kept on changing as I walked.

In Muslim regions, the men were Mohammad, the women wore a hijab, and there were mosques on the land. In Hindu regions, the men were Ram, the women wore saris, and there were temples enshrined on the land. In Christian regions, the men were John, the women wore traditional western dress, and churches were planted on the land.

Internally nothing changed. They were all the same to me.

It was riveting to see these external features constantly altering on the walk. I could see how humans – all of us – were part of mass organized movements, which foisted us into these little boxes and explicit constructs, so we could learn to obey and act according to their specific rules.

I no longer related to any of these external structures my eyes saw – I had moved away from them into occupying a boxless space.

# VII. MUNROE, AMRITAPURI, ALLEPEY, MARARI, AND KOCHI

*I* *SLEPT INSIDE A GRUNGY* dark room in an old collapsible building in Kollam for the night before my senses woke me to the sound of morning prayers resonating from a temple next door.

Soon after crossing the town, I was walking on National Highway 744 away from the Malabar Coast toward Munroe Island. The highway, even at an early hour, was heavily flooded with vehicles racing past one another.

The highways in Kerala were very narrow. When they were busy, and I was walking by them, vehicles came extremely close to hitting me many times. People drove at such high speed with no consideration for traffic rules or pedestrians.

While walking on this highway, I came closest to being hit by a vehicle.

The route to Munroe Island was not straight forward. I shadowed the recommended directions from google maps on my phone. They suggested I get off the highway at one point and take a left on the Kollam Bypass Road. That way, I could make my way through the back routes, via tiny villages to get to the Perumon-Munroe Island junction, where I could get on a ferry to cross Ashtamudi Lake to Munroe Island.

I was standing by the highway, watching the fast-moving traffic converging from both sides, waiting for a window of opportunity to cross the road without getting hit.

The traffic was driving expeditiously. There was no space between the vehicles for me to get an opportune moment to cross. Many trucks were moving along the highway amongst other vehicles, so I could not always examine behind a truck to estimate the number of cars following it.

I waited for a bit until I could sense the advent of an opportunity for crossing the road safely.

I had to run to get to the highway's middle, which had no divider on it – so that meant I had to continue running to get to the other side to avoid getting hit.

As soon as I reached the middle of the highway and was about to cross the second half, I realized a car was approaching. It was driving too fast, and I knew I would not be able to cut across the road without getting smashed by it. I could not go forward or stay where I was, as it would still hit me.

I had no choice but to go back – where another vehicle was advancing toward me. It all happened so quickly – I was baffled at one spot to see a scooter coming at my body.

The man riding the scooter punched his brakes instantaneously. If he hadn't, the scooter would undoubtedly have hit me. Three people were sitting on the scooter, including the driver. The scooter slid down onto the highway, with one of the guys falling off. The car on the other side also had to slam its brakes on and drifted in the other direction. All the traffic from both sides came to a sudden stop, as everyone pressed their brakes immediately.

Dead silence.

No vehicle touched me for some miraculous reason; I stood unharmed in the middle of the road. I rushed to pick up the guy who fell from the scooter. He was totally fine. The driver riding the scooter seemed shocked. I said to him, "Sorry, sorry ..." and inquired, "Are you ok?"

No words were spoken. Only a sense of trauma persisted.

An accident was averted. Nobody got injured. Not a scratch on any vehicle. The whole highway had come to a halt for speechless several minutes, and I safely crossed to be on my way.

It was a miracle that I was not hit, and nobody else got injured either. I was sure in the moments after that avoided collision that somebody was looking over me.

The scooter on one side and the car on the other missed my body by tiny fractions of an inch. It all happened so speedily, I had no time to act or react. Everything froze for those seconds after the accident had been averted. But it felt like forever.

It was intriguing that no sense of fear arose when I was about to get hit. None came up, and life continued, as usual, only minutes later.

I was lost again in my world while walking through the inland routes consisting of dirt roads, fading tiny villages, and wild patches of land before arriving at the Perumon-Munroe Island junction beside a splendid lake.

A concrete bridge with railway tracks on top was built next to the ferry terminal with its legs going all the way down into the lake, connecting this slice of the land known as Perumon to the island floating in the distance – Munroe Island, named after a British Colonel, John Munro.

A ferry was approaching Perumon as I arrived at the edge of the water. Soon enough, the ferry's flat wooden surface leveled with the land. The locals on their vehicles and the pedestrians could get off the ferry and back onto land.

As soon as the transfer from the ferry to the land finished, I followed the remnants of the rolling vehicles to board.

The ferry was run by an old diesel engine, which made a lot of noise while imperceptibly moving the ferry across the lake. I would come across several of these ferries along the walk. When the land came to an end, the only way to keep on walking was to board a ferry or sail in a fisherman's boat to cross the water and get back onto the soil.

Sitting on the slow-moving ferry, I could see a blue-colored train running on the bridge next to it and an extensive view of the lake beyond it. It was a gorgeous sight, and I was glad I followed the Israeli travelers' suggestion to visit Munroe Island.

It was a magical ride, and as soon as I set foot on Munroe Island, I felt I had landed on another planet altogether. With stillness, huge indigenous trees, uninterrupted marvels of green, and barely any humans in sight, it felt surreal to have made it to the island.

The few islanders I came across on my way were extremely friendly and welcoming, even more so than in other parts of Kerala. Without commercial activity going on, I had to walk around the island for a while, asking whoever came my way if they could direct me toward a dwelling where I could stay for the night.

After Varkala, which was flooded with travelers, Munroe Island was the opposite. I could hardly see anybody, and finding local islanders was not easy.

The island itself was so beautiful and magical that all my tiredness from walking that day evaporated. After asking around a few places, I found a family in the middle of the island who could host me.

It was a wonderful family of five – a man, his wife, their one kid, and the man's parents. They had built the house with their own hands. The man and his father were skilled at carpentry. The wife, whose name was Devika, managed most things around the house and was the one who cooked food for me for the two nights and one full day I stayed there.

They grew a lot of their food and tried to be self-sufficient. Munroe Island was one of the most peaceful spots I had unearthed by that stage of the walk, and I was naturally won over by its simple life as soon as my feet landed on it.

It was surrounded by water on all sides, one body of water being the Kallada River. Historic churches and old temples alongside prodigious hanging trees were just some of the added relishes for my eyes.

It was a perfect getaway for a writer. But for my pilgrimage, I think I would have stayed in Munroe Island for a longer duration to bathe in its tranquility.

## A. Day 15 – 200 km Later.

After a day inundated by the serenity of Munroe Island and loving being lost in the divinity of its nature, I continued my walk in the direction of the Malabar Coast toward Amritapuri, the premier *ashram* of the renowned spiritual leader revered by many as the hugging saint – *Amma*.

I decided to go to Amritapuri as I had met so many of Amma's devotees on the walk who had invited me there. As it was on my way, I thought, *It couldn't hurt to make a stop there – rather, it could be very insightful.*

I left Munroe Island in the morning from the opposite side to my arrival. Devika told me I would find a small ferry ride at 6.30 in the morning to get off the island on that side. I took her advice and left the house about 6 am to be at the Kallada River's bank by 6.30 am, but as I stepped onto the river bank with the sun spiraling above it, I could not see a ferry or any boats.

An islander sitting by the river told me that the ferry was not running that day and I could cross the river via the train bridge. It wasn't designed for pedestrians, but if you waited for a train to cross the bridge and before another train was approaching, you got a small window to nip over the river across the railway tracks drilled into the bridge.

Those tracks were part of the main route for Indian Railways, so it was a busy route, and I would have to make my way across speedily.

Luckily, as I was climbing up the uneven surface to get on the bridge, a young college girl was also climbing up to cross the river. I asked her, "Is this the way to go?" She shyly smiled and communicated with me through her facial expressions and hand gestures, suggesting that I wait.

So, I lingered next to her as we saw a train rush by. As soon as it had gone, she waved at me. I followed her tiny body on the railway tracks while the sun was emitting its charisma over the Kallada River, and then we heard the deafening horn of another train in the distance. The girl looked back at me and signaled with her hands to walk faster.

I obeyed. Soon enough, we spanned the river and were quickly sliding down from the bridge to the ground and be on our independent ways. I thanked her as we took off in our two directions. She responded with a pleasing smile.

By the end of the walk, I could not count the number of people who walked with me, directed me, and helped me along the way.

It was always the simple, ordinary people, living their day-to-day lives doing jobs the world no longer holds any respect for. The people, considered poor, labeled as not having much, and blamed for their incapacity "to do something" in life. We don't ever acknowledge the devotion in their hearts, or the limiting circumstances they are born into. Regardless of our judgmentalism, many of them were willing to provide a helping hand to a stranger, and it was heartwarming for me to experience that.

Sometimes, when I was transiting by remote villages, men would surround me and touch my body with out-and-out curiosity. They would inspect the tattoos on my skin and hold my hands while caressing my chest and arms.

Never did I feel threatened by their genuine curiosity. I knew it was their way of showing love, respect, and admiration for what I was doing as they sensitively gathered that I was on a pilgrimage through the seething heat of their land.

I never felt vulnerable when strangers were tangibly affectionate with me but felt loved. It always made me recognize that this was why I was doing this – to connect with people directly through the purity in myself.

To link back with the Malabar Coast, I had to follow inland pathways away from Munroe Island that rambled toward the town of Karunagappalli. Asking whoever came my way for directions, I was guided onto the Karunagappalli-Kottarakkarra Road after several hours of walking and headed straight to Karunagappalli.

I passed the 200-km mark that day. My body was just managing the escalating outdoor temperature along with the alarming humidity. It was becoming hotter every day, and with that, the challenge of walking was mounting. Dehydration and inflammation in my body, along with increased rigidity and immobility in my joints, caused a lot of physical discomfort, particularly when I did longer than 25 km in a day.

I consciously chose to keep myself detached from the physical pain and not let my mind be affected by it – otherwise, I would not have been able to walk. I knew from being connected with the voice deep inside me and the spirit raging through me that stopping was not an option; I had to keep going.

I only glanced at the hectic town of Karungappalli while passing through it on National Highway 66. I kept walking toward the coast, which is where the main *ashram* was beyond the village of Vallikavu close to the universities and institutes run by Amma's organization.

The *ashram*'s tall building was placed diagonally to a splendid bridge built over the Kollam-Kottapuram Waterway. The *ashram* was anchored in between the ocean on one side and a river-like waterway on the other.

It was not just a single building, but a vast campus officially denoted as *Mata Amritanandamayi Math*.

Earlier that day, I had contacted Christina (the woman I met in Kovalam), telling her that I would arrive in *Amma's Ashram* that day. Christina referred me to the administrative people, who asked me to come to the International Center on my arrival to get a room at the *ashram*.

It was a tough day of walking, with the heat overwhelming my body. I arrived outside the main gate with my body coated in nothing but sweat. I felt utterly exhausted from walking over that last obstacle, the bridge.

The International Center was right outside the main gate with a white-skinned older woman wearing a plain white *sari* sitting behind the reception desk. Some foreigners were waiting by the reception to be allotted a room. I had noticed something interesting right away when I arrived outside the elegant-looking building of the International Center. Right across the street, a small window was planted in a wall with the sign "Accommodation for Indians" above it.

I was confused for a second, not sure what was going on. *Why did Christina tell me to go to the International Center?* I asked myself.

I approached the receptionist at the International Center. "I am looking for a room. How can I get it?"

She asked me in a friendly tone of voice, "Can I see your passport?" I replied, "I'm Indian. I don't have a passport. The administrative staff told me to come here to get a room... but I'm a bit confused." Pointing my finger toward the window in the wall across the street, I continued, "It says over there 'Accommodation for Indians,' and I am Indian, so do I need to go there?"

She responded, "Yes, this is only for foreigners."

I could not understand the segregation based on Indians and foreigners, but without thinking much about it, I went to the window in the wall across the street. An unfriendly man was seated behind the window. "Can I get a room?" I asked.

He replied, "No rooms for Indians. Only dormitories."

He gave no answer when I asked him why.

So, I went back to the International Center to the receptionsit. "Hey. They only offer dormitories for Indians. I've been walking all day, and my body is quite injured. I would really like to get a small space of my own, if possible, as I need to rest in quiet by myself. Don't you provide affordable rooms for Indians?"

It was interesting to notice how her treatment toward me changed when she found out I was Indian. She replied, "No, we don't provide rooms for Indians."

I didn't react to her statement and realized I would be better off staying somewhere outside the *ashram*. Rather than getting into, "Why do you have this rule to segregate Indians and foreigners in an *ashram* that preaches oneness?" I decided not to retort and stayed out of it.

The reasons could have been anything – logistical formalities, money, struggle to handle large crowds of Indian devotees of *Amma*, who mostly belonged to lower socio-economic stratas, etc. I didn't know the reason for this example of segregation between foreigners and Indians.

Still, I simply decided to remove myself from that situation.

I had gotten used to such racist encounters while moving around India, where white-skinned people were treated differently to Indians by other Indians. Subtle power dynamics based on skin color, nationality, social hierarchy, and money played their role in these encounters. White was somehow considered superior and was subconsciously assumed to be richer and more formidable in its presumed positioning on the food chain.

The difference in the amount of money spent in constructing the receptions – the International Center on one side, and a small window in a wall on the other – was enough to convey the power dynamics at play in India everywhere, even in *ashrams*.

I left the *ashram* in a state of physical exhaustion. There were no other housing options around the *ashram*, so I had to re-cross the bridge and walk toward the main junction of Vallikkavu, where a local man gave me a 200 rs cage-like boxed room in his empty lodge. It was even cheaper than the dormitory option in the ashram.

It was the only other accommodation I could find. My body felt crushed by exhaustion from the day's walk, so I happily took what I could find, washed with water dripping down a broken tap, and lay down on a broken piece of furniture in a state of nothingness.

I returned to *Amma's Ashram* later in the evening as a visitor to meet Christina and check out the place. She had earlier messaged me, inquiring if I could check in. I told her I had decided to stay outside the *ashram* as they did not provide rooms for Indian nationals. It was not that I resented staying in a dormitory – I was used to staying in them on my travels. It was the irregularity of the situation, forcing me to identify myself based on my documents that I didn't want to be a part of.

I no longer adhered to the idea of segregation based on nationality, religion, or race – especially not in an *ashram*. It did not matter to me what the reasons may have been. As part of the nameless walk, I chose not to be part of any segregation measures.

Leaving behind the impression from my previous encounter at the *ashram*, I decided not to hold any grievances about its way of functioning, even though it was heavily based on segregation between foreigners and Indians.

It was not just accommodation. Other things inside the *ashram* were segregated between the west and the east. Food cafeterias and lines for hugging *Amma* were denoted as western and Indian.

It was fascinating how the segregation mindset manifested itself inside the *ashram*. As an Indian person who had lived in the west and understood western values very well, and at the same time didn't physically look like a local, I was treated differently inside the *ashram* just because of my external appearance.

This is something that I wish to see change – not just in India but in the world at large – so we stop caring about people's external manifestations, be it skin color, clothes, or anything else, for that matter. We are so consumed by physical appearance all the time that we flounder to see beyond it.

Today's relative world has become all about how we look, what we wear, and how others perceive us based on our outward features.

Even before conversing with a stranger, our conditioned minds have figured out the person based on our one-dimensional view of things. This view roller blades around inside our heads on stories we've been brainwashed into believing throughout our restricted lives.

We find reasons for dreaming up stereotypes to distinguish among us. We don't recognize that everything we think about others is a segment of the countless superficial stories we've been made to believe since birth.

It's easier for our minds to make sense of things based on these stories. We don't question them or try to break out of them. That would demand that we go deeper into our selves to interrogate our ways and belief systems in the hope of eventually letting them go. Instead, we continue to cling to the immaterial stories so zealously ingrained in our systems.

## THE WILD ONE

We are children of the wild.
With blood that is one, flowing through our veins.
What separates us is only us.
There is no separation in who we are.
We are one.
With the world.
With the universe.
With everything that coexists along with us.
Us is how we came to life.
Life is in all of us.
As one.

# VIII. INJURED BODY. BURNING SPIRIT.

*I* *STAYED IN VALLIKAVU FOR* a few days, spending most of my time
inside *Amma's Ashram.*

I met with Christina later in the evening after the consequential
hours of my arrival. She felt a bit guilty about what had happened. The
next day she had her husband, who was also an *Amma* devotee show
me around the *ashram.*

The Italian women I had run into earlier on the walk were also
present. They were delighted to see me. In addition, I bumped into
a few travelers I had met initially in Varkala while walking to the
*ashram* with the prospect of making some new friends. With its highly
communal framework, it was easy to meet people.

Folk from all parts of the world shared tables while eating delicious
food at both the Indian and western cafeterias.

A lot was going on there. It was less of an *ashram* and more of a
university. There were conferences on Ayurveda in their enormous hall
by day, free meals for visitors in the mess, a charitable hospital providing
treatments for the poor. In the middle of all that, prayers could be heard
resounding inside the beguiling temples dedicated to explicit goddesses.

Hundreds of people resided in the *ashram's* housing. Extensive
activities took place on the floors above the principal temple, the
ground floor of which was where *Amma* gave out hugs in an epic space.

There was always a buzz around the *ashram.* Devotees were restlessly
consumed with wondering when *Amma* would start giving out hugs,
which was the primary lure for most people visiting the *ashram.*

*Amma* was renowned for healing people with her hugs, which was quite testing for my mind to digest when I first heard it.

In the early afternoon of my subsequent day, I was standing by the temple's humongous entrance door, and I saw *Amma* walk onto the stage accompanied by devotees. All of them wore simple white *saris*, including *Amma* herself.

People started running toward the stage frantically. They were dazed and thrilled as they had been told she was not giving out hugs that day.

Fortunately, I was already inside the temple when she emerged, so I got a hug from her way before it all went crazy. The lines became as long as possible, with people waiting tirelessly in their separate Indian and foreigner queues for hours to receive their precious hugs. Many cried in her arms as they had been holding onto tears for their entire lives.

The energy around the hugs was so abundant that even before somebody went to receive a hug from *Amma*, they were sold on the idea that this was the most significant activity they could engage in.

What *Amma* did was truly admirable though. Hugging thousands of people daily did require somebody to be divine in their existence. *Amma* had a sense of purity about her, even though a lot of buzz and a substantial commercial element were attached to the entire scene. *Amma* certainly triggered a release for the many, who could shed their tears in her arms and let go of their grievances while sharing their suffering with somebody who could feed them with a mother's warm and nurturing care.

That was when I understood why she was referred to as *Amma* – mother. Who doesn't like receiving a cozy warm motherly hug?

*Amma* was a mighty rock star in many ways. After giving out hugs all day, she would sing *bhajans* later in the evening inside an enormous hall for the countless who would gather to see her perform. I was part of this gathering – just like a concert for her spiritual devotees. In that twinkling, I could see why so many people loved her and considered her to be a divine mother because she unquestionably produced a dazzling experience for her spectators without holding anything back.

---

I had an incredible few days of surrendering myself to random and obscure occurrences inside the *ashram*.

*Ashrams* are places where you observe all types of fascinating and peculiar people doing their own thing.

Seen by many in the western world as cults, *ashrams,* and the whole *guru* and follower matrix have been part of India's heritage for hundreds of years.

Visiting *ashrams* across India always presented my mind with many insights about the world of humans. *Ashrams* have a specific god-like human figure as their leader, who endows their followers with an explicit set of values, a purpose, and doctrines to follow. This creates a space where a community of like-minded people can be formed. In the community, people learn to live and work together to run the *ashram* while being devoted to their unique roles and adopted values. This ties the community together.

If we think about it, this is possibly how all human civilizations over history began.

Take the example of religious organizations. They have used their specific doctrines and symbolic images of gods to build their communities for as long as we can remember. And it is not just religion. Even countries are formed based on an idea.

It can be an idea about democracy, or dictatorship, or another system that organizes people as part of an idea. It doesn't matter what the system is. There's always a set of doctrines and laws relating to the idea's creation, which can further materialize into founding a nation, a village, a tribe, an *ashram*, a cult, a company – or anything.

Labeling our external ways of providing humans with a purpose and a place where they feel they can belong is a fundamental way of defining human history.

In the opening days of attending a business school, students are taught that for a company to grow, it needs to have a clear MISSION, VISION, and STRONG LEADERSHIP, and only then can it succeed.

The way they function, these *ashrams* are no less than a nation or a business. It shows us how humans always need something to strive for – it doesn't matter what it is.

Having a purpose and a role's duties to fulfill, delivers us satisfaction and a direction for our footsteps.

We do not like being lost. Being in the unknown scares us. Not knowing where we belong makes us feel insecure. Not having an identity troubles us. Not being bestowed by a set of doctrines make us feel ungrounded. Not having things organized and part of an appropriate construct drives us insane.

This is why our mind is always looking for something. It is never satisfied on its own. It must keep striving for something, or else it feels confused, lost, and directionless. It must always be distracted. It cannot accept the truth of nothingness.

It fails to see the nature of reality beyond all the amusements we have contrived over centuries of sightless expansion. It is a reality that stays true regardless of whether we exist or not.

## A. Day 18 – Fisherman's Boat

After a warm hug from a saint and a room full of unequivocal synergy amongst strangers, I departed from *Amma's Ashram*. Soon, I was walking by the Kollam Kottapuram Waterway. While gawking at the millions of boats stranded on the waterway and kissing each other's wrecked wooden wings, I marched on a swampy path, unsure where I was heading.

It was one of those days when I was back with the unknown, not knowing how long I was walking for or where.

Instead of following a marked path, I was flowing along with the wind. Shortly, I streamed past some fishing villages on the coast. So long as I was moving north, I was unconcerned about anything else. The locals glowered at me, and soon I had more than enough dogs barking belligerently at me.

Going through remote fishing villages on the coastal areas was turning out to be a nightmare, with the rising number of dogs that attacked me as I briefly passed their esteemed territories.

It was indeed testing my abilities not to react to the dogs, especially when a pack of them surrounded me. They growled at me with their spiteful teeth wanting to penetrate through my skin all the way to my bones. I had to use my stick routinely to protect my body when the dogs wanted to be as intimate with me as my skin. The best strategy was to keep on walking without looking into their eyes while utterly ignoring their presence. I knew if I let them sense any fear, they would attack me, so I made a conscious effort to let go of the thought that they could bite me.

Once I became detached from the possibility of what could happen if they attacked me, they didn't exist for me. I was no longer bothered by their aggression, even when their attacks occurred almost daily – and only increased when I was crossing through the State of Karnataka.

It was another intense morning of dog attacks, and then I was faced with another hurdle. After a few hours of walking along the coast, I was stranded with nothing but crashing waters around me. I was separated from where I needed to be, with no ferries or other means of crossing the water.

A small *chai* shop with just one person was the only thing at the tip of the land. A few drunkards were lying down outside the shop, and that was it.

I asked the guy at the *chai* shop how I could get to the other side. He told me, "*Yaha kuch nahi hai.*"

Few fishing boats could be seen on the water, so I asked him, "*Yaha kuch nahi hai?*"

"*Pata nahi, main poochta hun,*" he replied.

I sat by his shop to take a breather and drink a *chai* while he asked some of his fishermen friends in Malayalam if they could take me to the land on the other side. I could not understand why they were talking for so long about it, but that was always the case whenever I found myself in one of these situations.

A lengthy discussion in their local tongue would go on forever, while I stood to the side either doing nothing, or smiling, or using hand gestures while throwing in some broken Hindi words requesting them to help me out.

Somehow, I always found my way around any given situation, which demanded that I improvise while embodying the anonymity of every converging moment.

All I had to do was ask people for help genuinely, and if they said no, I didn't react insincerely but thanked them and asked other people. I knew there would always be that one person willing to help.

One of the fishermen agreed to take me, and after gulping down the last bits of that flavorful *chai*, I was sitting with some other fishermen on a small wooden boat cruising along using a strident motor engine. They were all very shy; people generally in South India were quite reserved and gentle. It was the opposite to most parts of Northern India, where, in comparison, people come across as loud and indiscreet.

The fishermen always wore a brightly checkered cloth hung from their waist around their lower bodies and a brightly colored shirt or t-shirt synthesizing with it. They also carried a long piece of usually white-colored cloth to cover their heads from the sun. When not tied on their heads, this cloth was retained around their necks like a scarf.

The boat soon dropped me on the other side, where some fishermen were hanging out under a shack. I had my first meal of the day in that shack in company with the other fishermen. The meal consisted of some local fish the fishermen had caught the night before. All the fishermen were staring at me, wondering, *Who is this guy? What is he doing here?* I had just disembarked from a very inaccessible village.

Every trice from that day onward until I arrived in Kochi was to fuse into a blur, as I was walking like a maniac.

All my internal rage mounted through my belly into my heart. My eyes correspondingly let out heavy tears as I progressed through Kerala's most ravishing parts. The last droplets of water were still behind my lids. When they flowed out of my eyes, nothing remained inside.

The backwaters of Allepey, the white sands of Marari Beach, and the archaic, symmetrical temples of Hindu gods were some of the enticing sites on my route to Kochi, whose beauty arrested my eyes too.

On the 25th day into the walk, having crossed 300 km and with my legs comprehensively injured, I entered Kochi, Kerala's financial capital. I followed the coastline to the enticing sight of Fort Kochi. This was the city's cultural hub and massively influenced by European architecture. It had been previously colonized by the Dutch, Portuguese, and the British.

It was an improbable shift in the world outside – it felt like I had been beamed to Europe while marching along the pebbled streets of Fort Kochi on my wounded, swollen feet. Jumbo trees and architecturally astounding buildings enticed me from all angles. I felt surreal from the influx of their energy.

Word of my walk and the book had been spreading in Kerala, thanks to social media. I had been invited to speak at the Krithi Knowledge Fest underway there. That was in addition to interviews lined up with journalists from newspapers, *The Hindu*, *New Indian Express*, and the *Malayalam Manorama News*.

It was like being on a walking book tour, even though that was not what I had intended the walk to be. For me, it was all just a nameless phenomenon with no surety about what was to come.

These occasions in Kochi synchronized with one of the most prominent contemporary art festivals in Asia and the most significant art exhibition of India – the Kochi Art Biennale.

I had docked onto a new world compared with what I'd been on throughout the whole walk. The days to come were to be all about dissociating myself from my physical pain and keeping on drifting into a world full of possibilities.

The day after I arrived in Kochi, I went to see an Ayurvedic doctor. My legs weren't in good condition, and I had purposely avoided seeing somebody. The discomfort had increased tremendously, so I had no choice but to seek help. I wanted to continue walking and needed some suggestions about what could help relieve the pain and swelling.

I saw a signboard for an Ayurvedic doctor while blazing through Fort Kochi the day I arrived. On seeing it suspended outside a strikingly-built traditional Keralan house, I had stopped by to inquire. It was managed independently by a Keralan man named Robin. He was casually sitting by his serene garden on a chair wearing his customary attire of a *mundu*[57]. It was orange-colored, contrary to the white I was used to seeing on men.

When I asked if he could look at my legs, he told me, "Today, I have treatments all day. Come tomorrow morning around 10."

"Ok, that should work," I replied.

I settled in a homestay room run by a lovely Christian family in Fort Kochi itself, and the next morning I went back to Robin's house for a consultation. I was also supposed to speak at the Krithi Knowledge Fest the same day. Fortunately, I had plenty of time on the clock to begin an Ayurvedic treatment with Robin that day itself, if it was needed.

Fort Kochi had a very chilled-out vibe that was pleasing for the senses. Strolling the narrow lanes that intersected the main streets, I made my way back to Robin's house. A ground-level edifice where Robin carried out the Ayurvedic treatments was next to the house. It was a modest setup with two rooms solely set aside for healing.

Both rooms had a wooden couch set into the floor and rising up to waist level for patients to lie on and for the doctor, Robin, to carry out the Ayurvedic treatments and massage therapies required.

Robin had a sense of sincerity about him. I just knew his understanding of Ayurveda and the human body was very profound.

He asked me to lie down so that he could inspect my body. A zesty smell from the blend of unusual aromas was spilling out from the

---

57  A *mundu* is a cloth that goes down from the waist to the ankles.

bottles of herbal oils and medicines inside the room. Tasteful artworks depicting Ayurvedic practitioners treating their patients were hanging on the alloy, orange-tinted walls.

I told Robin as he was about to inspect my legs, "I have walked here from Kanyakumari, and in a few days, I will continue walking further."

He replied with some astonishment, "Walking??" and then went on to inspect my legs. His fingers deliberately pushed into their inflamed muscles as he took a closer look at them. Soon, he said to me, "Your legs are severely injured. You shouldn't walk anymore."

"That's not an option. I need to keep going. Can you tell me what precautions I can take? Because I am not going to stop."

He said, "You'll probably cause permanent damage to your legs."

"Nothing will happen to me."

He understood that I was determined and would not stop walking, so he asked me to buy a pair of new shoes, knee wraps and offered a *kizhi* massage[58] for a few days.

In the end, he said, "What I'm suggesting will not be enough because your legs are injured; you need to rest them and not walk anymore."

"I will get the treatment and rest here in Fort Kochi for a few days, but then I'm going to continue walking. Can you start the treatment now?"

"Yes. I can give you a three-day treatment."

"That's perfect," I replied.

I was very aware that my actions were those of an extreme character and that this was not the first time I had been willing to go as far as it took. It had happened previously in the few years since I'd left New York and was on this maddening quest of figuring out life's ordeals.

Everyone I knew from my past had officially labeled me "crazy." But I did not care what anyone other than myself thought about me any longer. To me, all that mattered was nothing, and I was willing to go as far as it took until my spirit could bleed free.

Was it all worth it? Time would tell.

---

58 *Kizhi* is an Ayurvedic massage where herbs are boiled in a medicated oil and tied in a cotton cloth before treating the body.

Sure as hell, it was enlivening. I was living every moment of life, not worrying about what was to come or fearful of the unknown. Instead, I was learning to fully immerse myself in life while breathing to stay truly alive.

Willingness to damage my body so I could keep on listening to my spirit and the cryptic messages from the anonymous source seemed absolutely worth it – even if those extreme measures were pilfering from me.

# IX. ROAD TO MADNESS

*I* *STAYED IN FORT KOCHI* for about seven days, eclipsing a month since I began walking from Kanyakumari. Even though I tried to rest my legs as much as I could in those seven days, I was startled by all the exciting events sprinkled around Kochi.

My time was a mashup of speaking at the Knowledge Fest, engaging in book signings, doing interviews with journalists, and visiting mesmerizing art exhibitions – part of the Kochi Biennale – inside the historical buildings nestling around Fort Kochi.

I also reunited with some travelers I had previously met down South while getting to rally around some recent ones while moving around Fort Kochi. In addition to these synchronicities, I heard some brilliant artists' fresh voices.

From having read my interviews published in the newspapers, when I was in Kochi, Kerala's young people had started approaching me when they saw me. It turned out to be the most extravagant of times.

It was a sheer celebration of art, culture, humanity, and diversity in thoughts, ideas, and people.

I was delighted to have taken part in that exorbitant gathering of people from all parts of the world. It was a vivid reminder that life is meant to be lived with courage and shared with others whole-heartedly.

If we live our days not fully immersed in the outbreak of what every moment can bring to the table, we are missing the point. We fail to accept life for what it is without our fingers always trying to fiddle with it.

I was on a road to madness. Blinded by the pain surging outside the aspects of my self participating with zeal in whatever came my way, I was only becoming more distant from my past and seeing more of the world without blankets shrouding my eyes.

Being around Fort Kochi and exploring the inspiring spaces in the area was a memory of its own.

From regarding the eloquent, remaining site of supposedly the first European church built in India, St. Francis CSI – where they told me that the explorer Vasco da Gama had been buried; to seeing an old *synagogue*[59] in a part of Fort Kochi that was literally called "Jew town;" to being hypnotized by the sights of other iconic buildings with wild historical implications, Fort Kochi was undoubtedly one of the most obviously developed cultural hubs in India I had observed in my years of moving around the country. With the Art Biennale in full swing at the same time, it was as if somebody had purposely put a cherry on top of a luscious cake.

It was all too staggering. Everything was coming to life, and the world inside and outside was starting to show its light.

My senses were aroused, and my heart animated, and that was enough for me to keep going strong.

Fort Kochi was also one of those places after Varkala, where I felt I could stay forever. However, as soon as the swelling in my legs mellowed a bit, I was willing to continue. I received the Ayurvedic treatment for a few days and continually communicated with my legs, asking every cell and muscle in my body to heal itself.

I just knew that if I spoke to my body and asked it to heal itself, it would. So, at night, that was all I practiced. I communicated to my body, especially my legs, "You have all the strength you need," and "All your cells are regenerating and rejuvenating." I repetitively implanted these statements into my mind while vividly screening all parts of my physical body and visualizing my legs as downright fit and strong.

I didn't allow my mind to retain any thoughts such as "I am injured" or "My body cannot move ahead." I figured the only way my body could support my burning spirit was to truly connect with my body and ask it to brace itself. It was no longer just my mind's battle. If I wanted to keep moving forward, I had to fuse with my body genuinely.

---

59 A Jewish house of worship.

My mind's determination had brought me to Fort Kochi, but I knew that I could not continue walking without my body's full support. Instead of perpetually being inside my head, I tried to listen to and interact with my body as if it was a living entity. This led to creating a bond with my own body that would stay with me for a lifetime and showed me how my body could heal itself, if only I let it.

I no longer indulged thoughts such as, "I can't," or "not possible," or any other limiting ways of functioning. I understood that if I had to sustain walking with my body's painful state, I had to let go of my limitations and go beyond them.

To not displace my momentum, I left Fort Kochi with the unfamiliar approach of leading from my body and not just my mind. As suggested by Robin, I got myself new shoes, and a set of knee wraps to support my legs to lessen the stress on my feet and knees, both of which had endured a lot of strain from ceaselessly marching on fiery, concrete roads.

Not once did I mention what Robin had told me about the injuries in my legs to anyone else. I knew deep in my heart that it would all be ok. I just had to stay connected with my legs and serve them with nothing but constant affirmations while sincerely requesting them to support me.

On the morning of Day 32, I left Fort Kochi from the ferry junction next to the famous Aspinwall House. It was the biggest ferry I saw on my walk. It had two floors with loads of vehicles flooding on it to get to the land on the other side, Fort Vypin. I merged with the vehicles encircling my body. It was teeming with immense amounts of gratitude, love, and inspiration from all the conviviality I had received from people in Kochi.

My stay in Fort Kochi was my longest in one place in the whole time of the walk. My days there were predominantly about engaging with the external world purely. I had the intention to share and receive with an open heart.

Leaving the encores of the cultural hub of Fort Kochi behind, I was back in the openness of the wild with only my spirit expanding in its might.

After getting off the ferry in Fort Vypin and then walking on National Highway 63, I was very much attuned to my legs. I knew they were exacting retribution for the act of walking as they didn't want to be in motion. They wanted to rest, but I was telling them that the only way I could do this was if they stayed with me no matter how much discomfort they were in. I could not persist in walking with them resisting me – they had to work with me.

Instead of walking like a maniac shoving my legs forward – which is what I had been doing until I reached Fort Kochi – I ensured I worked with my body more harmoniously. I delivered it space to breathe wherever necessary, so it could let all its bodily tension dissolve, and my mind could be at ease.

My focus became my breath as I began walking in a deep meditative state unconditionally in synch with my breath and body. I was becoming increasingly aware of my every movement and my body as a whole. I knew exactly what my body was going through all the time.

Walking away from the Southern part of Kerala and leaving behind the prime tourist destinations, I was now winding through regions without much tourism. Finding accommodation was to become a challenge, along with the continuous rise in the heat and humidity as March approached, and temperatures easily touched 35° Celsius by the afternoon.

Even though the external conditions were not favorable, and my body was retaliating, I didn't know why I had such a strong sense of determination to keep walking. People had no expectations of me, nor was I on a mission. It was all just a nameless ride, and I could have stopped whenever I wanted, but something deep in me just wanted to keep going.

It was all an unknown and nameless act. From the instant I received the enigmatic message directing me to go on this walk, I did not try to make anything happen but just let it all happen.

Days into gliding away from Fort Kochi in a northerly direction, I had to start approaching homeowners to let me stay at their places for the night. Meanwhile, I was also learning to listen to my body more and more. It was asking me to rest and not over-injure myself. As a result, I shortened my distances and maintained an average of about 15-20 km per day to sustain the walk's continuity and furnish my legs with some time to heal themselves.

I stayed in a family's gray house on my first night after leaving Fort Kochi. To find the house, I went to a church and asked the people leaving after prayers about finding a place somewhere to stay for the night.

There was always that one guy who would tell me where I could go. This one suggested I go to a house positioned near the church.

I went to the house he suggested, and as I was standing outside its gate, I started howling out "Hellooooo!" in a loud but friendly voice.

A Keralan man came out of the door to the main gate to ask me what I wanted.

I told him that I was walking through Kerala and asked if he could host me for the night. His eyes became curious. He asked me the usual questions I was very used to answering by then – who I was and why I was walking.

I willingly answered his questions. He then asked me, "How did you find this house?"

I replied, "A man from the church sent me here."

He agreed to let me stay as he realized I was harmless and genuine in what I was telling him.

He unlocked the main gate to let me in, and I was soon walking past the old walls of an archaic house and showed a room where I could settle for the night. Only the man and his wife resided there. He said to me, "We used to give out rooms to passersby, but not anymore. That's why the man from the church sent you here. You seem like a good guy, so it's ok."

I responded with a big smile on my face, "Thank you very much!"

One of my best meals of the walk was in that household, cooked for me by the man's wife. It was a revitalizing change from eating out all the time and a gentle reminder that nothing can beat home-cooked meals.

Having already walked plenty through Kerala, I was now comfortable with the *Malayali* people, who were generally quite relaxed and welcoming in nature.

My mind had picked up selected *Malayali* words from my constant interactions with locals. My untrained ear for the Malayalam language sensed some similarities between it and Sanskrit words. I was not sure if they meant the same thing, but there were some parallels in the pronunciation of the consonants. The word I used the most was *sukhamano*, the most basic of all *Malayali* words – "How are you?"

I thanked the family for letting me stay with them for the night, which was one of pure stillness.

With no goal or destination in mind, I was back on the road the next morning. After making my way through the solitude of villages, I soon crossed National Highway 63 to walk along the Malabar Coast with the sound of waves vibrating inside my placid ears.

I found a room further on from Cherai Beach, where I halted for two nights. There were some tourists around this area, but nowhere near the numbers I had seen in other Keralan tourist destinations. Just a few faces here and there, but no more.

The road ahead was getting more solitary, with long hours of walking on my own under the baking sun. With fewer and fewer people out in the open during the daytime and no tourist destinations in the offing, I was on my own for most days.

Regularly watching my breath with complete awareness while walking was beginning to take me more inward. Even with my eyes open, I was aiming to be more with the inside than the outside. The outside was still very much alive, but it was all whirling into a dream-like state with my mind accessing the deepest parts of my body and my spirit fully awakening to take me into a euphoric state of being.

## A. Day 35 – The Eagle Found its Nest

Not scared of walking alone, I struck along the coast past Cherai Beach in the silent company of the sea. I was confronted with dog attacks all morning until I arrived at the brink of the land past the village of Kuzuppilly, where I conversed with a local man while he tagged along with me on his morning walk.

"What are you doing?" he asked me.

"Just walking."

As we walked and talked, he told me, "I worked in the Gulf for over 40 years, and now I am back in Kerala to retire."

I responded with a smile on my face and said, "Like most *Malayali* people."

Every local I had interacted with in Kerala had some connection with the Gulf region. Either they or their cousin, uncle, son, daughter, brother, sister, or somebody else in the family lived and worked in one of the Gulf countries.

It was too common not to notice. Cash machines specifically for receiving money sent from those countries were in all corners of Kerala.

"Money from the Gulf countries over the years has been a big reason for boosting prosperity in Kerala," a businessman I had met on the walk told me. "But it has become competitive to get jobs there because of the economic slowdown in the Gulf countries and rising competition from folks from Africa and Nepal, who are willing to work for way less than *Malayali* people."

He also told me, "Young Keralans don't fancy the Gulf dream as much as the older generations did – they want to do something in Kerala itself."

"That's good to hear!"

He responded, "Yes, it is good, but many challenges are surfacing because of it, as numerous people are doing similar things, such as opening a bakery, a café, or a car dealership."

"Yes, I have noticed a lot of bakeries and car dealers everywhere."

As a result, I was not surprised to hear the man accompanying me when he'd told me about his time in the Gulf.

He walked with me for a few miles to the point where the waters rumpled the land. Fortunately, because of trading activity in that area, the local boat ride for pedestrians was functional. The boat was packed with people working in the region, and he made sure I got on it without any trouble. Only when the boat started navigating did he go on his way while politely wishing me the best for everything.

These boat rides were surprisingly gratifying to be on. They delivered a breather from all the walking and gave me a chance to reflect on myself while dousing myself with the water's restorative virtues.

After my feet landed on the ground again, I decided to get away from walking along the coast, where the dog attacks were only increasing, to reunite eventually with National Highway 66.

In the upcoming days, I crossed Kodungallur and Perinjanam to arrive at the Thriprayar Sree Rama Temple. Many young Keralan men stopped me on the way wanting to talk, as they'd read about me in the newspapers or heard about me from their friends. Their eyes lit up on seeing me ramble past their towns or villages.

It was on the morning of Day 38 when two brothers on their scooter stopped next to me.

They said to me enthusiastically, "We've heard about you ... wow! We cannot believe it's you."

I smiled while looking straight into their jubilant eyes.

The older brother driving the scooter said to me, "Can you please wait here? I want to give you a gift."

I replied sincerely, "I don't accept gifts. I can't add any weight to my bag."

He insisted, "It's very small – doesn't weigh anything."

I said, "Ok. I'll stroll on. Come find me."

They rode away on their scooter, and I continued walking. Ten minutes later, they returned and presented me with a tiny glass eagle.

The older brother placed the eagle in my palm and said to me, "This is something we want to give you to show our appreciation for what you are doing. You have made our day! Thank you so much."

I felt my heart skip a beat at that moment because of their benevolent gesture.

I happily received their present and told them, "You know, the eagle is a special symbol for me. My first tattoo was of an eagle. It represents freedom."

The older one replied, "My parents gave this to me when I became a pilot and told me how they thought I was a brave person."

"Wow! That makes it more special. Thank you for this moment. I will never forget it."

We went on our ways after that timeless moment of true camaraderie, and I thought to myself as I kept walking ahead, *This is what life is for. This is what I am walking for – to share such precious moments of purity with people I have never met previously.*

----- ✪ -----

Later that day, I arrived at an ancient temple devoted to the famous Hindu god *Rama,* built on the placid Karuvannur River's bank. It had a grand entrance at the front with towering steel pillars, creating a walkway with shops on both sides for temple goers.

That day I was disoriented in my walk. I had no clue where I was going. A local guy came by to my rescue and guided me to the entrance gates of the Thriprayar Temple.

Just outside its entrance gate in the colossal passage at the front, a *dosa*[60] eatery was at the corner, where the owner served me a light meal for the day and gave me a room in his lodge upstairs. After indulging

---

60 A *dosa* is a rice pancake made of fermented buttermilk.

my palate with crispy *dosa* – that my stomach received cheerfully along with coconut *chutney* – I filed past the *Rama* temple's medieval gates.

The temple was vast and had its foremost statue of god *Rama* situated in the central part inside the vintage walls of a square edifice, whose base rooted directly into the soil around the main temple. I went inside the main temple to sit in silence and connect with the divine.

I was praying not to *Rama* – nor any symbol – but the nameless power beyond us, requesting it to provide me with vigor in my legs, which were struggling mightily.

The temperature was increasing so much that I was sweating while sleeping inside the caged boxes, even at night time. My body was becoming exceedingly dehydrated – so much so that my muscles were cramping all the way to the inside of my bones. I had started buying hydration salts from medical stores to mix with water. That helped a little, but I could only do so much to combat the worsening conditions.

I had covered over 350 km by that day and sat inside the *Rama* temple wholly relinquished to the energy beyond me, asking it to hold me tight and not let me collapse.

Moments after being inside the main temple, I made circles around it. Moving along the burning grounds at noon with my bleeding feet and naked chest and unable to feel any pain. I was speaking directly with the divine, downright lost in the madness of the act I was pursuing.

It was unmitigated madness, and I was thoroughly absorbed in it with no separation whatsoever.

# X. LET THE FIRE BURN

"*SEENE MAIN JALTI HAI ek aag. Iss aag ko hi toh jalne do.*"
This is an expression in Hindi. My mother tongue. It became the mantra I recited during the pilgrimage. I sang it repeatedly on the walk. It emerged from me during the long hours of walking on my own. I would hum it in time with the rhythmic movement of my feet while remaining lost in the divinity of my maddening crusade.

Its melody corresponded with the fire burning through my spirit, which kept on rising and igniting my chest ferociously.

When translated into English, it does not have the same intensity and rhythmic power as it does in Hindi. Its words generated strength in me whenever I needed it.

"A fire is burning in my chest; let it keep on burning," is its translation in English. It was only when I chanted it in Hindi repetitively – with my heart fully devoted to it – that my mind grasped the true essence of the vitality aroused in my body from months of dwelling deeper within myself.

In the company of nobody but myself for days of being lost over the immovable land, I was no longer the same person who began the walk only months ago. I had moved past the idea of self and the identity as "Kartikeya" imparted to me by my parents. No identity existed for me any longer; I had realized that what remained of me was not in my body but beyond it.

I knew that even if somebody caged me inside a box, dissected my body, or hurt me however they wanted, they could never break my spirit. It had become unbreakable.

My selfless identity no longer engaged with the relative world's stories; it was kindred with the totality of the absolute. My selfless identity was learning to exist by being truly independent of everything – and learning to see the world with more clarity while understanding the roots binding it all.

⬯

I left Thriprayar Temple on the morning of Day 39 after having spent my night lying down in a dripping body inside a black box, observing the pain searing my legs.

Trailing alongside the villages next to the calming Karuvannur River, I walked for a few hours until I linked back with National Highway 66 and crossed the town of Engandiyoor. While coasting along the highway, I saw a signboard with the words *horticulturist* and *plant nursery* printed on it.

I walked inside the gates and eventually stood outside a lovely house. A lean Keralan man, wearing a traditional *lungi* over his dark skin and sporting glasses on his face, toddled out of the door.

"Who are you?" he asked inquisitively.

I told him my whole story and asked, "Can you give me a room for the night?"

He thought about it for a second and said, "Follow me. Leave your bag here on the verandah." We walked behind his house to another building. He said, "I'll rent out this place ... it's currently empty."

We went inside. It had several unoccupied rooms, and out the back, he did additional farming.

"Is this your farmhouse?"

He replied that it was and showed me an empty room, with nothing inside it - no furniture or anything.

He said to me, "I can give you this if you want."

"Yes. This will work."

He was a polite man who welcomed a stranger into his house with an open heart. His wife was a courteous woman, and together they had two sons, who were delighted to meet me. I stayed the next day with them as well.

The man told me a lot about himself. He voiced concerns about his struggle with negative thoughts and that he used to work in Dubai and was now back in his house, which was his ancestral property. He encouraged his highly intelligent and creative sons to interact with me. One of them was in the eleventh grade, and the other, in university. They were a fantastic family, and it was unbelievable to have found their house just randomly walking along the highway.

I had a whimsical day in their house the next day while indulging in the taste of delicious home-cooked meals with the family, using ingredients grown on their farm.

The family was not intrusive either, which was a refreshing change, and I got some much-needed space to be with myself and do nothing but solely be among the trees encircling the farm.

I was back on the road the next day, my 40th day into the walk. The man woke up before sunrise to walk with me to the highway and wish me his best.

He said to me as I was leaving, "You are welcome to come back again."

"Yes. Hopefully, I will come back one day. Thank you for everything," I replied.

We hugged, and I swiftly got back into coasting along the highway.

I walked for a few hours before taking a break at a local eatery where a young Keralan man got me some food. As we were eating together, he told me how he'd traveled all across India the previous year, but now he was back here in his hometown because his brother was sick and in hospital.

He suggested that I go to Guruvayur, a pilgrimage town named for the ancient Guruvayur Temple in its center. It was dedicated to *Lord Vishnu*, who was worshipped in the temple through his avatar, *Krishna*.

I took his suggestion, and after thanking him for the meal, I departed for Guruvayur. I had to take a right turn away from National Highway 66 to cross over the Chettuva Bridge across the Kunduvakadavu River and ultimately turned left on the Chavakkad-Kanjani Road to ramble straight on.

After being funneled past some affluent residential colonies with palatial houses, I soon arrived in the religious town of Guruvayur.

It had an extremely lively ambiance as a festival was to commence that night.

I could not keep track of all the festivals that had greeted me on the way, so I stopped inquiring about them and instead just surrendered myself to whatever happened.

I stayed in Guruvayur for a few days. Because of the ongoing festival, the town was flamboyantly decorated and abounded with people. Additionally, because of its religious affiliation, it had many rules in and around the temples. There were boards saying things like, "Only Hindus allowed inside the temple," or "Men and women have to stay in separate rooms." It was a very orthodox town whose locals were concerned about their rules.

In the nameless state that I was in, I found such rules interesting. Only human beings – of all the animals on the planet – busily devise and fight about such things.

We love to have rules relating to our ideologies, laws, and faith to define our existence.

It is always, "This way," or "The other way." We seem unable to live within an abstract creation. Instead, we constrict ourselves by functioning as part of a specific society and producing illusory rules to keep ourselves in check and conform to whatever idea we've been made to believe in since birth – depending on where we were born on the planet.

How demanding is it for humans not to live by any rules, either socially or self-bound?

We only know about functioning by these rules, so we never question them or harness our courage to see past them.

While I was exploring the town of Guruvayur, I followed many of their rules but consciously chose to ignore some and not to participate in them.

For instance, when I saw some temples with the sign, "Only Hindus allowed inside," I intentionally chose not to enter them. They would not have stopped me because I had a Hindu name on my identification card. Still, I didn't like the idea of such a rule, dividing people based on their religious identity, and not letting people enter a place meant for praying to the divine.

Even though I was given a Hindu name by my family, I had let go of my attachment to that identity a long time before. My only identity had no label attached to it. If someone asked me, "Are you a Hindu?" I replied, "No. I am a nobody who doesn't submit to the ideals of the labels relating to where I was born."

I frequently wondered, *When will humans understand that nothing we've accomplished in this relative world is real? We fight about things that won't matter once we die. So, why are we busy fighting among ourselves while being attached to our imaginary creations – whatever they might be?*

## A. Day 41 – 400 km Later

I had covered over 400 km by the time I arrived in Guruvayur, which was ecstatically glowing from the lighting, vibrant decorations, and full complement of locals absorbed in preparing for the festivities to occur after the sun's melting away.

Guruvayur had many accommodation options, as Hindu devotees and pilgrims frequently visited by. I stayed in a pilgrim residency for one night before moving into a quieter place away from the main Muthuvattoor-Guruvayur Road, which narrowed and led straight to Guruvayur's main temple.

The residency I stayed in was owned by a respectful man who had read about me in the newspaper. He was happy to offer me a room at an affordable rate, considering I was walking past his town. The news about my walk was quite handy for strangers showing their support in whatever way they could. I thought it was marvelous for people to be so helpful and kind.

In the evening, when the sun had mellowed, I followed the walkway toward Guruvayur Temple. Inside the temple is where the celebrations were to occur. I didn't know what festival it was, but I eagerly enjoyed my time irrespective of that.

Golden lamps had been laid down the street's middle to the temple's entrance gate. Hindu priests were lighting them, while others were creating *rangooli*[61] in between the lamps. Shops on both flanks of the

---

61  *Rangooli* is an Indian art form using colored sand or powder to decorate floors.

walkway had glimmer lighting dangling over their board signs. There were stereos at regular intervals pumping out loud music. The number of people walking on the streets had increased dramatically from the day before.

By the time I entered the temple, it was like another world altogether. Priests were playing rare instruments. Decorative pieces depicting various forms of Hindu gods covered with shiny lights were installed around the temple. Traditionally-dressed, large crowds, mostly Keralans, were entranced by the festivities. It was a fascinating fusion of everything showcasing the altering colors the sacred land had to offer.

I relished my time observing and being part of the madness that prevailed over the holy site. Even when I was back in my room, the music and celebrations could be heard all night. They went on until the morning, leaving me awake for most of the night.

I stayed another day in Guruvayur before commencing the next phase of the walk on Day 42, which entailed walking through farmlands, coconut plantations, and vast patches of green.

Trailing away from Guruvayur, I also saw an Elephant Temple with an Elephant Sanctuary next to it, where many elephants resided.

I had always found elephants to be such elegant creatures. I paused to watch them as they whirled their trunks and swayed in a leisurely fashion on their thick legs while gleefully playing with water. The baby elephants were the cutest of the lot. I spent some time observing those gracious beings, full of wisdom and solidarity.

I was fascinated by how the elephants surrender to human dominance. They are like ants to the elephants and could be squished by their solid, powerful legs if the elephants desired. But somehow, they give in to the mistreatment and cruelty dished out by humans, who pray to Ganesha's idols[62] while simultaneously chaining the animals representing the same god.

How ironic to see that in a country that loves breathing through hypocrisy by adhering to a persistent disparity between its spoken words and implemented actions.

I spent nights in the village of Perumbadappu and the town of Ponnani before arriving in the municipality town of Tirur, which was also a business hub in the Malappuram district.

The two days before arriving in Tirur were filled with interesting encounters. On transiting through little villages, I met some amiable men, who offered me money and refreshments for the way. One man handed me 500 rs, while another got me food and water saying, "*Main allah se aapke liye duya mangunga. Aapko kuch nahi hoga.*" Another man helped me get a room inside a lodge next to the highway in the town of Ponnani. In the night time, as I was sleeping, somebody tried to enter my room.

There was a loud banging on my door in the middle of the night. I felt nothing in me on hearing it. I was not scared, and without reacting to it, I went back to sleep. This was the second time somebody tried to enter my room, but I was altogether unmoved for the first time.

---

62  *Ganesha* is a vastly celebrated god in India who has an elephant head.

The early hours of 6 to 9 am were the most ideal for walking. After that, the rise in temperature made it difficult to keep going. I increased my walking speed during the early hours, which allowed me to cover a greater distance than later when my body started feeling tired. When the sun's severity increased, my pace involuntarily declined.

I had walked over 450 km by the time I arrived in the town of Tirur, which was busy everywhere and easily sensed to be a trading center. Although it was a place for business, it was also a treasure trove for the lovers of the Malayalam language. It was the birthplace of Thunjathu Ezhuthachan, the man celebrated as the father of the Malayalam language.

The Thunchan Parambu memorial and research center had been built on top of what was considered consecrated sand. It was in the memory of this devotional poet and linguist.

A local man from Tirur told me about him. When he saw me walk by the street where his house was, he joined me, inquiring about who I was.

It was March. The days of walking long distances in the heat were taking a toll on my body. By the time I stopped to rest somewhere for the night, I did not feel like going outside the room as my body would object, as it had only a few remnants of vigor left in it. I had to start forcing my mind to get my body to take proper rest days to give it time to heal – or else my body would have collapsed.

Although a day's rest would not do much for the kind of stress my body was in, it was better than no rest, and it certainly allowed my mind to keep distant from the never-ending bodily pain.

I stayed indoors for most of my day in Tirur, observing the pain in my legs and trusting the swelling in my body to reduce. I had to start consuming pain and anti-inflammatory medicine. I didn't want to ingest them, but given the inflammation in my body plus the dehydration, I had no choice. I had been walking nonstop for days without resting, so my legs could not heal themselves.

This madness continued for many days to come, with my body fleeting along the coastal line on the Anangadi-Parapanangadi Road next to the thumping sea while dogs prepared to eat me.

On the path running next to the train line through the town of Parappanagadi, I witnessed the glories of the ecstatic Kadalundi Bird sanctuary. Soon afterward, I was sailing on a boat with the fisherman from Chaliyam Village to disembark at Beypore port. This was a prominent landmark thought to be a fragment of the relic port town of Beypore.

Although Beypore was considered one of the oldest Keralan ports to be trading still, it was inundated with fishermen, residing in plenty of the lodges built there.

None of the lodges in Beypore would let me stay, and I encountered a lot of hostility from the lodge owners. I came across a similar situation further into the walk as well. Straight away, the person sitting at the front desk of these cheap lodges would turn me down when I inquired about a room.

They didn't want an outsider to stay in their place. They said, "No," by telling me they had no rooms available. The places were usually empty, so I always knew they were lying to me, but I never argued. I just thanked them and continued walking.

Unable to find a room in Beypore for a night, I had no choice but to continue walking until I could find something. It turned out to be one of those days when I walked for uncountable hours. I covered over 25 km with an injured body – passing the 500 km mark before entering the City of Kozhikode on Day 47.

A coastal city known for its significance as an olden-day trading center for spices, Kozhikode was an exciting place where I received a subtle welcome from its people. This was the city where allegedly the Portuguese explorer Vasco De Gama had landed in India back in the 15th. Century.

I marched into the City of Kozhikode around 1 pm by scaling bridges with trains on one of my sides and vehicles on the other. Being in the presence of many, huge concrete towers was a radical shift from the morning's village tapestry.

Even with shoes on, I could sense blood trickling out of my feet, which were swollen so frequently the feeling had become customary.

The anticipated days in Kozhikode were going to be very interactive. I had been invited to speak at a venue called the Design Ashram, a trendy space run by a talented bunch of the city's young architects and designers. They offered accommodation for travelers and hosted speakers to address a gathering of the local crowd under the shade of a Peepal tree, which had been planted inside their heritage property's courtyard. It was on Gujarati Street, named after the *Gujarati* traders who had migrated to the land back in the day.

Containing the fire raging through my chest, I keyed into Kozhikode. I was willing to share a spark from its fire that had been burning in my chest for eternity.

## NOTHING BUT FIRE

Fire was all I had.
Fire was all I had become.
Fire was all I could see.
Fire was all that was breathing through me.

# XI. DAY 48 – BACK WITH CHAOS

*I* WOKE UP WITH SOLEMN eyes and made my way out onto the balcony of the room in a tourist home, where I stayed for my first night in Kozhikode. It was an old place, which I saw as soon as I crossed Kallai Bridge to enter the City of Kozhikode.

Sunshine reflecting off the other side of the road hailed me along with echoing trains behind me; the train station for Kozhikode was just a few blocks away.

I had my breakfast of *dosa* and *sambhar* at the noted franchise of Indian Coffee House just next door. Soon afterward, I transported myself to a more central part of the city near Indira Gandhi Road that was crammed with shopping malls and large complexes.

There was a drastic change of pace in my external environment with traffic and people hastening into one another and four-to-five floor concrete buildings overseeing it all. It was a chaotic mess possessing the unique signature of India. Whenever I found myself in this chaos, it always aroused my senses thrillingly.

My first full day in Kozhikode was occupied with all styles of engagements. I had two extensive interviews with journalists representing prominent Malayalam newspapers, *Deshabhumi* and *Janmabhumi*. The journalists came looking for me in my new lodge, my second home by then.

Before the interviews, I consulted an Ayurvedic doctor. This was the second time since Kochi I'd done that. I had not thought about consulting an orthopedic doctor because I felt they would not let me continue walking – and I did not want to take that route.

I had found the clinic online, and, as it was not far from where I was staying, decided to go there.

The doctor was a polite Keralan woman. On seeing her, I immediately told her about my walk. As soon as she saw my legs, she commented: "They are very swollen." Another man was standing beside her during the consultation, the Ayurvedic massage therapist. He carefully inspected my legs with his hands and then expressed his concerns. "Your joints are very dehydrated. If you keep walking, you could permanently damage them ... It's too hot to be walking so much. The weather is not suitable for that."

I stayed quiet for a few seconds and then stated my request, "Could you give me some oils and medicines that can help? Because I am not going to stop."

They replied, "Yes, we can do that. But they will not help much because you need to stop and rest."

"Can you provide me with some treatment for a few days?"

The man answered, "We could ... but it's too hot now, and it's not good for your body to take treatments in this heat ... you need to stop walking."

"Ok, just give me the oils and medicine then."

They figured I would not stop, and even though we'd just met, they felt concerned for me. They were very sympathetic, but somehow, I knew I would be ok. I just had to keep moving.

The following hours went by in company with journalists who interviewed me for an extended time before I had to leave for Gujarati Street to speak at the Design Ashram.

The Design Ashram hosts received me courteously and first gave me a tour of their entire venue. It had working spaces for architects and designers, accommodation for travelers, gallery capacity for art exhibitions and events, a sensitively designed café, and a room full of antiques procured by the man who had offered it to the designers and architects for running everything from. It had been delicately crafted with copious attention to detail by a team of talented creators working under one roof.

"We host architects, musicians, travelers, and artists all the time," one of the hosts, Sherin told me. She was a brilliant, young Keralan woman with lustrous skin and silken dark hair falling to her mid-back. She was delighted to show me around all of Design Ashram and specifically commented: "This is the first time we've had somebody who is traveling by foot."

I smiled at her remark and replied, "Well, I'm glad I can bring some add-on to your speaker list."

"We are pleased to have you here," she responded.

———⊗⊗⊗———

A large group of young people from Kozhikode gathered in an overflowing courtyard under the Peepal tree.

I spoke into the silence from a stage while beholding the eyes of the listeners. While they received the words emerging from my lips, I could sense the tracings of their hearts.

Following the talk, I engaged in one-to-one conversations with attendees while undertaking a book signing, as I had brought along some copies of my first book.

I was so delighted with everything that life kept bringing into my day-to-day that I forgot about the pain in my body and continued breathing through time fearlessly and exchanging with others the rawness of what I was feeling in every moment of its creation.

Regardless of where I stood – in front of a large gathering, a few people, or nobody, for that matter – nothing affected the inside of my skeleton anymore. It remained constant regardless of the changing situation outside my body.

Moment to moment is what became of my life in its raw demeanor.

———⊗⊗⊗———

It was late at night by the time I returned to my lodge. I was feeling fatigued all the way to the inside of my cells, but nonetheless, a sense of joy prevailed. Many of the locals I met in Design Ashram had invited me for dinners and suggested I visit exclusive spots in their city, but instead, I gave my body time to rest.

I went on a few strolls around the area where I stayed to taste the appealing food that everyone from Kozhikode kept on boasting about.

As the city used to be a hub for spice traders, it made sense that it had excellent food options.

On the recommendation of a local named Stanly, I did visit a restaurant named the Paragon to try their famous Mango Curry, which was a hallmark of exquisite food – as I was told. Stanly was the one who suggested my name as a speaker in Design Ashram. He was friends with a girl I had met in Kochi, a photographer who had previously seen me in Delhi.

She had approached me when she saw me sitting in one of Fort Kochi's cafés. She was originally from Kozhikode and told me that she would put me in touch with her friend Stanly for when I would be passing by Kozhikode. "Stanly will help you out," she said to me, and that is exactly what happened.

The randomness of how things manifested themselves during the walk was inexplicable. I would meet somebody, and they would know somebody who would know somebody else, and that person would somehow hear about me, contact me and help me out.

It was a phenomenal networking effect that governed everything. To have become a part of it and experience it first hand was something outrageous for my logical mind to grasp. So, I let go of the rational way of functioning and instead embraced the notion that "Everything is possible."

After a few days of slowing down internally while observing the organized chaos rifling through Indira Gandhi Road, I was forced by my body to take an extra day of rest in Kozhikode. It was the first time in the walk when I woke up one morning to leave the lodge and be back on the road, but my body could not move. It was almost paralytic, and that was the day I had to take a strong dosage of anti-inflammatory and pain medicine to get my body somewhat ready for the coming days.

A state of numbness in my body endured as that day progressed while something within me changed. The observer resting inside my mind was disassociated from my body for a prolonged time. My consciousness was no longer constrained within my body but was suspended outside it.

It was the strangest thing to observe in myself. It was not just momentary either. It was as if I was looking at a body that was not mine anymore; whoever was watching this body was outside it, not inside it.

The mind's observer completely removed itself from my body that day. Whatever my body was doing, sleeping or walking – or anything else – that observer was viewing my body's movements from outside it.

I was lying down in a paralytic state when that now separate observer was looking at this body that was still and refusing to move. It was just the oddest thing to experience. The next day onward, my body started following the observer, which commenced walking away from Kozhikode on Day 52.

This observer was what bore my body forward.

The sensations that had been with me until then disappeared along with my body's ability to be governed by its senses. No physicality remained with this observer anymore. It stood apart from my body and expanded its consciousness without being affected by anything my body felt, while simultaneously fully aware of everything.

I can't describe how it felt, but it was the most eccentric way of being I had ever experienced and it stayed with me for the remainder of the walk.

All of life's illusions were becoming clearer to this nameless entity that was now free from my body while I moved forward with a novel sense of being.

Past Kozhikode, the walk was not the same anymore. I was shadowing through an inexplicable space, in which I lost sense of everything and breezed through momentary lapses of time that were to occur in my days until I stopped moving my feet.

## A. Humans – Cause for Destruction?

Walking along National Highway 66 away from the City of Kozhikode, I was back on the road with my body not seeming like mine anymore. It had metamorphosed into an instrument following the presence of an observer, guiding me to experience life in the most intricate way possible.

Everything was animated and fully alive, with my mind freed from my body and stripped from the concepts of time and space.

I was not trying anymore. I was simply in a state of being. Either walking or sitting, it did not matter what my body was doing. I was detached from it, drifting along the coast in a spaceless space by the road while breathing to keep my body alive.

A pure sense of nothingness prevailed through me – I could not understand how I kept walking for the coming days without any rest.

I saw the site of an accident on the highway a day after I was back into the walk. A Toyota Innova had been extensively wrecked. Nothing was left of its front. A traffic jam continued for a few miles on both sides of the highway. The seats which were no longer attached to the car were fully covered in blood. Half the car was non-existent.

I was unsure if the passengers survived or not, but I prayed for them as I continued walking.

Soon I glided through the coastal town of Vadakara and the Union Territory of Mahe, which, with its French colonial heritage, was considered a district of Puducherry. It was one of India's eight Union Territories. It used to be a French colony and was commonly referred to as Pondicherry.

I was unaware that other Indian districts were considered part of Puducherry because they'd previously belonged to the French. I was astonished at first. Puducherry is located far away from Mahe on the South-east coast of India, where it shares borders with the State of Tamil Nadu.

At first, I was puzzled on seeing the words "Union Territory" linked to Mahe. I had never heard of that Union Territory before. White-colored buildings influenced by French architecture were everywhere in Mahe alongside French Revolutionary statues. It all called for a mind-trip.

Considering I was already in a bizarre space where everything was dream-like, the noticeable shift in the land's tapestry as I passed through Mahe just after seeing the devastating accident site on the highway only added to the craziness.

It was all too impelling. The towns I was crossing. The nature I was seeing. The rivers I was beholding. The people I was noticing. My mind that was broadening. My body that was melting. The spirit that was flaming. The heart that was beating. The eyes that were envisioning. The trees blooming. The vehicles honking. The trains speeding. The birds chirping. The sun glowing. The dogs attacking. The food sizzling. The stars shining. The moon flashing. The singing. The road burning. The trash that was confronting. The land that was grounding. The truth that was holding. The freedom that was enticing.

Everything had consolidated to become a part of me, and I had become a part of it. It was the most alive I had felt in my entire life; existence no longer had any meaning attached to it.

With continuing expansion in every moment, I kept on trailing past the Union Territory of Mahe until I was back with the ocean and grounding my feet in the sand of Muzhappilangad Beach. That is where I saw the oddest thing. Locals were driving their cars on the beach for fun – and boosting local tourism. As a result, the beach's natural setting had been destroyed.

I stayed at the house of a Keralan man who lived by the beach and hosted travelers. He was retired but had traveled across India. He and I discussed the beach drive-on concept.

"It's an idiotic thing to do," he said, and I agreed. He continued, "You are a writer? Yes? Please do write about this."

I responded with firm resolve, "I will."

It was testing to see what humans had done to a beach, which was stunning in its natural setting. Instead of leaving it untouched or preserving it, they had converted it into a racing arena. The sand had been ruined by vehicles driving on it, and if people wanted to walk on the beach bare feet, they could no longer do that – it had been trashed.

I thought to myself, *Aren't roads enough for vehicles? Now they're allowed on the beaches as well, where they ruin the beach's natural scenery?*

I had seen many things in my time moving around India, but one thing stayed constant everywhere in the country – people's disrespect for their land and nature. Even in Kerala, which was considered one of the most environmentally friendly states in the country, I noticed a similar disregard among humans for their motherland.

It was a land they were prepared to kill for – if someone threatened to take it away – but they were not willing to respect and protect it with their everything while they had it as their own.

———◦∞◦———

On Day 58, after walking for over 600 km and becoming one with the burning road, I entered the City of Kannur. Primarily a trading port, Kannur was my fourth big city in Kerala after Thiruvananthapuram, Kochi, and Kozhikode.

Colonial architecture was ubiquitous there. The historical presence of St. Angelo Fort, a signature lighthouse, palaces for the Muslim royal family, and numerous other colonial impressions coalesced to shape the city.

I drifted along in Kannur not as an explorer anymore, but as someone who had no sense of self or any grip left on his physicality.

Close by Fort Road, I stayed in a lodge near the railway station. A cluster of journalists and photographers from Malayalam newspapers had tracked me down with a desire to interview me.

The journalists interviewed me in the dingy lounge area where I was staying. There was only one couch, but a large group of us, including all the journalists and photographers. So, we all sat on that one couch, and they asked me plenty of questions about the whats and whys – all questions I had heard before.

I answered them with full honesty. The journalists could not believe that I was walking in such torrid conditions. I told them, "I have no reason to make you believe anything. You will believe what you want to believe. I am simply telling you what is there to tell."

Eventually, they asked me to come outside with them to click a photograph of me walking with my backpack through the dynamic market close to where I was staying with small traders and shops selling an array of articles from spices to clothes. It was all very spontaneous, and I played along with whatever came my way.

On the morning of Day 59, I continued my walk out of Kannur. Yet again, I was at one with my robust companion – the road.

The previous day's interviews were published in the local newspapers across the region where I was walking. As a result, I was stopped quite frequently by people on the road that day.

It was amusing to see people sitting on their wooden stools by their shops or homes reading the news about me, and then on seeing me walk by, they would run up to me saying, "It's you! This is you!" while pointing at the newspaper.

They would ask me to sit with them straight away while they translated the articles published in Malayalam into either English or Hindi so I could understand what they said. Some elderly *Malayali* men would hug me and say, *"Bhagwan tumhare saath hai beta."*

I didn't care much about what the articles said. Rather than conversing about the interviews, I would talk to whoever stopped me on the road to share a brief moment of human-to-human camaraderie. I had gotten very much used to strangers just walking up to me and embracing me by then, as I knew that was their way of showing affection. Their not hesitating before touching me was a sign of it being a pure gesture.

I was as surrendered to that as I was to the walk. Both were now causalities that stood beyond my physicality; both were enacted as part of my being, which derived from a newly found space where nothing ceased to exist.

# XII. A NEW STATE. A NEW LIFE.

*IN THE COMING DAYS,* I drifted away from the main highway toward the grasslands seeded by the paradise of spreading agriculture. After sliding through the village of Kunhimangalam and the locality of Payannur, I arrived in the town of Nileshwaram. It was Day 62 of the walk.

I took a few days of solitude by the beach of Ozhinvalappu, nestled next to Nileshwaram, to retract from the world outside and levitate up to the extraordinary observer of my mind, which was still as detached from my body as it could be.

After those days in solitude, it was clear that the pilgrimage's upcoming days would bring about everything possible. It was time to be totally unconcerned about the external world, and create space for the observer to see through every piece of my still-persisting being.

On Day 66, I reappeared on the road and approached Kerala's border. I knew it would arrive soon as my eyes had glimpsed a glitzy, green-colored highway sign with the names of several up-coming cities.

Among the names was Mangalore, a major seaport on the Arabian Sea. It was a vital commercial center in the State of Karnataka, which would be the third southern state in India I walked through after Tamil Nadu and Kerala.

Before leaving the State of Kerala behind and traversing through the State of Karnataka, an ancient fortress, Bekal Fort struck my eyes. It was assembled in red stones on the coast overlooking the Arabian Sea, flattered by an extensive stretch of sand with trees encasing the land's curve beautifully. The terrain enveloping the remains of Bekal Fort brought some respite to my mind.

As I distanced myself from Bekal Fort, another fort, Chandragiri Fort, emerged. It was next to the waters of the enchanting Chandragiri River – named after the fort itself – and spread its composure throughout the surrounding rich biodiversity, including an indistinct image of a far-distant mountain range, the Western Ghats on the eastern side of the river.

The magic lured into my eyes by the seeds of earthly creations took me hostage, but I soon found myself in the last municipal town of the northernmost part of Kerala, Kasaragod. I stayed there overnight before merging along with the rubble of the liquefying concrete road the next day.

After 70 days – and over 700 km – I saw another green-colored highway sign next to some toll booths. This time it flashed the words, *Thank you for visiting Kerala*. I solemnly navigated past the toll booths where lines of colorful trucks fused into one another. I had nothing but gratitude in my heart for everything I had received from Kerala's wonderful people and sacred land.

An ecstatic feeling arose within me from all the improbable internal and external calamities of the preceding days – not because I had walked so far.

How could a person ever be the same after experiencing such invaluable moments, time and again?

Those moments had exhorted every part of my being to transform itself and move beyond its perceived potential to harness the mind's limitless potential.

If we aren't willing to embrace the constantly changing self – while filtering out the external noise of our human-devised expectations – and dive deep into the unknown the world has to offer, how can we ever set foot outside our mind's locked doors? That is the only way to unleash an abundance of imagination and universal teachings within those doors.

The external world suddenly changed as soon as I entered Karnataka. The highway broadened to four-lane capacity. A physical divider in the middle isolated the traffic moving in opposite directions. A load of space spread beyond the highway's edges for me to walk on. I was finally relieved of continually having to deal with vehicles trying to drive through me.

Another noticeable change was that Karnataka had a lot more industrial and commercial activity than Kerala, which hardly catered to any industries. Karnataka's tapestry and human occupation were also more spread out. Its setting was not as compact as Kerala's, where I encountered tiny villages at short distances.

As a result, I walked for more hours on the road without glimpsing human settlements. That would make the approaching days of the walk most demanding ones – and simultaneously the most expansive.

## A. Day 71 – An Illusive Wonderland

I spent my first night in Karnataka by National Highway 66. My daily walks were lengthening and with diminishing human interaction, but those that did happen were very fruitful. There was little difference in people's receptivity in Karnataka and Kerala – they were equally hospitable. The only thing that changed was their language – *Kannada*.

After sailing over the Netravathi River, I landed in the illusive wonderland of a place called Mangalore on the morning of Day 71. Mangalore was very cosmopolitan with an additional historical element pulsing through it. Enormous old churches and temples were visible everywhere. By the time I was walking through the city center on K S Rao Road, there were gigantic shopping malls and fancy outlets for designer brands lined up on both sides. It was an exceedingly inconceivable alteration for my mind to grasp after Kerala's agricultural villages.

The changing parallel realities and constant paradoxes relating to the land I was moving through evoked my brain's continuous neuronal firing. That, plus my overflowing state of nothingness, made me experience an indefinable spectrum of veracity, no longer related to the human world. It was as if it was a separate living creature.

I stayed in Mangalore the next day, close to National Highway 66. Campuses of large IT companies were in the area. I felt indifferent to the external concrete world – perhaps because I had already seen plenty. My body had surpassed its physical limitations long ago and was now plainly injured and fatigued from walking in such extreme conditions.

I was no longer provoked by the external human world and was solely resonating within my blissful self.

On 31st March 2019, I walked away from Mangalore to lope along the coast, where I stayed in an old family property close to a quaint beach. A local guy rented his place to me for a few days. It was in a predominantly Christian village with no tourism whatsoever. At night, it was as silent as it could be, though the ancient walls imparted a sense of hauntedness.

This was the last time I took a few days for introspection during the walk. I welcomed April by rejoicing in the strong currents hitting the coast. The owner warned me to be careful of the waves, which were very robust and dominated me. As a trained scuba diver in my past, the ocean never intimidated me, but the waves in that section were undoubtedly powerful. It required a lot of effort to stay vertical when going into the water.

I continued trailing along the coast in the days to come with a grave feeling that something big was approaching, which would require me to give my everything with no chance of holding anything back. I was unsure where this feeling originated from, but somehow, I just knew that something was coming my way.

What accompanied this feeling was a deep sense of fearlessness in myself. I no longer felt overwhelmed by what was to come but felt fully assured in my self that I would be able to handle it.

This assurance did not arise from arrogance or ego, but a place of surrender. I truly felt I was no longer holding back anything in myself and would somehow be taken care of by the sacred land I was walking on.

I had full faith in the unknown, knowing that it would help me whenever I sincerely needed it.

On Day 76, I began what was to be the last phase of the walk.

Expanding in the rawness of my being, I was now starting to experience the deepest of my vitality. The walking paths became increasingly unpredictable, as the wilderness brought unexpected difficulties. While walking, I struggled to find food and water. The little stores and eateries I came across regularly in Kerala were much further apart in Karnataka. That brought me up against my bare needs for physical survival. My body got dehydrated almost instantly because of the rising temperature, and I had to walk to slake my throat's aridity.

I was so deeply in myself that my cells started remembering ancient primitive times and brought up visions of our animal past. I felt like an animal again, willing to kill other animals with his bare hands if the situation demanded. The biology of wanting to procreate was also ascendant, and I could comprehend that my whole body was now in a primal state.

I felt like I'd been teleported back to hunter-gathering times and was a hunter or a caveman out in the wild seeking food, water, and shelter.

Hunger for food and thirst for water induced hallucinations. The observer watched and remained detached. It did not bow to my physical needs and chose to move away from them to let my spirit evolve.

Karnataka's dog attacks jumped exponentially compared to those in Kerala, especially by the empty narrow roads not far from the sea close to fishing villages, outsiders rarely visited. I was attacked by packs of them regularly, almost every 100 yards. They were no longer dogs to me, but wolves attacking to kill me.

They charged ruthlessly at me with ferocity in their bloodshot eyes – some of them extremely bulky in size too. I had to stand my ground and not be afraid of them while they maliciously charged. Sometimes, a fisherman came to my rescue. But in most cases, I was all on my own, so when the dogs bailed me up and barked at me, looking for a reason to attack, I would use my stick to defend myself while cautiously struggling to keep going.

After a few days, I hovered through the serene beaches of Kapu and Malpe. They were local tourist attractions near the holy town of Udupi. With its sanctified Sri Krishna Temple and Anantheshwara Temple devoted to mighty Shiva, Udupi pulled many pilgrims to its doors.

Drained from confronting dog attacks on the coastal route, I felt I had to reunite with the highway where there were fewer dogs – but April's heat felt harsher than ever there. My body was left to breathe through its heatstroke without respite from cooling sea breezes.

Further up from Udupi on the Panvel–Kochi–Kanyakumari Highway after walking for over 800 km, I crossed the town of Kundapura feeling as wild as never before, breathing through a different dimensional reality altogether. I then halted near Marvanthe Beach on Day 81.

That was one of the most spectacular highway routes I had seen in India. On one side, the road touched the sea and human-made, titanic rocky surfaces at regular intervals piercing into the sea – and on the other, the Suparnika River danced along.

In comparison to Kerala, this part of Karnataka was almost empty, except in villages. Even when walking on the highway, I barely saw any vehicles. Maybe that was a result of the heat – or it could have been for other reasons. I was not sure, but I was stranded on my own for miles with no humans in sight and covered extended 25-plus km distances each day while seeing astonishing landscapes.

Breathing through fire, on Day 83, my body transitioned from rising with the glorious sun in the town of Byndoor to navigating by a shrieking, relatively empty highway to arrive in the port town of Bhatkal.

Bhatkal was another one of those historical towns where I could easily sense its deep connection with Imperial history. It was invariably visible in its classified architecture and disparate intertwined religious grounds.

The people of Bhatkal were very friendly. I stayed in a lodge near the frantic Bhatkal Circle on National Highway 66 for a night before continuing early the next morning to glide over the Venkatapur River. I accompanied green hills on my right side along with train tracks, where trains kept running by at routine intervals.

I had to make my way inland away from the highway by penetrating through farmlands to arrive in the hallowed town of Murdeshwara on Day 84. By this day, I had walked over 900 km and was greeted by the imposing, grey-colored Murdeshwar Temple. An imperial statue of Lord Shiva touching the vastness of the sky was behind the temple.

Murdeshwar was a sacred spot for many Hindu devotees and Shiva disciples. It seemed almost surreal to be burning in the heat and my body's internal raging on the 11th of April 2019 while being there on an eternal pilgrimage.

The huge rise in temperature had forced people to avoid being outside in the blistering wind and churning humidity that came with the month of April. I was aware that my body was fighting heatstroke in addition to all its injuries. Despite that, I kept on going while continuing to observe the pain from a distance.

I found a pilgrim's lodge at the corner facing the main Murdeshwar Temple Road. It linked directly from the highway in a straight line stretching right to the soaring temple. It was undoubtedly one of the tallest temples I had seen. Its rectangular form reached for the sky while fielding as many as twenty floors.

I climbed the stairs of the pilgrim's lodge to get a bed for the night. The lodge's manager, a joyful *Kannada* man, was standing behind the reception and said to me excitedly, "I saw you walking here from Bhatkal. You walked all the way here?"

"Yes. I walked all the way here from Kanyakumari." His eyes showed how stunned he was – and he couldn't respond.

By this time, when I told people that I had been walking for nearly three months and had started from Kanyakumari, they could not believe me. The distance was now too long, and because I was walking through such harsh climatic conditions alone, it was tough for them to digest what I said.

They would always inquire, "Just walking? No cars? No trains? Nothing?" and I would say, "Yes." But then I could see the bewilderment on their faces and how their minds were internally conflicted about accepting what I said.

I was not articulating many words by this time into the walk – hardly any, for that matter. I was experiencing life through the silence within myself without feeling the need to converse with others. I found speaking almost unnecessary and could convey everything necessary through my eyes and expressions without indulging in a wordy debate.

The storm in me had settled. The fire in my chest had been tranquilized. I was breezing through a space of equanimity and clarity after having let go of so much of my existential past. I was breathing through every moment that was rising in me slowly and deeply.

I was in a state of awe and nothingness with no affiliation with anyone or anything, experiencing life as it was without any interference from me.

I took a day to meditate and reflect within the freshness produced by the stone walls of Murdeshwar Temple. Surprisingly, the temple was not crowded, and I could easily sit in silence while the priests performed their usual rituals and chants.

Later in the afternoon, I took a moment to gaze at the remarkable statue of Lord Shiva, placed further away from the main temple with its separate entrance. Simply observing the symbolic representation of the highest form a being can attain, I remained unaffected by the sun's rays bathing the statue of Lord Shiva while blissfully seated in a lotus posture and ascending beyond myself.

I could not precisely describe the kind of space that I was in by that time. I was in the world – but at the same time, I was not. I was completely alive – but at the same time, I was not. I could feel everything – but at the same time, I couldn't. I could be everything – but at the same time, I couldn't. I could love everything – but at the same time, I couldn't. I could observe everything – but at the same time, I couldn't. I could listen to everything – but at the same time, I couldn't. I could see everything – but at the same time, I couldn't.

I was in everything – but at the same time, I was not.

Whatever that indescribable space was, it was surely the most intensely I had ever connected with myself – to a point where my whole sense of self had dissipated, and the only thing that remained was nothing.

# DEVOTION WITHIN

I was immersed in the light of devotion.
Not to a body or a symbol.
But a nameless creation.
Carried over by the seas and the hills.
Looking over me.
Guiding me.
Protecting me.
Holding me.
Breathing through me.
Within me.

# XIII. LAST MILE

WITH A SWIRL OF blessings spiraling through my heart, I left the town of Murdeshwar on Day 86 entirely in tune with my body and perfectly clasped by a highly determined spirit that needed no fuel anymore as it was effusively burning on its own.

It was a long day of walking effortlessly over 25 km through jungles, quiet highways, and large water bodies near the town of Honavar, which is where I stayed for the night before departing the next day.

I rested at a family's house in a village for the night before making my way toward the celebrated destination of Gokarna. That was another pilgrimage town famous for its sacred Shiva Temple of Mahabaleshwar and its enticing, sensuous beaches that hosted travelers from around the world.

It was the 15th of April 2019 and my 88th Day into the walk. By then, I was accustomed to the newly discovered rawness of my being and was breathing through space beyond my mind's imagination. I left the home of a welcoming *Kannada* family before sunrise to go along the Arabian Sea's coast.

I knew I would confront dog attacks as soon as I went inland, which is what happened. Disregarding their outrage, I kept on walking while keeping in mind the suggestion of the lovely *Kannada* man who had hosted me. He had advised me the day before, "If you keep going by the coast, once you meet it again, a ferry usually runs at the end, that can take you from Nirvana Beach to Om Beach on the other side."

Om Beach, he told me, was the most visited beach in Gokarna. He also warned me that now the tourist season had ended, it might be challenging to find a place to stay.

I took his advice and paced through some dense belts of jungle and little towns to reunite with the sea and march along with it.

It was one of the most arresting expanses of land with trees everywhere and white sandy beaches calmly sitting behind them. Eventually, I followed a coastal pathway of red muck with trees encircling my body. I was nearing the land's confines and catching the sound of my footsteps through the silence of it all.

No ferry or any boats could be seen when the land came to an end. I was unsure of where to go. So, I went looking for people in the area who could guide me. I found a group of young men as I was wandering about in that no-man's-land. When they saw me, they asked me what I wanted.

I told them, "I need to get to the other side of the land to Gokarna ... can you help?"

One of the guys, who was short and skinny with glistening dark skin signaled to me with his hands to follow him.

I shadowed his lean figure, which took me away from the beach into the jungle and eventually reached a tribal village. He said to me, "This is my village," and took me to his house to introduce me to his mother, who was a delightful woman. Her eyes exploded in light as soon as she saw me enter their hut.

I sat with her for a few minutes on the floor, as she put her palms on my face while her eyes became animated with sheer warmth.

Soon after, we continued trailing through his village on slender pathways, then crossed a vast open field before going through another village and finally hit a concrete road. The man tried to convey me a message with his hands pointing toward a hill that this road led toward. He didn't speak Hindi or English, but I gathered from his broken tongue that he was telling me that I needed to climb over that hill. A ferry could be found at the bottom.

I thanked him and began climbing the hill, which would not be my only one for the day. My body was tearing as I climbed it, and even though the views were spectacular, I was struggling to scale it. Somehow, I coped with the climb up and down that hill and landed in the village of Aghanashini. A small ferry was boarding just as I neared the water – as the man had said.

I didn't know it then, but this was to be my last ferry ride on the walk.

I boarded along with a few others and was soon borne to the land on the other side. All the commuters went toward the sole road to the car park's right, but I chose to follow the other direction toward the sea with topsy-turvey hills for obstacles.

Without thinking by that point, I followed a narrow, muddy path that was supposed to lead me somewhere. I was not sure where, but I was hoping to get to Om Beach.

My body was bleeding while I followed the narrow tracks that guided me up and down a hill. I realized that there was nobody around me; I was all on my own. Regardless, I continued following the path, whose natural setting was unmistakeably the most expansive place to be.

Ageless trees enfolded my body, the ocean breeze drummed my face, and gigantic rocks surfaced by the empty beaches. It was all just magical.

With no one in sight, I did not think of turning back but continued forward, even when my body was rebelling. As I climbed down from the first cliff to cross a small beach, I discovered I was out of drinking water, and my throat was parched. I had no more strength left in my injured body, as I had already walked plenty that day. By this time, the sun was precisely overhead and fully potent.

Something in me did not want to stop. It wanted to keep going. It was not afraid of what could happen – there was no sense of fear in me.

I inhaled long, deep breaths to use my lungs at their full capacity and walked in a state unlike any before. My breath had been my most significant aid for the duration of the walk, but that day it was turning out to be more than just a tool – it was my sole companion producing life in me.

The surface of the next hill on the path was entirely rocky. Although it would not have been a tough hike on some other day, that day, I had nothing left in me. Still, I knew I had to keep going. My feet were bleeding, and my body was dry. The rocks were discharging heat, so touching them was like holding fire. The hill was steep, with waves roaring their authority at its edges. If I fell, I couldn't make it.

I climbed that hill like a turtle in a state beyond physicality. My body had given up a long time ago, and my mind's observer stood outside my body, inspecting it vigilantly for any budding fear. None appeared. Past and future did not exist. I was utterly submerged in those moments of pure expansion through and beyond me.

When I reached the clifftop, I looked at the sea and saw no separation between it and my being. I was one with it all – the land, the sea, the air, the trees, the soil, the rocks. They were all part of me, and I was part of them.

I walked through this timeless state of being with no fear and a complete sense of nothingness in my spirit and ultimately landed my blood-sodden feet on the shore of Om Beach in time-forsaken hours.

I knew in those moments that this was why I was called to do this walk. That exact moment was what freedom became of me. There was no separation in anything. No loose ends were tied to me anymore.

That was the day for which I had been born – when I would experience life in full capacity with nothing left in my body to furnish myself with. I had walked over 950 km by then, and my body crumbled as soon as it arrived at the only place that was open at the far end of Om Beach.

The first thing I did was to drink water to irrigate my dried veins. It was as if I was drinking water for the first time in my life. Everything expanded in its originality. I can never forget the power of this day throughout my entire life. It was to be the most defining moment of my selfless self I had been trying to let go of while on the pilgrimage.

I was nothing.
Nothing was I.
And so, that moment became a crusade for the divine.

I woke up the next day, sure that I would soon stop walking. I felt at ease with that thought as the day before had given me more than I could receive.

I was staying in a small room close to Om Beach, the only place open. The tourist season had ended, and it was almost empty, so the owners happily gave me a room for the night.

I mostly just watched the waves approaching the shore and being reclaimed by the sea. I felt magical and indebted for everything I had received in the last few months on this nameless walk, which I knew would soon end. I could no longer hear that voice in me, asking me to keep going.

On Day 90, I continued strolling away from Om Beach.

Following the stairways through a hilly park to a vacant path with the rosy glow intensifying in the backdrop and no soul around me, I made my way toward Kudle Beach. Narrow pathways led me between the boundary walls of many buildings. I reached the beach just as the sun's presence reflected on the sea.

Nobody was on the beach. I had to climb another set of stairs to reach the top of the hill, leading down toward the main town of Gokarna.

Something changed from that day onward. I relished my new self while I passed along natural paths, and past closed Ayurveda and yoga places – the tourist season had ended – and finally united with the main town of Gokarna.

Gokarna was a multicolored town with charming little houses and temples everywhere. Many women wore clothing that I was unused to seeing local women in. It was very tribal, and I had seen it a few times when passing through some tribal villages, where women with their luminous dark skin wore these striking one-piece dresses, gloriously revealing their entire backs. A thin string around their necks held the dress while covering their chests in a triangular shape that then fell to slightly beneath their knees.

I saw the Mahabaleshwar Temple from the outside. Local priests and women were preparing for a festivity. I didn't enter and caressed the temple's aged walls with my palms and slowly idled toward the main Gokarna Beach, just in front of the temple.

Finally, more people were around, which reminded me that I was still in India.

I had arrived in the contented space of wanting to end the walk soon and felt like enjoying its last bits by giving my full attention to every impermanent flickering. I walked past the town and stayed overnight in a place just outside it. Next day, I moved along the inland routes of Karnataka, where I had my last battles with dogs. There were also some interesting encounters with tribal women in villages in the jungle belt past the Gangavali River. They were clothed in their conspicuous, colorful attire and were delighted to see me walk by.

Beyond the jungle was the town of Ankola, the last town before I reunited with National Highway 66. On Day 93, I covered over 32 km in a single day and crossed the walk's 1000 km mark. I passed nothing on the way, except a naval base. I had no choice but to keep on walking until I entered Karwar, my last city in the State of Karnataka.

Karwar was one of those peculiar port cities with a lot going on in it – war museums, old forts, religious buildings, and the divine Kali River flowing alongside before it ultimately merged into the Arabian Sea.

I stayed a night in Karwar and united with the road on Day 94 for my pilgrimage's concluding day on the 21$^{st}$ of April 2019.

A long walk lay ahead, but this was the day I decided – without actually having to think about it – that it was time to stop walking as soon as my feet planted themselves on the soil of Goa, which would be my fourth state in the walk.

It was almost impossible to describe everything that I had been through in those few months walking on my own through the southern parts of India. However, a vast feeling of nothingness filled me when I crossed the border of Karnataka. It was as if nothing at all had happened in the previous few months!

The person who began the walk a little over three months before had been left behind somewhere on the way. With no attached name or label, a new being was now making its way into the mighty unknown. It was ready to face everything that was to happen with a pure sense of freedom.

Because of the central government's elections in April, many police officers were deployed for security purposes at the State border between Karnataka and Goa. As I crossed the border, I was stopped and questioned by them.

I told them about the walk, and they could not believe that I had walked from Kanyakumari. On hearing my story, the chief officer offered a meal with him. *It could not have been a better ending*, I thought to myself. After that affectionate gesture by the Karnataka police, I drifted along the highway to enter the State of Goa.

On seeing a board positioned on the side of the highway with the words *Welcome to Goa* inscribed on it in white letters, I was ready to stop walking.

My spirit was blazing through me in the purest of forms, and I knew I had gained everything I could from this chapter of life. It was time to move on.

The border police went so far in their hospitality that they stopped a bus on the highway and instructed the driver to take me wherever I wanted.

I had no sense of attachment to all this as I sat inside a bus for the first time in many months, not knowing what was to come but willing to embrace its anonymity.

The bus dropped me off in the Canacona region of South Goa, where I hitchhiked on a scooter with a guy who dropped me off near Patnem Beach.

I had officially stopped walking and took a few days in that quaint area resting in a hut within a cocoon of coconut trees close to Patnem Beach, which like Gokarna, was empty as the tourist season had ended.

I didn't think about what had happened in the previous three months, so I could simply exist in the present moment I was in. I was experiencing a bizarre sense of reality – I had walked off my whole past and was now in an inexpressible state of harmony.

## A. Hello Governor?

The next day I received a call from the Office of the Governor in Goa, inviting me to meet with the Governor, Mrs. Mridula Sinha. She had heard about me walking all the way to her state and was interested in meeting with me, considering that I was also an author.

After a few days of some much-deserved rest for my severely injured body, I got a ride to the Governor's mansion in Panjim, Goa's capital city. It reflected the deep colonial heritage of the Portuguese, who ruled the State of Goa until 1961.

Goa was popularly known for its beaches, partying, wildlife, and pleasurable lifestyle, among other things. It was supposedly where the first hippies arrived in India in the 1960s and 70s, seeking an unconventional way of being.

The weighty metallic gates of the Governor's mansion were in a whirl for this man with no name, who had somehow managed to get a shirt on the way to meet with the Governor in her mansion overlooking the Arabian Sea.

While waiting in the grand hall, I was interviewed by some journalists. Soon afterward, a man dressed in flawless gentleman's attire asked me to follow him. It was all very formal. We walked across generous balconies to enter the meeting room, where Mrs. Mridula Sinha was waiting to meet with me one-on-one. We conversed for over an hour about writing, among other things, as Mrs. Mridula Sinha was a writer herself. We also talked about her home state of Bihar, where she was born.

I sat across from her on a couch, while she sat elegantly like a queen displaying her delicate but simple *sari* and determined attitude.

She was elderly and wore glasses, but her eyes carried a lot of wisdom.

While we were conversing about a variety of topics, she told me that she was writing her take on her and her husband's relationship – and he was writing a similar book about his outlook on their relationship. Once they each finished the separate versions, they planned to combine both perspectives into one book.

"Wow. That sounds brilliant. It would be a fascinating read."

---

After walking through South India for over three months, sitting in front of the Governor of Goa felt like a vivid dream.

I felt clear in myself and was so ingrained into the present moment that I had no idea what the future held for me. I had realized from walking so much that the outset of the present moment matters the most in life – nothing else is as real as the moment we are in.

The moment we are in defines our character and our ability to transform ourselves beyond what we think is possible.

The initiation of each moment that breathes through us speaks through us. It brings us closer to the light that shines in our hearts and the fire that bleeds within us.

As time passes, we can forget to bring our attention to these perishable moments where life happens in us – it does not happen somewhere else away from us.

We forget that all the joy to be experienced in life lies in these little moments. What is life worth living for if we can not be joyous in our every moment?

No matter how painful or blissful things may seem, deep joy in life – regardless of what might be happening externally – reflects the truest and the rawest form of our fundamentally free selves.

# GLOSSARY OF HINDI-ENGLISH TRANSLATIONS.

## PART 1

*Tum yaha kaam karte ho?*
> Do you work here?

*Haan, aapko room chahiye?*
> Yes, do you want a room?

*Jullay ... Aapko room chahiye? Kitne time ke liye chahiye?*
> Do you want a room? For how long do you want a room for?

*Acha hai na bohat?*
> It's very good? Huh?

*Aap aa gaye? Saath main dost bhi laye ho?*
> You're back? And you've also brought a friend along with you?

*Bohat acha.*
> Very good.

*Chalo.*
> Let's go.

*Aur kya haal hai? Theek hai?"*
> How are you? Fine?

*Zanskar kehte hai bohat khoobsurat hai.*

They say Zanskar is very beautiful.

*Main nahi gayi par uncle gaye huye hai.*

I have never been, but uncle has been there.

*Haan, haan ... Jaldi betho ... we leave soon.*

Yes, yes... sit down quickly... we leave soon.

*Yeh bags kaha rakh sakhte hai?*

Where can we keep these bags?

*Bas pohachne wale hai Lamayuru.*

We are about to reach Lamayuru.

*Bhaiya Kargil tak chodd sakte ho?*

Brother, can you drop me at Kargil?

*Aapko kal Zanskar jaana hai?*

You want to go to Zanskar tomorrow?

*Kal?*

Tomorrow?

*Paaji room toh ho sakta hai... par perfect condition nahi hai, abhi construction complete hi huya hai.*

We can arrange a room... but it is not in perfect condition. The construction was completed just recently.

*Aapko rehne ki jagah chahiye?*

You want a place to stay?

*Haan.*

Yes.

*Aa gaye wapas!*

You are back!

*Jullay Aunty. Aap kaise ho?*

Jullay Aunty. How are you?

*Ek dum badiya. Maine aapka room tayyar rakha huya hai.*

I am very good. I have kept your room prepared.

*Kaha kaha gaye aap?*
Where did you all go?

*Bohat khubsoorat hai waha par.*
It is very beautiful there.

*Woh to hai!*
That's for sure!

*Seva dene main bohat powerful experience hota hai. Isme tumhari khud ki bohat growth hoti hai.*
While serving you have a lot of powerful experiences. And you grow plenty from it.

*Itna kya likh rahe ho aap?*
What are you writing so much?

# PART 2

*Jaa rahe ho? Apna dhyan rakhna.*
You are leaving? Take care of yourself.

*Aap bhi kya bol rahe ho. Yeh toh humara farz tha.*
What are you saying! That is what we are supposed to do!

*Kitna patla ho gaya hai.*
You have gotten so slim.

*Aa gaye bhatak ke.*
You're back from wandering about, hey.

*Kaha jate ho aap?*
Where are you going?

*Kisse milte ho aap?*
Who are you meeting?

*Kya likhte ho aap?*
What are you writing?

*Apna dhyan rakhna.*
Take care of yourself.

*Kabhi kuch aur bhi pee liya kar.*

Drink something else as well sometimes.

*Iska dimag kharab ho gaya hai? Kaha se aise ideas aate hai?*

Has he lost his mind? Where does he get these ideas?

*Kuch bolo mat... apne aap time ke saath idea drop ho jayega... hum bolenge toh aur karna chaheyga yeh.*

Don't say anything... with time he will drop the idea... if we say more, he will want to do it more.

*Tu pura pagla gaya hai.*

You have totally gone mad.

# PART 3

*Aap Shailja ko kaise jante ho?*

How do you know Shailja?

*Yaha kuch nahi hai.*

Theres nothing here.

*Pata nahi, main poochta hun.*

I don't know. I can ask.

*Main allah se aapke liye duya mangunga. Aapko kuch nahi hoga.*

I will pray to Allah for you. Nothing will happen to you.

*Bhagwan tumhare saath hai beta.*

God is with you, son.

# ABOUT THE AUTHOR

$A$N *ACCIDENTAL WRITER AND* social media influencer who has built an online community of thousands from across the globe, Kartikeya Ladha first gained international recognition after the launch of his first book, *Dream Beyond Shadows*, in late 2018.

The book, his first, was well received in India and worldwide, creating a path for Kartikeya to encourage thousands to embrace creativity and courage in their lives, to pursue their dreams and, in the process, to empower and inspire the people around them.

Kartikeya was born in Gwalior, a historic town in India, and grew up immersed in the richness of India's vibrant customs and family life. He was educated in a rigid educational system, at The Scindia School, a relic of the British Raj era. After completing high school, he left India to attend Northeastern University in Boston, U.S.A., where he concentrated on Management and Entrepreneurship. After graduation, he moved to Brooklyn, New York, and worked for a solar start-up company as a door-to-door salesman, soon becoming a team leader.

In one of the most successful community solarization programs in the United States, Kartikeya knocked on doors in Brownsville, an area tagged by TIME magazine in 2012 as "Brooklyn's Most Dangerous Neighborhood." He educated hundreds of households about climate change and motivated them to take positive action for the environment by embracing renewable energy. Kartikeya quickly became the company's highest earner and enjoyed all the delights of fast city-living, until an inner voice surfaced from the darkness, compelling him to renounce his long-held plan of building a life in America, and instead to seek the truth of human existence.

His quest for the absolute truth led him to walk an unknown path that inspired travels to faraway lands worldwide. He went beyond life's usual norms to unearth his calling in this magical world, by initiating an unending discovery of himself as a human being, while serving his life's heart-felt mission.

*Dream Beyond Shadows* became an Amazon Bestseller in India after capturing people's imagination with countless insightful stories based on Kartikeya's experiences during a life changing expedition to Peru, South America.

Wanting to give life to a new work that exemplified the rawness of "what it means to be a human being," Kartikeya continued his explorations, returning to his home county, where he traveled into the heart of the Himalayas, facing extreme conditions and challenging his mind to gain powerful insights for its re-creation. This was followed by a solo pilgrimage on foot from Kanyakumari to Goa, where he walked more than 1000 km in three months through South India.

Kartikeya's travels within India inspired his second book, *Life Unknown – A Passage through India,* which continues the themes of *Dream Beyond Shadows* and goes further, taking the readers into the deep unknown, to face the darkness in life in order to be able to recognize the ever blazing light that shines within them.

"The moment you let go of the idea of who you are, you let go of all the expectation that hinders you from achieving your full potential"

Author website: https://www.kartikeyaladha.com

Follow:
Instagram @kartikeyaladha
Facebook @newageauthor

# ALSO BY THE AUTHOR

KARTIKEYA LADHA

Recounted through an epic life-changing journey,
this book affirms for many seekers in the world.
–INDIE SPOTLIGHT

# DREAM
# BEYOND
# SHADOWS

## NO ORDINARY TOURIST

THOUSANDS
OF COPIES
SOLD
WORLDWIDE

AMAZON BESTSELLER

Lightning Source UK Ltd.
Milton Keynes UK
UKHW012223170821
389016UK00004B/1055